# Step Into My Parlor

## The Chilling Story of
## Serial Killer Jeffrey Dahmer

Ed Baumann

Bonus Books, Inc., Chicago

95  94  93  92  91                                        5   4   3   2   1

Library of Congress Catalog Card Number: 91-76192

International Standard Book Number: 0-929387-64-3

**Bonus Books, Inc.**
160 East Illinois Street
Chicago, Illinois 60611

*Printed in the United States of America*

*Composition by Point West, Inc.*

'Will you walk into my parlour?' said the Spider to the Fly,
''Tis the prettiest little parlour that ever you did spy;
The way into my parlour is up a winding stair,
And I have many curious things to show when you are there.'
'Oh no, no,' said the Fly, 'to ask me is in vain,
For who goes up your winding stair can ne'er come down again.'


—From *The Spider and the Fly*
  Mary Howitt (1799–1888)

# CONTENTS

# Foreword

Serial killers in our midst. No two are alike. If that surprises you, consider, while reading this exceptional book by veteran crime writer Edward Baumann, the life-styles of these two examples of murderous homosexual horror:

• John Wayne Gacy, the killer of 33 young men and boys in a Chicago suburb. An extrovert, he sought social and civic attention, putting on a happy clown's face to entertain at block parties; working a precinct to get out the vote. Everybody's pal. All the while the remains of his victims rotted in the crawlspace of his home.

• Jeffrey Dahmer, an exceedingly dull but equally deadly character about whom this book is written. A stay-at-home guy in his stench-ridden Milwaukee apartment, when not trolling for his victims or bombed out on beer,

Dahmer, unlike Gacy, comes across as a classic "disorganized" serial killer.

The smiling, glad-handling Gacy used a rope trick to bind his unsuspecting victims, ultimately strangling them. Though his crimes were discovered in 1978, he continues to await execution on Illinois' Death Row, where he's been since 1980.

Dahmer's deadpan lure was the money he offered his 17 male victims, many of them pickups off the street or in gay bars. In return all he asked of them was to pose suggestively for him in the privacy of his apartment. This done, he'd extend a sedative hidden in a drink. Strangulation and dismemberment followed.

This book casts a powerful new light on the complex mind of America's lastest serial assassin.

Written by Edward Baumann, whose riveting tales of true crime in books and magazines are known to mystery buffs nationwide, it explores Dahmer's search for sexual identity and his ghastly admissions of homosexual murder and mayhem, beginning as a high school graduate in his native Ohio. Ironically, his crimes began the same year, 1978, that Gacy's ended, because of Gacy's arrest.

Baumann's work pulls no punches. Yet he is refreshingly subtle. No victim is trashed as a mere statistic. Baumann's words breath life back into all of them, and we see each as his family and friends did.

Baumann masters the dialogue of the Dahmer story, recreating the mood of disgust and wonderment felt in those first minutes when cops burst inside Dahmer's death chamber, arresting him.

The chilling story moves forward from there, shifting from a noisy Milwaukee police interview room to the courtroom, with new disclosures along the way of murder, bittersweet relief for relatives at finally knowing the truth and talk of scandal.

It is for the FBI, whose special agents study and profile serial killers, the task now of making sense and meaning from of the Dahmer story.

With help from such unexpected sources as John Wayne Gacy, Edmund Kemper III, killer of six coeds, his mother and grandparents and Dahmer himself, law enforcement in general and the FBI in particular are closing the gap about what makes serial killers tick.

Having committed wanton crimes these slayers continue to tell of their terrible deeds, in prison interviews with FBI behaviorial analysts. The Bureau has formalized the study of serial killers, hoping through its acclaimed behaviorial science unit in Quantico, Virginia, to identify those still committing them by analyzing their crimes.

"In most cases you will find a bad childhood, says FBI supervisor Robert Scigalski. "In their minds they don't have power; they don't have control," he said of one motive behind multiple killings. "The ultimate in power and control is to end another person's life."

According to the FBI, "organized" serial killers are apt to plan their crimes, use restraints, commit sexual acts with live victims, use a vehicle to commit crime and display control over a victim to induce the victim to show great bodily fear.

The organized murderer also is more intelligent and possesses job skills. He engages in "controlled" conversation with victims, hides bodies and follows news media accounts of his crimes.

"Organized offenders have a high birth order, often being the first born son of a family," the FBI reports. "Although the organized offender has an average or better than average IQ, he often works at occupations below his abilities, yet prefers a skilled occupation. His work history is sporadic.''

''Disorganized'' killers, on the other hand, are just that. The term ''lowlife'' seems to accurately depict them.

They aren't so smart and tend to leave weapons at crime scenes, according to the FBI. They also perform sexual acts on the dead, keep bodies around, ''depersonalize'' or dismember victims and don't use or have a vehicle for criminal purposes.

And they tend to kill when the urge strikes them. The FBI study of their crime scenes are ''random and sloppy'' and their violence sudden, with little conversation with the victim.

He is also likely to be socially inadequate. ''Often, he has never married, lives alone or with a parental figure and lives in close proximity to the crime scene,'' the FBI study concluded.

But there are always exceptions.

John O'Brien

# CHAPTER 1

---

# THE SACKS BY THE SIDE OF THE ROAD

The kind of weather usually reserved for the Dog Days of August had already seized control of Southeastern Wisconsin by mid July of 1991—muggy, stifling, oppressive, parched-lawn, dust-blowing, lung-aching, wet armpit hotness. The chest-tightening kind of heat where the sweat from your forehead fouls up the inside of your eyeglasses, and your underwear sticks to your hind end when you get up out of a chair, and you see people tugging self-consciously at their rears.

But through the heat waves simmering off the sunbaked pavements loomed the promise of a bonus month for murder mystery fans. Over in Racine County on the western shore of Lake Michigan the long awaited trial of Joachim E. Dressler, a scholarly looking, former Army intelligence man, was about to begin. It had all the ingredients of a Grade B Boris Karloff movie with overtones of homosexuality, bloodletting and bondage thrown in for good measure.

It was to be the grand finale of a gory story that began to unfold just a year earlier as John Dahl, a local dairy farmer, was driving his daughter-in-law, Ruth Dahl, home from a Friday morning shopping trip.

As they tooled along Highway K, in the western part of the county, they observed several of their holsteins sniffing curiously at a couple of yellow plastic bags that had been tossed alongside the fence bordering their pasture on the north side of the road.

"I noticed those damn bags when I drove by last night. I figured they might have blown off a passing truck or a car, and landed by the fence," Dahl commented.

"There might be something in there that could harm the cows," his daughter-in-law suggested. "Let me out here, Dad, and I'll get them away from the fence."

Dahl pulled the car off to the side of the road and Ruth got out on the passenger side. Walking gingerly over to the fence she gave the bags a nudge with her foot, rolling them down into the ditch.

"One of them's kind of heavy," she remarked. "I wouldn't be surprised if it had a dead calf or something in it. It tees me off that someone would dump it there."

Back at the house she mentioned the yellow bags to her husband, Howard. "I can't understand why people would do something like that," she said disgustedly.

"Why don't we send Chad back to get rid of it?" he suggested. "He can take it to the dump."

Chad Cadman, their sixteen-year-old farmhand from nearby Franksville, hopped aboard a front-end loader and rumbled back to the spot just west of Britton Road where the bags lay ominously in the ditch. He lowered the bucket as near to them as he could get and climbed down from the seat. Bending over, he got a firm grip on the tops of the two sacks and groaned audibly as he hefted them into the front end of the loader. He had just about gotten them aboard when one of the sacks ripped and, to his horror, a human foot tumbled out onto the ground.

Through the gaping hole in the bag Cadman could see there was more—white skin, with a patch of hair on it. Leaving the grisly bundles where he found them, the young farmhand climbed back aboard the tractor and hightailed it back to the barnyard.

"What in the world's the matter, Chad?" Mrs. Dahl inquired as he rolled into the drive. "You're white as a sheet."

"I think it's human," he blurted out, and burst into tears.

Ruth Dahl put her arms around the shaken teen-ager to comfort him as she turned to her husband. "Talk to Chad," she said. "I'll call the sheriff's office."

The Racine County Sheriff's Department sent out its heavy artillery. Lieutenant James Scheriff and Lieutenant James P. Ivanoski, chief investigator, ascertained that the "commercial grade" plastic sacks did indeed contain the partial remains of what had once been a white male. They presented the grisly find to Ron Turner, the deputy medical examiner.

"There's two legs and a pelvis in one of them, and the upper torso in the other," he advised them, after sorting out the contents. "The head, arms and hands are missing. No sign of clothing. Whoever it was was stripped naked."

The assorted body parts were taken to the Milwaukee County medical examiner's office, where a postmortem examination was performed the following morning. At the conclusion of the autopsy Racine County Medical Examiner John Esayian notified the sheriff's investigators, "It's the body of a white male, in his middle twenties. He died of traumatic injuries—several stab wounds in the chest and one in the back. There's also a tattoo that might help in identification."

Oh, yes. One more thing. The victim's internal organs were missing. The liver and heart had been removed, and the genitals were cut off.

The complete lack of blood at the scene indicated that the victim had been slain, beheaded, dismembered, disemboweled and emasculated elsewhere. Furthermore, it had happened rather recently, since decomposition had not yet set in.

In questioning farmer Dahl, the sheriff's investigators deduced that the bags had been dumped by the side of the road some time between 9 a.m. and 6 p.m. the previous day, June 28. "There was nothing there when I went by that way chopping alfalfa around nine o'clock in the morning," he insisted. "I first spotted the bags when I drove past at around six o'clock at night."

Ivanoski, a bullnecked, mustached twenty-one-year veteran of the sheriff's department, assigned all fifteen of his investigators to work on the gruesome homicide. They were assisted by the Wisconsin Department of Criminal Investigations and Milwaukee agents of the Federal Bureau of Investigation.

The first thing they had to try to do was identify the body, which would be no easy task, given the fact that the head and hands were still missing. They would not be able to rely on dental records or fingerprints. They began by checking to determine whether there had been any recent reports of anyone missing in the area.

There had, indeed. James Michael Madden, a twenty-four-year-old, clean-cut young man from the Milwaukee suburb of Whitefish Bay, had last been seen going from house to house in rural Racine County, soliciting donations for Citizens for a Better Environment. He failed to show up for his ride back to town Wednesday night, and his supervisors reported him missing when he did not come in for work Thursday morning.

At that very moment, in fact, Madden's worried father was going from farmhouse to farmhouse in the area, knocking on doors, and telling residents in a quivering voice, "My son is missing. Have you seen him?"

In going over the young canvasser's route, Sheriff's Deputy Thomas Gehl determined that Madden was last seen around 7:30 p.m. Wednesday near U.S. Hwy. 45 and Five Mile Road, about three miles distant from where the torso and legs were discovered.

Meanwhile Sergeant William Vyvyan obtained a physical description of the missing man, including the fact that Madden had a tattoo on his body. It matched the one on the torso, which the killer apparently overlooked in disposing of his handiwork. "The dismembered body is unquestionably that of James Madden," Vyvyan advised Ivanoski. "We're sure of the identification, lieutenant, even though the head and arms are still missing. We're confident it's one and the same person."

The tentative identification cast a pall over the Citizens for a Better Environment offices in Milwaukee. "We're devastated by this violent and horrible act, Rose-Mary Oliveira, the administrative director, told investigators who called to get what background information was available on Madden. "It's too horrible an experience to comprehend at this time. What can I tell you? Jim was an avid environmentalist. He was devoted to the cause."

She said Madden, who was extremely well liked by

his colleagues, had joined the state organization two months earlier as one of thirty full-time environmental canvassers in Wisconsin. "It's a very chilling effect on the openness of society to have something like this happen," she said. "We do the same thing that candidates, religious organizations and Girl Scouts do. It's not just us at stake."

Residents of Milwaukee's silk-stocking suburb of Whitefish Bay, where Madden had lived with his parents and three brothers were equally stunned.

"Jim was a very friendly, well-mannered guy. He was the type who'd always shovel other people's sidewalks and mow their lawns," one neighbor told investigators, who were trying to establish a motive for the slaying.

"Yeah, he was very civic minded and community-oriented," another remarked. "He didn't go out much. He spent a lot of time with his family. We'd see him out training Valerie, his dog."

Wisconsin authorities were still trying to get a handle on the perplexing case the following Monday when the head, legs and torso of Sonya Raue, a twenty-three-year-old housewife, were found wrapped in plastic bags in a garbage truck in Lockport, Illinois. A disposal company crewman called police when one of her legs tumbled out of a garbage bag as his truck was compacting the trash he had collected.

Investigators were suddenly faced with the numbing possibility that a madman might be roaming Southern Wisconsin and Northern Illinois, hacking humans to pieces and disposing of their body parts in plastic bags.

The similarities in the two dismemberment murders were obvious. Lieutenant Ivanoski contacted Police Chief Robert Miller in Lockport, eighteen miles southwest of Chicago, and the two lawmen compared notes. In the end they decided that it was just a horrible coincidence, but there was otherwise no link between the two slayings. Mrs. Raue's twenty-seven-year-old husband, John, would later confess to her murder.

Back in Racine, Ivanoski called his investigators together for a brain session. "From what we have at this point, it appears that Madden's death was a localized incident, that he ran into a psychopath, and that the psychopath killed him and cut him up," he speculated. "The results of the autopsy indicate that someone used a large, very sharp instrument to dismember the body. A sharpened knife, sword, or even a meat-cutting machine could have been used. I would say that we're looking for at least two weapons here. The torso wounds indicate the knife used to stab him was much smaller than the object used to cut up his body."

Hundreds of tips poured in after the victim's identification had been confirmed. Most were from people who thought they'd seen Madden on his rounds.

Every tip was meticulously checked out, of course, but there wasn't a positive one in the batch. By the end of the second week all Sheriff Robert Rohner's investigators had to go on were two sacks of James Madden, and they weren't full sacks, at that.

On Monday, July 9, a somewhat shaken resident of the town of Raymond phoned the sheriff's office to report, "My dog just brought home the upper part of a human arm! It must be from that guy you're lookin' for."

Sheriff's investigators converged on the area with a Labrador retriever trained to pick up the scent of fetid flesh. A short time later the Lab sniffed out the lower part of an arm and attached right hand in some underbrush about a mile away near Franklin, just over the line in Milwaukee County. This brought Milwaukee County Medical Examiner Jeffrey M. Jentzen into the bizarre case. He confirmed that the arm, with a tattoo related to the one on the torso, belonged to Madden. Since the arm parts were found about five miles from where the headless torso had been discarded, authorities now widened their field of search.

The next day searchers flew over the area where Madden was last seen, as well as where the body parts were found, looking for more yellow plastic bags that might contain the rest of his remains. They were also looking for bits of clothing, and anything else he might have had in his possession on the night he disappeared.

Back on the ground the town of Raymond resident put in another call to the sheriff's office. "My damned dog did it again," he reported. "He just come trotting home with the guy's other arm in his mouth." A deputy was dispatched to the home to collect the latest piece in the puzzle.

Authorities now had everything but the severed head. That would come next. A man out for a stroll with his ten-year-old son in the town of Raymond came upon the ghastly relic in a grassy field along Eight Mile Road near 108th Street.

A pathological examination of the head disclosed one bullet hole—and the startling fact that Madden's brain had been scooped out.

All of the external body parts had now been accounted for, and authorities were able to positively confirm identification through dental records, fingerprints, and the tattoos. But there was still the puzzling absence of the internal organs to ponder. Had the murder been part of a Satanic ritual? Sheriff Rohner refused to speculate. "Right now the investigation is going in many different directions," he said, in the understatement of the day.

To aid in the investigation the FBI was asked to de-

velop a personality profile of the killer, based on information at hand, to determine whether Madden had been the
victim of a serial killer, as some people feared, or an isolated attack, as Lieutenant Ivanoski suspected.

The *Milwaukee Sentinel*, meanwhile, obtained a profile of its own from Robert M. Holmes, a University of
Louisville professor of criminal justice and nationally recognized authority on homicide, deviant sexual behavior
and pornography. Holmes, who had visited Wisconsin
nine months earlier to address the state's Criminal Justice
Education Association at its annual conference in Stevens
Point, told the newspaper:

"The person who killed and dismembered Madden
probably was a transient, who will kill again, but not in
the same area. He was probably a single, white, homosexual male, in his mid to late twenties, with limited intelligence and education. He lived alone and performed the
act as a random 'lust kill' for extremely perverse sexual
gratification."

The professor, who had profiled more than 150
killers for police agencies nationwide, boasted a 99 percent success rate in accurately describing characteristics
of killers who were later caught.

"You're looking for a very dangerous person," he
cautioned. "He probably is not a local. If he's a transient,
he'll move on. It's going to happen again."

The professor's profile did little to set the minds of
America's Dairyland at ease. With ringside seats at the
kind of bloodletting featured in horror fiction, they feared
whom the psychopathic killer might encounter next.

"People are nervous," asserted Dahl, on whose 250-
acre farm the initial discovery had been made.

"Everybody's talking about it and is concerned,"
agreed Imelda "Mel" Fine, who ran Chet & Mel's Club

45, a tap room not far from where Madden had been soliciting for his environmental cause when he disappeared. "They always will be until they find him. It's scary."

And with each day the investigation dragged on, Sheriff Rohner's men felt they were a little bit closer to finding "him." Through extensive interviews and canvassing the area they had ruled out scores of possible suspects. They were also able to retrace Madden's steps throughout most of his last day on earth, as he made his way from farm to farm.

The last sighting they could verify had him walking along Five Mile Road, about five miles west of Interstate Highway 94, near a driveway leading to the isolated home of a local elevator repairman, set well back on a sprawling seventeen-acre plot.

Lieutenant Ivanoski's men had already interviewed neighbors of the property owner, forty-two-year-old Joachim Ernst Dressler. Curiously, Dressler's wife, Kathleen, had been hospitalized for surgery and the couple's two small children were away with relatives on the day Madden made his final rounds. Joachim Dressler—Joe to his neighbors—had been "batching it" on his secluded property at the time the environmental solicitor vanished.

On Thursday night, July 26, as sheriff's detectives chatted with Dressler's nearest friend and neighbor, Sherwin O. Beyer, they could see he wanted to tell them something but seemed reluctant to spit it out. With a little gentle coaxing he eventually revealed something he said Dressler had confided to him:

"Joe told me in strictest confidence that he accidentally shot a man while they were looking at his guns. He said he showed this man his rifles, and the gentleman fired a couple of practice shots. Then, as he was showing him his pistol, it went off. He said the gentleman was dead before he hit the ground."

According to Beyer, Dressler found the body too heavy to move. "That's why he dismembered it. To avoid tying the bullet to him, he removed the brain and ran it through the garbage disposal and into the septic tank."

The confidential information was hardly courtroom evidence. But, along with the fact that the last time Madden was seen in one piece he'd been walking near Dressler's driveway, it certainly warranted a peek inside the elevator man's house. Furthermore, once detectives zeroed in on Dressler, they were able to link the distinctive yellow plastic bags that had contained Madden's body parts to his farm.

The information was laid out before Assistant District Attorney Robert Flancher, who prepared a formal request for a search warrant. The instrument was signed by Racine County Circuit Judge Stephen A. Simanek the following Saturday.

Warrant in hand, the sheriff's men, along with agents of the FBI and the State Division of Criminal Investigation, paid an unannounced visit to Dressler's secluded residence Monday morning, July 30. During a twelve-hour search of the home they confiscated some 300 items. Among them were guns, knives, printed material, books, hair and bone samples, fibers, and what Ivanoski described as "several instruments that could have been the ones that dismembered the victim's body."

For a time the single-family dwelling must have resembled a beehive, with thirty investigators and agents going over the property, inside and out. "Handle everything with extreme care," Ivanoski urged the search team. "Everything's going to the State Crime Lab guys in Milwaukee for analysis."

The search failed to turn up the murdered man's clothing, but did uncover several items that could have been human organs. That would be up to pathologists to determine.

On Tuesday the searchers returned for a second sweep of the house and farm, to make sure nothing had been overlooked. Additional items removed from the property included pornographic pictures, magazines and books, handcuffs, ropes, saws, ammunition and a panel from a tanning booth with the name "J. Madden" and the number "27" taped inside.

Dressler, a German immigrant who had come to the United States as a child some thirty years earlier, was detained for questioning while the search progressed. He had no previous arrest record. He denied any knowledge of Madden or the disappearance, and insisted the solicitor had not called at his home.

But he was certainly the hottest suspect police had, and the sudden focus on the gentle, soft-spoken German took his neighbors quite by surprise.

"He's the intellectual type. He's into public television and reading," one neighbor, Karen Jones, offered. "He has a sort of a rigidity about him, but he's very civil, very hospitable. He's also into gourmet cooking, and he's been known to lay out huge dinners for people and provide all the drinks. He loves to do that sort of thing. He enjoys French and German cooking."

Another neighbor told investigators, "I sold him his land twelve years ago. To me he's a gentleman." He said Dressler, who worked as a $17.81-an-hour mechanic for a Milwaukee elevator maintenance firm, rented his fields out to soybean farmers.

Dressler's fascination with firearms was well known to residents of the area, who said he kept a vast array of rifles, shotguns and pistols in his home. "He didn't have them on display. They were just stashed around the house," one neighbor explained. "He's not a hunter. He just likes guns. You know, he believes in his Constitutional right to bear arms."

While Dressler may have believed in the Constitution, he did not believe in God. He was an avowed atheist. His wife and their two children, ages five and seven, attended church in nearby Hales Corners, however. Upon being released from the hospital, Mrs. Dressler checked into a Racine hotel while the investigation centered upon her husband. The children had been sent to stay with their grandparents in Florida.

The detectives questioned Dressler's wife about the distinctive yellow plastic bags found in the home—the same type used to wrap the victim's body parts.

"I purchased them myself, from my sister," she told them. "They were being sold as part of a fund-raiser for Burleigh Elementary School in Brookfield."

Indeed, investigators determined that the Burleigh school had been the only source of that particular kind of bag in the Midwest.

Authorities subsequently seized a bank safety deposit box, in which they found Madden's driver's license, checks, jewelry and other personal belongings.

Police efforts to either exonerate Dressler or link him to Madden's murder took a further turn against the suspect on August 9, when results of the crime lab tests began to trickle in. These, along with the contents of the bank box, provided the link authorities needed.

Sheriff Rohner sent deputies and SWAT team officers to the Dressler home to place him under arrest.

On receiving no response to their knocks, the lawmen entered the house and found Dressler, a tall, thin man with dark hair, a mustache and glasses, asleep in an upstairs bedroom. He was handcuffed and brought to Racine, where he was arraigned before Judge Simanek on a charge of first-degree intentional homicide. He was then transferred to the Racine County Jail in lieu of $250,000 bond.

With Dressler's arrest Lieutenant Ivanoski and Lennie Weber, an assistant district attorney, disclosed publicly for the first time that items taken from the suspect's home included numerous videotapes showing humans and animals being tortured, killed and mutilated. The lawmen also found photographs of dead bodies, along with a collection of newspaper clippings about Madden's disappearance hidden in an overhead heating duct.

"I viewed the videotapes, called 'The Faces of Death,' and they were very difficult to watch. They showed the killing and mutilation," the veteran lawman commented.

According to a criminal complaint filed in court, in the last hellish moments of his life Madden was bound and handcuffed after he came to Dressler's door, soliciting environmental funds. Dressler then hung the young Milwaukeean upside down from an electric hoist in his garage, shot him in the head, and drained the blood from his body. He then decapitated his victim with a razor sharp knife, broke his skull open with a hammer, and removed his brain. The victim's chest cavity was opened from his neck to his waist, and his heart and vital organs were removed. The body was then severed at the waist with surgical precision, and the arms, legs and genitals removed.

"Mr. Dressler was fascinated by pornography, and young, pretty men—a category Jim Madden unfortunately fell into. I consider this man as dangerous a criminal as this court will ever see," Prosecutor Weber asserted.

Lawmen and people who had known Dressler for more than thirty years could not help notice that the accused murderer hardly fit the "profile" of the killer prepared by the Kentucky college professor—"probably a transient, who will kill again, but not in the same area... a single, white, homosexual male, in his mid to late twenties, with limited intelligence and education...[who performed a] lust kill for extremely perverse sexual gratification."

Dressler's arrest shot a gaping hole in the prof's "99 percent record for accuracy."

Now, one year later—on an oppressively hot July day in 1991—Dressler was finally going to trial. Devoted aficionados of grisly gore could hardly wait for the gruesome details that were sure to be brought out in court.

Then something happened that suddenly made Joachim Ernst Dressler look almost like a choirboy by comparison...

# CHAPTER 2

---

# THE APARTMENT
# ON 25TH STREET

For some time now folks living around 25th and State Streets in Milwaukee's West Side low rent district had noticed a rather unpleasant aroma wafting from one of the apartments at 924 North 25th—the one where that nice looking white fellow lived. As a matter of fact, that wasn't all they noticed. Strange things seemed to be going on there.

In the early morning hours of Monday, May 27, concerned neighbors called 911 when a brown skinned Asian boy of about fourteen, with jet black hair, burst out of the building stark naked, bruised and bleeding from the elbows, knees and buttocks.

Eighteen-year-old Nicole Childress was visiting her aunt at the time. She and her cousin, Sandra Smith, also eighteen, had gone out for ice cream and were just returning to Sandra's apartment. As they pulled onto 25th Street the headlights from their car caught the child standing, naked and dazed, in the middle of the street.

They got out of their car and went over to see what they could do, just as the tall, blond-haired man who lived there, thirty-one-year-old Jeff Dahmer, dashed up out of the darkness and yanked the boy to his feet. "He's drunk. He does this all the time," Dahmer said disgustedly. As he spoke the youth reached out weakly toward the women.

"You stay away from that boy," Childress said, stepping between her aunt's next door neighbor and the naked youth. "There's something wrong here. I'm gonna call the police."

"Hey, the police don't need to get involved," Dahmer said, trying to appease the women. "This is my friend here. He does this all the time."

Smith stood by, defiantly placing her arm around the naked boy's shoulder, while Childress ran to a nearby pay phone and dialed the police emergency number.

"Milwaukee emergency operator seventy-one," a male voice answered.

Childress, visibly upset over the bizarre drama unfolding before her eyes, blurted out nervously, "OK, hi. Um, I'm on 25th and State. And there's this young man. He is buck naked. He has been beaten up. He is very bruised up. He can't stand. He just fell down. He has, he is buck naked. He has no clothes on. He is really hurt. And I, you know...I just seen him. And he needs some help, so I called."

"Where is, where is he at?" the dispatcher asked, hesitatingly.

"On 25th and State. The corner of 25th and State," she repeated for the third time.

"He's just on the corner of the street?"

"Yeah, he in the middle of the street. He fell out. We try and help him. Some people try and help him."

"OK, and he's unconscious right now?" the dispatcher affirmed.

"They...he getting him up. But he is," she answered.

" 'Cause he is bruised up. Somebody must have jumped on him and stripped him or whatever."

"OK, let me put the Fire Department on the line," the dispatcher suggested. "They'll send an ambulance. OK?"

"OK," Childress agreed.

"OK? Just stay on the phone, OK?"

"OK," she agreed once again. All the while this was going on, her cousin was trying to intercede in the tug-of-war between the neighbor and the naked boy. Finally the fire department dispatcher came on the line, and she had to start all over again.

"Um, yes, could you send an ambulance to, on the corner of 25th and State?"

"What's the problem?"

"OK," she explained. "There's this buck-naked young boy or man or whatever. He, um, is buck naked. He's been beaten up real bad. And he fell down, and people is trying to help him stand, and he can't stand. He is buck naked. He has no clothes on. He is very hurt!"

"Is he awake?"

"He ain't awake. They trying to get him to walk, but he can't walk straight. He can't even see straight," she emphasized.

"Ah, OK," the fire dispatcher interjected.

"And every time he stand up, he just fall out," she continued.

"At 25, 25th and State?"

"Yeah," she asserted, getting tired of repeating the location while the situation grew worse by the second.

"All right."

"That's one-way," she added, noting that State was a one-way street going west.

"OK," the dispatcher acknowledged.

"Bye," she said, hanging up the phone, feeling as though she had just been run through a wringer.

The 911 dispatcher recorded the call at 2:01 a.m. At 2:06 the dispatcher radioed Car 36, which had just completed another assignment. "Thirty-six, you got a man down," his voice cracked out over the police network. "Caller states there's a man badly beaten and is wearing no clothes, lying in the street, two-five and State. Anonymous female caller. Ambulance sent."

Car 36 responded, "Ten-four."

When no emergency vehicle had arrived within five minutes after Childress made the initial call, another neighbor impatiently called the sheriff's office. The sheriff's dispatcher simply relayed the message to Milwaukee police.

"A caller reported that there was a subject male dragging a naked male that looked like he was beat up, ah, severely, ah, between 25th and 26th Streets on State," the sheriff's dispatcher advised Milwaukee emergency operator 0-4.

"OK, we'll get someone out," the 911 operator responded.

The two cousins, meanwhile, flagged down a passing patrol car, number 68, just as number 36 pulled up and the fire department ambulance arrived. Two of the police officers and a detective got out to survey the situation, while a fourth remained in his patrol car monitoring radio calls.

Dahmer, a tall, soft-spoken, straight-backed man with blond hair and mustache, grabbed the fallen youth by the hand as the police officers approached and asserted, "Here he is! Here he is!" as though he had just found him.

"What's going on here?" one of the patrol officers asked.

Both women were chattering at once while attempting to shield the bleeding youth from Dahmer, who quickly assumed control of the situation.

"Ah, look," he smiled nervously. "We've been drinking Jack Daniels, and I'm afraid he's had a little too much."

The Asian youth was mumbling incoherently, and one of the officers propped him up unsteadily against the side of the squad car, as his partner asked, "How old is this kid?"

"He's nineteen," Dahmer answered. "We live together, right here at 924. We're boyfriends, if you know what I mean."

The cop nodded sagely. "What's his name?"

"Ah, well, his name is well...uh...his name is Jim something," Dahmer stammered.

"This is just a boy," the Smith woman argued. "He's badly hurt. Anyone can see that." Pointing to cuts on the youngster's elbows and knees, she demanded, "What are you going to do about it?"

"Why don't you just butt out?" one of the officers suggested.

Childress tapped the plainclothes cop on the shoulder to get his attention. When he tried to ignore her, she persisted. "Wait a minute. Don't you even want our names? We're the ones who called 9-1-1."

"Hey! I've been a detective for eight years," he glared

in annoyance. "And I don't need an amateur poking her nose into my business."

Childress turned to her cousin and said in frustration, "He isn't listening to us. He's listening to Jeff. He won't listen to what we have to say. He..."

"We'll handle this," one of the officers interrupted. "I think you and your girlfriend maybe oughta get lost— or I'm gonna take you Downtown."

The women took the hint, and headed for Smith's apartment next door, while Dahmer shepherded the bleeding youngster back into his apartment building. Two of the police officers went in with them. The youth went along meekly, seemingly resigned to the fact that nobody was going to help him any longer.

Inside the third floor apartment the officers observed that artists' renderings of men in various poses adorned the walls. Dahmer showed them several Polaroid pictures of an Asian youth posing in what appeared to be brief underwear or a bikini-style swimsuit, to confirm that the naked subject was indeed his roommate.

It could have been the boy, who now sat dazed and bleeding on the couch, oblivious to his surroundings, or it might well have been someone else. As a native Hawaiian once jokingly pointed out to a group of American tourists, "You all look alike to us."

The photographic evidence was enough for the two police officers. They didn't want to hang around any longer than they had to. The place didn't smell too appetizing.

They shook their heads in amusement and went back into their squad cars. One of them radioed the police dispatcher at 2:22 a.m. to report that their assignment had been completed. "Ah, the intoxicated Asian naked male ...ha-ha...was returned to his sober [pause for effect] boyfriend, haw-haw... My partner's gonna get deloused at the station [more laughter]." That was an inside joke among cops, but not a wise thing to put on the air, since police radio transmissions are tape recorded.

Sandra Smith was sobbing when she and her cousin walked into the house. "What's the matter with you, girl?" her mother, Glenda Cleveland, wanted to know.

"That little boy's hurt. He's really hurt, and the cops wouldn't do anything about it. We tried to tell 'em something was wrong, Mama, and they didn't even want our names."

"Good Lord," Cleveland gasped. "I can't believe the police couldn't see that something' wrong. Something's very wrong."

Cleveland, thirty-six, and the two younger women sat around and talked about the incident they had just been a part of. This was hardly the best neighborhood in town, it was true, but what had happened just outside their front door was beyond the occasional fighting, drug deals or gunshots echoing in the night.

"I'm gonna call the police station and find out what this is all about," Cleveland declared. She dialed police headquarters, and would not take no for an answer. "My daughter and my niece flagged down a policeman when they walked up on a, ah, a young child being molested by a male guy," she explained. "And, ah, no information or anything was being taken. I was wondering, I mean, I'm sure further information must be needed. It was Squad Car No. 68."

After some switching around, while she repeated her story several more times, she was finally transferred to the 3rd District police station, where one of the officers who had responded to the call was put on the line.

"Yes, ah, ah, there was a squad car. No. 68, that was

flagged down earlier this evening, about fifteen minutes ago," she began.

"That was me," he said, muffling his name so it couldn't be understood.

"Yeah, ah, what happened? I mean, my daughter and my niece witnessed what was going on," she explained. "Was anything done about this situation? Do you need their names or . . . "

"No, I don't need . . . " he interrupted.

". . . information or anything from them?" she finished her sentence.

"No, not at all."

"You don't?" she gasped, as though she couldn't believe what she had just heard.

"Nope. It's a, ah, an intoxicated, ah . . . boyfriend of another . . . boyfriend."

"Well, how old is this child?" she demanded incredulously.

"It wasn't a child. It was an adult," he insisted.

"Are you sure?" she asked emphatically.

"Yup."

Mrs. Cleveland wouldn't give up. "Are you positive?" she pressed, pointing out that her daughter had seen the "child" on the streets previously.

"Uh-hmm," he said. "He's ah, he's ah—that's all been taken care of, ma'am."

"Are you sure?" she demanded, beginning to sound anguished.

"Ma'am, I can't make it any more clear," the police officer said, showing signs of exasperation. "It's all taken care of. That's, you know, ah, he's with his boyfriend and, ah, his boyfriend's apartment, where he's got his belongings also . . . "

"But isn't this, I mean, what if he's a child and not an

adult?'' she interrupted. ''I mean, are you positive this is an . . .''

''Ma'am,'' he broke in.

''. . . adult?'' she went on.

''Ma'am!''

''Uh-hmm.''

''Like I explained to ya, it's all taken care of. It's as positive as . . . as I can be.''

''Oh, I see.''

''OK, there's a . . .''

''But . . .''

''Ah, I can't . . .'' She tried to get a word in, but he continued, ''do anything about somebody's sexual preferences in life.''

''Well, no, I'm not saying anything about that, but it appeared to have been a child. This is my concern,'' she explained.

''No, he's not,'' he argued.

''He's not a child?''

''No, he's not. OK?'' Mrs. Cleveland sighed audibly as he went on. ''And that's a boyfriend-boyfriend, ah, thing, and he's got belongings at the house where, ah, he came from. He's got very, ah, nice pictures of himself and his boyfriend and so forth, so . . .''

''Oh, I see,'' she said, glancing at her daughter and niece, who were nodding in agreement as she tried to press her point.

''OK?'' the police officer asked, pushing to bring the conversation to an end. ''OK, well, I'm just, you know, it appeared to have been a child,'' she said. ''That was my concern.''

''I understand,'' he said. ''No, he's not. No!''

That was it. A ''boyfriend-boyfriend'' thing. Just a

domestic squabble between a couple of gays. End of discussion. G'bye, ma'am.

Two and a half miles away, at the Northwest Side home of a Laotian immigrant family in the 2600 block of North 56th Street, Somdy Sinthasomphone could not sleep and her pillow was wet with tears. Her fourteen-year-old son, Konerak, had not come home that night. He had never stayed out so late before, and she was worried half to death.

Somdy and her husband, Somthone, a farmer, had fled their native Laos in 1980 and brought their nine growing children to Milwaukee in search of a better life. Konerak was only three at the time, and it didn't take him long to develop into a typical American boy. He picked up English fast, and was popular among his freshman classmates at Pulaski High School.

Like many of his American friends, the bright-eyed, smiling teen-ager even had a girlfriend.

On Sunday, May 26, he had gone to meet some of his buddies at Mitchell Park for a soccer game. The park was a popular gathering place for boys his age, who played soccer almost daily when weather permitted.

When Konerak didn't show up for the game, one of his friends called his twenty-two-year-old sister, Keisone Phalphouvong. "I have no idea where he might be," she said. "Have you tried his girlfriend's?"

"Yeah. She doesn't know where he is, either. She hasn't seem him."

"Well, I don't know what to tell you," his sister said. "I'll tell him you guys called when he gets home."

But Konerak never came home to the plain white house with the tall sunflower growing in the front yard. His family never saw him again. They spent the entire day

Monday looking for him, calling every one of his friends they could think of, checking his hangouts.

"I don't know where else to look," his sister told her worried parents, who spoke little English. There was only one thing left to do. On Tuesday morning, May 28, Konerak's family reported him missing.

"We've called everywhere," his sister, Keisone, told police. "My brother has never been in trouble and he wouldn't have run away from home. He has never been gone from home."

She gave police a description of the brown-skinned youngster. "When he left home he was wearing blue jean overall shorts and a white T-shirt," she added.

On Thursday, May 30, four days after the youth disappeared, the telephone rang in the Sinthasomphone home. The caller was a man, who spoke in a deep voice. His message was brief and to the point:

"Konerak is in danger right now!" Click! The caller hung up.

His family again called police, and told them of the ominous call. Unless they knew who made the call, police advised them, there was nothing they could do.

The next day Konerak's picture appeared in the *Milwaukee Sentinel,* along with a story saying the youth was missing, and that his family had received a threatening phone call.

When Nicole Childress saw the article, she almost jumped out of her chair. The boy in the newspaper photo was the same person she had seen stagger naked, battered and bleeding from the apartment building next door. It was the same boy police had obligingly given back to Jeff Dahmer after diagnosing the incident as a homosexual lover's spat.

"Aunt Glenda, look at this!" she cried, showing the paper to Mrs. Cleveland.

"Oh, my Lord! That's the little boy," she gasped.

Mrs. Cleveland grabbed the phone and called police. "The boy whose picture's in the *Sentinel*," she told them. "He's the same one who..."

The police officer on the other end of the line listened patiently to her story, thanked her, and said they'd check on it. Mrs. Cleveland, her daughter and her niece waited—and waited. But nobody came by. Two weeks passed. Cleveland called again. Still no one came by.

Had police bothered to make out a report, and routinely run Dahmer's name through the computer on the night Nicole Childress and Sandra Smith called about the boy who had run naked out of his apartment, they would have discovered that two years earlier, Jeffrey Lionel Dahmer was convicted of sexually assaulting Konerak Sinthasomphone's then thirteen-year-old brother.

# CHAPTER 3

---

# BEHIND DEATH'S DOOR

In the wake of the naked boy episode, residents of the integrated neighborhood two miles west of Downtown began to give Jeff Dahmer such a wide berth he might as well have undergone a charisma bypass.

"When you walk down this street, every day you see people who are a little off," one block member explained. "You become accustomed to a little weirdness in this neighborhood."

Others, like Pat Laur, didn't bother to call the police any more when things happened. "It used to be if we heard shots or a scream at night we were all ears and looking outside to see how it was," she remarked. "And now if we hear a scream, we really don't kind of hear it. It can be kids screaming around, or it can be people screaming around. It can be any number of things happening—but we don't hear it."

Folks might have been able to turn off their ears, but they couldn't plug up their noses. There was still that God-awful smell hanging like a huge net around the building at 924 North 25th Street that was enough to gag a maggot.

People who lived in the Oxford Apartments wrinkled their noses as they pulled their stoves and refrigerators away from the wall, looking for dead rats or mice, or maybe even an urban possum that had gotten caught behind something and died.

It was so powerful on certain days that some people had incense burning in their apartments, around the clock, to mask the awful stench. Eventually they all agreed that the smell was strongest when they passed apartment No. 213. Jeff Dahmer's apartment.

The smooth-talking Dahmer worked for the Ambrosia Chocolate Company, down near the river on North Fifth Street—but it definitely wasn't samples from his job that people smelled.

"This is getting worse than bad. Somebody's gotta say something," Vernell Bass told his wife, Pamela, as they sat down over a breakfast they could hardly enjoy. "I swear, it smells like somethin's dead in there."

"I'll talk to him," his wife said. "It's getting so bad a person can't sleep at night."

Dahmer had earlier told a neighbor that his fish had died. The next time she passed Dahmer in the hall Pamela Bass stopped him and said right out, "Jeff, something in your house is really stinking."

"Yeah, I know," he said, flashing a quick smile. "It's rotten meat. My refrigerator's gone out."

"Well, you ought to do something about it," she said curtly. "I don't see how you can stand it."

"I'll take care of it, Pam," he promised. "Soon as I

get home from work. I gotta run now, or I'll miss my bus.'' Like many who lived in the low rent neighborhood, Dahmer did not have his own wheels.

For a time after that, it seemed, the putrid aroma was less permeating. But there were other things that made people aware that Jeffrey Lionel Dahmer was existing in their midst.

Aaron Whitehead, who had the apartment directly below, would be awakened in the middle of the night by loud pounding and scuffling noises overhead.

"One night," he confided to a neighbor, "I heard what sounded like a kid up there. He was crying like his mother had just walloped him. Then I heard a big falling sound—just like he was being hurt, or something."

"He's a strange one, all right," the other tenant agreed. "I swear I heard sawing goin' on up there the other night. One o' them electric power saws. He must be building something, but I swear, how's he expect people to sleep?''

Whatever Dahmer was doing, he had no fear of interference. Ever since that night when the police officers took his word over that of the two young black women, his neighbors had kept a respectable distance. The repugnant smell coming from his rooms helped, of course. Nobody really had the stomach to get too close to the guy.

Then, on Monday night, the twenty-second of July, as Police Officers Robert Rauth and Rolf Mueller were driving through the neighborhood on routine patrol, all of the nightmares of holy hell broke loose.

# CHAPTER 4

---

# DAY I
# JULY 22

Officers Mueller and Rauth were cruising along the 2500 block of West Kilbourn Avenue shortly before midnight, with the car windows rolled down because of the heat, when they spotted a black man tearing down the street like Beelzebub himself was chewing on his tail. Swinging wildly like a pendulum as his arms flailed the air was a pair of handcuffs, clamped firmly around one of his wrists.

Suspecting he might be fleeing the law, Mueller and Rauth tried to head him off, but the minute he caught sight of the squad car he stopped running and went right up to them.

"What's shaking, Bro?"

"Hey, man, I ain't never been so glad to see the police in my whole life," he panted, holding up his arm as he spoke. "Can you get this thing off me?"

"That all depends. How the hell did it get on there in the first place?"

"See that building over there?" he said, pointing to the apartment in the middle of the block on the east side of 25th Street. "There's this white dude in apartment number 213, he's got a big-assed knife stashed under his bed. He said he was goin' to cut my heart out."

"All right, calm down. Nobody's going to cut your heart out. What's your name?"

"Edwards. Tracy Edwards."

"You live in that building over there?"

"No. I just moved up here from Mississippi four-five weeks ago. I live in the 1500 block of Kilbourn."

"That where you were heading when we stopped you?"

"You got that right!"

"All right, Tracy. Give us this again. One more time —how you got that handcuff on your wrist. From the beginning, if you don't mind."

"OK. My friend, Jeffrey Stevens, and me, we were walking around the Grand Avenue Mall downtown, when we ran into this white dude, says his name is Jeff."

"Tonight?"

"Yeh, that's right. A couple of hours ago. He invites us over to his apartment for a party."

"Just like that?"

"Yeh. But, you know, we both seen him around before, at the mall and walkin' through the neighborhood here. He seemed like a normal person. If I had any self-doubt I wouldn't have went."

"What happened to your friend?"

"He went down to the lakefront to find our girlfriends and they was gonna meet us there. This Jeff said his girlfriend would be at the apartment, but I found out later he gave my friend a wrong address. He and I took a taxi. When we got inside his apartment, he made me his prisoner."

"He the one who put the handcuff on you?"

"That's right. He acted like he didn't want anyone to leave him. First he starts praising me, then he's threatening me, on and off for four hours. It was like I was confronting Satan himself. The guy just changed from Mr. Right to Mr. It. It was a four hour period of hell, exactly."

The thirty-two-year-old Edwards started to sob as he relived the experience. On first entering the apartment he didn't notice anything unusual, save for the sickening smell.

"The minute we got in there I wanted to leave, because the apartment stank," he said. "But he gave me a can of Budweiser, then a rum and Coke. I figure it had a knockout drug in it, because he kept asking me if I was high yet. I noticed there were photos of men, some naked, others dead, on the walls. He also had an aquarium with fish that attacked each other. He had me watching the aquarium, and suddenly he attacked me and put the handcuff on me.

Brushing a tear from his cheek he continued.

"He threatened me, and made advances. Suddenly he had this big knife in his hand and pressed the blade on my breastbone, right here, by my heart. He said, 'You die if you don't do what I say.' His face was completely changed. I wouldn't have recognized him. It was like he was the devil himself."

Edwards said the man forced him into the bedroom, where he made him watch the movie, *The Exorcist*, which was playing in the background.

"He said I should watch the film. It was his favorite

film. But I could only see the pictures on the walls. Naked men. Completely mutilated, horrible.''

''All this happened in that apartment over there?'' Mueller interrupted.

''This is kind of heavy stuff you're giving us.''

''It's true, man,'' Edwards insisted. ''The pictures, naked men, some looked like they were completely eaten up by acid. And there's a huge barrel that stank worse than everything else in the apartment.''

''Did he have the handcuffs on both your wrists?''

''No, I'm not dumb,'' Edwards said, holding up his free arm.

''So you're telling us you managed to get away. Is that it?''

''He said he would cut my heart out and eat it; but first he wanted to photograph me, because my body was so beautiful. When he turned his head for a moment, I hit him in the face with my free hand, kicked him in the stomach and ran out.''

''Which is when we came along,'' Rauth noted.

Edwards nodded. ''Will you please take this thing off me now?''

Rauth and Mueller removed the handcuff, but made it quite clear that they suspected him of overtaxing his imagination.

''I'll tell you what we're gonna do, Tracy. We're gonna go over to the man's house and see for ourselves.''

''You'll find it just like I said,'' he insisted. ''Apartment number 213.''

The two policemen swung their squad around the corner and pulled up in front of 924 North 25th Street. The four-story Oxford Apartments building looked almost like a branch post office, or even a district police station, with its solid yellow brick facade, trimmed hedges, and the American flag flying proudly from a stout metal pole on the well manicured lawn.

They climbed two flights of stairs, and found themselves standing in front of a wooden door bearing the numbers 2-1-3. "The guy's right about one thing. It sure as shit stinks in here," Mueller said, as he gave it a knock.

A blond haired man in his early thirties opened the door and looked at them curiously.

"Are you Jeff?"

"Yes, I am. Is anything the matter?"

"I'm Officer Mueller and this is Officer Rauth. Do you mind if we come in?"

Dahmer, who was sucking on a can of beer, stepped aside and permitted them to enter. They explained that there had been a complaint, and they wanted to look around. He gave his permission. It was almost as if he had a death wish.

It was basically a two-room apartment. On entering, the officers found themselves standing in a combination living room-dining area, with a refrigerator, stove and sink taking up the entire wall nearest the door. To their right was the bedroom and bath.

Rauth looked under the bed and found the knife, right where Edwards said it would be. Checking the dresser, he found one of the drawers crammed with photographs of mutilated dead bodies, photos of various body parts, and graphic photographs of homosexual acts. This was enough to give the two policemen probable cause to go over the rest of the small apartment.

Mueller opened the refrigerator on the apartment's south wall and stepped back in disbelief. On the bottom shelf, next to an open container of baking soda, was a severed human head.

This was no routine assault and battery complaint.

The two officers put the cuffs on Dahmer and radioed for reinforcements.

Edwards, the lucky one who got away, was still standing outside when other police squads began to pull up, with their emergency lights flashing.

''God sent me to get this guy,'' he said.

# CHAPTER 5

---

# DAY II
# JULY 23

It was over. Whatever horrible, grim, dark, ghoulish secrets Jeffrey Dahmer harbored deep within his soul and kept locked behind his apartment door were about to be hung out for all the world to gag at.

Within minutes the 25th Street apartment was crawling with cops. A quick look-around revealed human body parts hidden in boxes, closets, drawers and coolers, and a fifty-seven-gallon blue plastic drum filled with what appeared to be formaldehyde, in which three headless torsos were marinating.

While the apartment was messy, it was not what one would call dirty. Dahmer just hadn't bothered to pick up after himself. Looking around, police noted a video camera mounted high on the wall in one corner of the living room, aimed at the entry way. Beneath it a lava lamp went through its changing forms on a table. A large, four-foot-wide aquarium filled with fish was on one side of the window, and on the other side the wall was adorned with a large black and white print of a well-built, bare chested male athlete, wearing nothing but a sheet hung loosely from his hip, and an abstract painting, mostly in reds, blues and greens, that Dahmer said portrayed Lucifer. On the east wall was a sofa with a bleach container and some electric tools on the floor in front of it. Nearby was a can of Lysol disinfectant.

The door to Dahmer's bedroom was protected by several deadbolt locks. Curiously, the locks were on the *outside* of the door, indicating they could have been used to imprison anyone in the bedroom with no means of escape.

Four boxes, each containing four one-gallon bottles of muriatic acid, were on the floor by the sink and refrigerator. On the freezer police found Polaroid photos of men's bodies in various stages of mutilation. Inside the freezer were several large sacks secured with garbage bag ties. Police undid the ties and found two more severed heads.

"Jesus, that makes three," Mueller noted. The place was a veritable morgue.

Elsewhere in the apartment they found unfilled prescriptions for Doxepin, an anti-depressant, and Lorazepam, an anti-anxiety medication.

There was only one closet in the tiny apartment but it, too, turned out to be a regular pathology lab. Tucked into a far corner was an iron soup kettle containing decomposed hands, and a set of male genitals. There were also several bottles of ethyl alcohol, chloroform and formaldehyde, and on the closet shelf above the kettle—two human skulls. That brought the body count or bodyless count, to be more specific—to five.

Police picking through Dahmer's bedroom were also having a field day. His dresser drawer was a treasure trove of photographs of men in various stages of nudity. Some had unknowingly posed for photographs after death—after their arms and legs had been neatly sawed off. On the wall over Dahmer's bed were several pictures of naked men. His Polaroid camera was on the bed, ready for instant action. Under the bed, where the knife had been found, was a discarded beer can.

And, oh, there was more. There was a computer box, but it no longer contained a computer. When police opened it they discovered a photo diary of death plus two more skulls.

"Let's see. The head in the refrigerator, and two in the freezer, plus two skulls in the closet, and these two make seven," Rauth remarked. "And still counting," Mueller added. "You think you've seen it all, working this neighborhood here, and then something like this comes along."

"How long you been a cop?" Rauth asked.

"Ten years," Mueller said. "This makes me wonder if I want to go for eleven."

He pulled open the top drawer of a filing cabinet. It contained two more skulls. The bottom drawer harbored an assortment of human bones.

"Before we get through here, I'll bet my star that we're going to clean up a lot of missing-person cases," Detective Lieutenant Roosevelt Harrell surmised. "The guys have already turned up some ID cards and other papers."

"You ever see anything like this before, lieutenant?" a patrolman asked, wrinkling his nose in a futile attempt to block out the odor.

"I've seen multiple deaths before, yeah—but this is definitely one of the most bizarre cases I've ever been in on. In fact, it could turn into the most gruesome case in the city's history."

Through the night and into the day police worked. A hazardous waste team was brought in to remove the barrel of torsos, on the assumption that the liquid was some type of acid, and the boxes of God knows how many mortal remains. Wearing bright yellow rubber suits and air masks, the disposal team removed some ten boxes of gore from the apartment. They also taped the door shut and carried out the refrigerator, which had served as a cold-storage mausoleum for human heads.

Why Dahmer had kept the heads preserved in the cooler was beyond comprehension. Unless he used them for homosexual purposes, as several of the cops crudely suggested.

After the hazardous materials team had removed the items, detectives wearing rubber gloves continued to comb the apartment, wondering what they might discover next. The hazardous materials guys wore air masks— lucky bastards.

Neighborhood residents, who stood by with their arms folded, watching police cart away the macabre evidence from the dormitory of death, were dumbstruck. Dahmer was somewhat of an outsider, being the only white resident of the building, but he never gave the other tenants any trouble.

"He seemed normal," noted thirty-eight-year-old Pamela Bass, who lived right across the hall from him. She was the one who eventually complained to him about the odor, and he said his refrigerator had broken down. "A nice white boy. He'd come over for coffee and sit at the kitchen table and talk sports with Vernell."

"Yeah, I've known the guy for a year and a half now," mused her thirty-six-year-old husband, Vernell. "I used to go in his apartment on occasion, and I always noticed the stench in there. I saw that big barrel in there, too, and I asked him, 'How'd you ever get that big thing home on the bus?' 'cause I knew he didn't drive. He never give me an answer.''

"Sometimes you could hear sawing noises coming from up there at all hours of the day and night," added Larry Marion, the building manager. "But I never thought anything of it. Except for the smell that people complained about, he never caused no problems. He always paid his rent on time, and he never turned his stereo up too loud."

"I know," Bass agreed. "The wife and I heard the sawing, too. I asked her, 'What the hell is he building up there?' I figured maybe it was a bookcase or something. God, I can't believe this."

"Believe it," said Aaron Whitehead, whose bedroom was directly below Dahmer's. "You wouldn't believe some of the stuff I heard going on up there. Last Thursday, and again Sunday morning, around 1 or 2 a.m., when the bars closed, I heard wrestling noises and bodies hitting the floor. I got out of my bed because I thought they'd come right through the ceiling. I went in the dining room and sat down. It didn't last more than ten minutes. Then it was all quiet up there."

Whitehead heard the noises again Monday night, when Edwards made his life-saving break for freedom. "I heard someone running down the hall and I thought, 'What's going on?' Now I know it was that guy getting away.'' "Hey, I saw that guy come flying out of the building with one handcuff on," said next door neighbor Earl Peterson, joining the conversation. "He was hollering 'Help!' He flagged down the police and brought them back to the building."

Around the backside of the apartment neighbors called police attention to an unpleasant stench surrounding the garbage dumpster in the cobblestone alley. A police officer poked around in the mess with a stick, and turned up a brown piece of bone clinging to a watermelon rind.

"Looks like a chicken bone," someone surmised. But a television newsman declared knowingly, "That is a human shoulder bone."

Several people began to pick up bones scattered all over the lot behind the building. When one resident showed a bone to a police officer, the cop said, "Throw it away! They're everywhere." By the next day neighbors had formed three large piles of bones outside the Oxford Apartments building. Two cops wearing plastic gloves picked them up and took them to the Medical Examiner's office.

In addition to the curiosity seekers and sightseers, there were those with harried looks on their faces, mingling with the crowd. Mildred Lindsey and her two sons, Michael, twenty-five, and Reginald, twenty-two, were tearfully showing family photos and passing out flyers.

"Has anyone seen my son around this building?" she asked, displaying a picture of nineteen-year-old Errol Lindsey. "We live just two blocks from here. Errol went out to have a key made at the shop on 27th Street on the night of April 7, and he never came home. He would have walked right by here on the way. It's like he just vanished from the world."

Her son, Michael, added, "We've been looking for a clue or a sign. When I heard about this, this was a heart stopper. I just got a bad feeling about it."

A uniformed police officer was assigned full time to

record information about missing persons from people outside the building.

By 4:30 Tuesday afternoon, police had carted away virtually everything from the apartment, including pots and pans, the refrigerator and the stove.

Milwaukee County Medical Examiner Jeffrey M. Jentzen, who examined the human relics before they were removed, said five of the skulls were matched up with skeletons, while various boxes contained assorted parts of six others bodies, "all in various stages of deterioration." None of the body parts had belonged to Caucasians. All were from black males, or possibly Hispanics or Asians. "Our office will be using fingerprints, visual identification, such as scars, tattoos or other distinguishing marks, dental records, X-rays and DNA testing to identify them," he said.

Once police had finished their grim work in Dahmer's apartment, the yellow "Police Line—Do Not Cross" tape that blocked public access to the murder scene was taken down and all hell broke loose. As many as a hundred frenzied spectators surged into the building, and wandered up and down the halls in hopes of seeing where it all happened. They yanked the back door leading to Dahmer's floor clear off the hinges. The door to Dahmer's apartment was sealed shut with tape, but that did not keep the curious from gathering in the corridor and staring at it, so at some future date they could brag, "I was there."

"This is history!" one of them bubbled excitedly.

Dahmer, by now, had been taken to police headquarters where he almost relished being the center of attention. Now that the game was up, he seemed only too relieved to get the whole thing off his chest. He told police that he had killed as many as seventeen young men, in Ohio, at his grandmother's home in West Allis, and in the house of horrors on 25th Street. Police Lieutenant David Kane listened in astonishment as the soft-spoken serial killer described how he drugged and strangled his victims, then dismembered them, and boiled some of their skulls for safekeeping.

"How did you come to know these fellows?" he was asked.

"I would meet them in taverns or shopping malls, and bring them to my apartment to be photographed," he related. He went on to explain that he "usually strangled" them after having drugged them. Then he would sever their heads, and get out his saw and take off their arms and legs. He often boiled the heads in a pot on the stove in order to remove the flesh, so he could retain the skulls.

"I took Polaroid photographs of a number of them while they were still alive, then after I had killed them, and pictures of their heads and body parts after I had dismembered them," he added.

Moreover, in addition to preserving some of the dead men's body parts to enhance his apartment's decor, he claimed to have engaged in cannibalism. Dahmer had cut one man's heart out, and was preparing it for dinner at the time of his arrest, he told police. Earlier, he said, he had cooked and eaten another man's biceps.

Had he actually lived off his victims? The only food police found in the apartment was several cans of beer, some potato chips, and a jar of mustard.

"I never did see him bring any food home," Pamela Bass told investigators. "I live right across the hall, and I guess I knew him as well as anybody."

Once the bizarre story was flashed out over the wires, police began getting calls from around the world. Deputy Inspector Vincent M. Partipilo had his hands full fielding calls from England, France, Germany and Australia, and there was very little information at that point that he could divulge.

He was also being swamped with calls from law enforcement agencies across the country hoping to match missing person descriptions with the grisly assortment of body parts found in Dahmer's apartment. "We have just been inundated with calls. I think anyone who has had a missing person in the last two years has called," Partipilo asserted.

"At this point we're not certain where the murders were committed, or how many there actually were," Police Chief Philip Arreola announced to a fast-growing contingent of newspaper, radio and television reporters. "We don't know if anyone else was in on this, or if the individual worked by himself."

Meanwhile police were busy familiarizing themselves with the man they had in custody.

A former resident of Medina, Ohio, Jeffrey Lionel Dahmer was named after his father, Lionel H. Dahmer. He had come to Milwaukee after serving with the Army Medical Corps in Germany from 1979 to 1981. The Army kicked him out because of alcoholism. After coming to Milwaukee he took a job as a laborer at the Ambrosia Chocolate Company. He was fired on July 15 for excessive absenteeism.

Dahmer also had a prior arrest record. He'd been cited for indecent exposure at the Wisconsin State Fair in West Allis on August 8, 1982, for urinating in front of a group of children. Four years later, on September 8, 1986, he was arrested for lewd and lascivious behavior. The charge was reduced to disorderly conduct, and he was sentenced to one year's probation.

There was one other incident that police knew about.

In 1988 an Illinois man named Ronald D. Flowers filed a theft report with West Allis police. The twenty-five-year-old Flowers told authorities that he met Dahmer in a gay bar on Milwaukee's Southwest Side. He said the two of them went to the home of Dahmer's grandmother, where Dahmer lived at the time. Flowers claimed to have been drugged, and said that when he awoke in a Wauwatosa hospital the money from his wallet and his gold bracelet were missing.

Police questioned Dahmer, who told them that he and Flowers had gotten so drunk after arriving at his grandmother's that they both passed out. The next morning, Dahmer claimed, Flowers was still under the weather, so he walked him to a bus stop and gave him $1. It was one man's word against another, and there was a witness who claimed to have seen Dahmer walking Flowers to the bus, so no charges were ever filed in the matter.

But it was the attack on Konerak Sinthasomphone's brother, who was thirteen at the time, that should have signalled authorities that here was a man who bore watching. According to court records, Dahmer had given the Laotian youngster $50 to pose for a picture in his apartment. Once he got the boy inside, he drugged him with spiked coffee, photographed him posing on his bed, and fondled him.

Dahmer pled guilty to second degree sexual assault and enticement of a child for immoral purposes, and was sentenced to eight years in prison.

But he never went. The sentence was stayed and he was placed on five years' probation. He served one year in the House of Correction's work release program, before being released in March of 1990.

The terms of Dahmer's probation required that his

probation worker meet with him twice a month in his home, but that never happened either. Her superior excused the worker from making the home visits because of her large caseload, plus she didn't like the neighborhood. Had the probation officer visited Dahmer's home as required, she surely would have become suspicious at the obnoxious odor, and things might have come to a far different conclusion.

"This incident is a damning indictment of the judicial system," Chief Arreola asserted on learning that the probation officer had been given a pass. "Here we see the dramatic and tragic results."

At the time of his arrest, Dahmer's father in Medina, Ohio, wrote a letter to Judge William D. Gardner asking that his son be ordered to attend an alcohol treatment program upon his release. "I have tremendous reservations about Jeff's chances when he hits the streets," the father said.

Judge Gardner also received a missive from Jeff himself, pleading for leniency. The letter was dated December 10, 1989.

"Sir, I have always believed that a man should be willing to assume responsibility for the mistakes that he makes in life. That is why I entered a plea of 'guilty'. . ." he wrote. "During my stay [in jail], I have had a chance to look at my life from an angle that was never presented to me before. What I did was deplorable. The world has enough misery in it without my adding more to it. Sir, I can assure you that it will never happen again."

It never did happen again—quite that way. Until Tracy Edwards made his miraculous break to freedom, none of Dahmer's other victims lived to tell about it.

They ended up in bits and pieces in his refrigerator or in buckets. Or perhaps in their host's stomach.

Incredibly, while television viewers from coast to coast were getting a look at the clean cut serial killer on their evening newscasts, most people in Milwaukee and the surrounding suburbs had no idea what Dahmer looked like. The two major newspapers and the city's television stations had agreed not to use Dahmer's picture, at the request of police, because authorities feared showing the photo might jeopardize police lineups. When Dahmer's face appeared on network news shows broadcast in Milwaukee, the local stations blurred it out.

Meanwhile reporters from Chicago, New York, Minneapolis, Madison and other cities were converging on Milwaukee to lend eye-witness coverage to the mushrooming story, while the two papers took calls from newspapers in London, Liverpool, Paris and other European population centers, hungry for the latest tidbits.

Attorney Gerald P. Boyle, hired by Dahmer's stunned father to represent his son, encouraged him to cooperate with police in the ongoing investigation.

"There are a couple of things Jeffrey has told me to say today," Boyle told a mob of reporters clamoring for news. "He wants to continue to talk to the authorities, to assist the authorities in identifying the victims. And he said, quote, he has no one to blame but himself, not the police, not the courts and not the probation department. He said 'There comes a time when you have to be honest and this is the time.'"

As far as the media was concerned, Boyle was a breath of fresh air. Unlike some lawyers who demonstrate an inborn ability to be arrogant, pompous, surly and insufferable all at the same time, he appeared to be quite open with the police and the press. The cat was out of the bag. Why try to be cute?

With the grim discovery in Milwaukee, Chicago police ran a routine check on Dahmer, to see whether he might have been involved in any homicides there. They were satisfied that he was not, although they determined that he had been a recent visitor to the city. On June 30, as a matter of fact, he reported to Chicago police that he'd lost his wallet on Belmont Avenue.

With the knowledge that Dahmer had been in their community, Chicago homicide detectives started checking missing person reports, in an effort to determine whether any of them might have ended up in Dahmer's refrigerator or on his shelf.

For Belmont Area Violent Crimes Lieutenant Richard Stevens, twenty-three-year-old Jeremiah ''Jeremy'' Weinberger was a distinct possibility. Weinberger, who lived with his father above a North Halsted Street cafe, had been reported missing July 6.

He was last seen late the previous evening leaving Carol's Speakeasy in the Old Town area of North Wells Street with a tall, slender, blond-haired man wearing a gold T-shirt, green plaid shorts and loafers. His father, David, reported him missing when he failed to report to his job at the Bijou Theater the next morning.

A former roommate, Ted Jones, who worked with Weinberger at distributing gay and lesbian adult videos, told police he had been at the Speakeasy when Jeremy left with the stranger.

''Jeremy said the man wanted him to drive to Milwaukee with him for the weekend,'' he related. ''He came up to me and said, 'Well, should I go with this guy?' I said, 'Well, let me see what he looks like.' And then when I met the guy he seemed, like, all right, but who's to say what a killer looks like?''

Young Weinberger's friends spent the next two weeks searching for him, and circulating flyers containing his picture. They even sat down with a police artist, who drew a composite sketch of the man they had seen him leaving the Speakeasy with.

While Dahmer's picture was obliterated from the television screen in Milwaukee, Weinberger's friends had seen it on the evening newscasts in Chicago and contacted police. He looked a lot like the guy they had last seen with Jeremiah.

Based on that information, Lieutenant Stevens forwarded a photo and physical description of the missing man to Milwaukee police. "If it turns out that he's one of the bodies, we'll be up there to assist," Stevens said. "Right now we're just waiting for word, some information that would tie this together."

Others were waiting for word, as well. Tony Hughes, a black, thirty-one-year-old deaf mute, was last seen May 24, leaving Club 219, a South Side Milwaukee bistro popular among homosexuals, in the company of a tall white man with glasses. Hughes, who communicated by reading lips or writing notes, had lived at 13th and State streets—in Dahmer's part of town—before moving to Madison eleven months earlier. He was home visiting his family on the night he disappeared.

When he did not come home his concerned mother, Shirley Hughes, talked to friends who had been with him at Club 219. Ever since then she had been carrying a piece of paper in her purse, on which she had scrawled a description of the man seen walking out with her son: "White male, wearing glasses, between 30 and 40 years old, hair less than shoulder length, slightly balding."

"I know my son would not be away this long without calling," she told police.

There was also grave concern in the Northwest Side home of the onetime Laotian farmer, Somthone Sinthasomphone and his wife, Somdy. One of their sons, now sixteen, had once been one of Jeffrey Dahmer's victims, and they were shocked that he had been let out on the street so soon afterward.

And now they were worried sick over fourteen-year-old Konerak, who had not been heard from since May 26, when he headed for Mitchell Park to play soccer. Members of the family sat with their eyes riveted to their television set, hoping for the best, fearing the worst.

Jeffrey Dahmer and the ghastly going's on in his apartment were also the overwhelming topic of conversation in Milwaukee's gay bars Tuesday night. Some gays were making sick jokes, like it used to be that casual sex with a stranger could lead to AIDS, but now you could lose your head. Only they weren't laughing when they said it.

"We've got a lot of people who've talked about it around here, and they're scared," the bartender at C'est La Vie told police who brought around mug shots of Dahmer, asking whether anyone had seen him hanging about the place recently.

"We've had two other kids that have been missing. One of those is Steve. I don't know his last name," John Clayton, C'est La Vie's owner, interjected. "And another one is—I don't know his name—they call him the Sheik. The tall, thin black fellow who always wore a turban."

Taped to the wall at the 219 Club, where Tony Hughes was last seen leaving with a blond stranger, was a flyer bearing the photo of Jeremiah "Jeremy" Weinberger, the missing twenty-three-year-old from Chicago. His friends had even come to Milwaukee looking for him.

While police went about their work downtown, and an exhausted Dahmer turned in for the night in his lonesome cell, crowds continued to gather outside the building where it all happened. Those who had been there all the live-long day were joined by curiosity seekers who had spent endless hours at work talking about it, and had to drive by and get a look for themselves.

By 10 p.m. the neighborhood had become so congested with traffic that police set up barricades at each end of the block, closing 25th Street between State and Kilbourn to all motor vehicles.

"I think it's awful," observed Don Clark, one of Dahmer's neighbors, in assessing the situation. "This man lived among us—regular people."

Glenda Cleveland, the concerned neighbor who could not convince authorities that something was wrong when the naked Laotian boy ran bleeding from Dahmer's apartment, could not resist calling police one more time Tuesday.

After identifying herself she asked forcefully, "Now are you going to come out here?"

# CHAPTER 6

---

# DAY III
# JULY 24

The first of Jeff Dahmer's eleven known victims was identified Wednesday. He was twenty-three-year-old Oliver Lacy, a former track star from the Chicago suburb of Oak Park. Lacy was last seen July 12, in Milwaukee's trendy Grand Avenue Mall, where he had stopped to buy some ice cream for his mother.

Catherine Lacy identified her son after examining his wallet, which turned up in Dahmer's apartment, and viewing two photographs of Oliver's severed head.

The identification put to an end to widespread speculation that the string of bizarre homicides were homosexual in nature. Although Dahmer might have been, not all of his victims were. Oliver Lacy was all boy. He had left the Chicago area four months earlier to be with his fiancee, Rose Colon, and their infant son, Emmanuel, who were living with his mother in Milwaukee.

As a track star at Oak Park-River Forest High School, he could run the 100 meter dash in ten and a half seconds, and helped his team bring home the state championship in 1987. After graduating from high school he was offered a track scholarship to Texas A & M, but his grades were not high enough to get him into the university.

A handsome young man who showed qualities of becoming a model, Lacy had been working as a custodian downtown for Pioneer Commercial Cleaning Inc., since moving to Milwaukee. He had stopped off at the shopping mall after work on Friday to pick up the ice cream for his mother, but never came home.

"When he wasn't home Saturday, I felt something was wrong because my son would always call me," his recently-widowed mother told police when she reported him missing that same day. Since then she had telephoned police headquarters every day to inquire as to whether there was any word on Oliver.

How Lacy ended up in Dahmer's apartment was anybody's guess, but Dahmer was known to have offered handsome young males $50 or more to pose for his camera. Perhaps Lacy thought it might lead to a modeling career.

Like other mothers whose sons had failed to come home, Mrs. Lacy had feared the worst. She was there in the crowd of curiosity seekers outside the apartment building on 25th Street as police carried out the grim results of Dahmer's handiwork the previous day.

"I somehow hoped my son was the one that got away," she said. "I went there hoping I might see the apartment, maybe find my son's clothing, or the two necklaces he wore. I felt something hit me real hard when I got to that building. I got like...my heart pounded in my chest."

On Wednesday morning the persistent Mrs. Lacy went down to the medical examiner's office, where items removed from the murder apartment had been taken to be inventoried. Sure enough, among Jeff Dahmer's keepsakes was her son's wallet and identification cards. After she identified the billfold she asked to see Oliver's body, but police told her that would be impossible. Upon finding his wallet, police had confirmed Oliver's identification through fingerprints. His body had been preserved in Dahmer's freezer. Police had some pictures, but they warned Mrs. Lacy that he'd been decapitated and his body had been dismembered. Nevertheless, she insisted on seeing the grisly evidence with her own eyes.

"I need to find out. I want to see for myself," she said. "I'll never rest until I know for sure."

She stared at the lurid photographs and sighed, "Yes, that's Birdie. That's my baby."

Did she have any idea how he ended up in Dahmer's house of death? "I don't know how this person lured my son," she wept. "He wasn't the type of person who would let someone put their hands on him. He didn't use drugs, and wasn't a homosexual. He had lots of girlfriends in high school."

He was also a wild kid during his freshman year, confident that his athletic prowess would get him through —the hell with homework. He was wrong, and at the end of the semester he was bounced off the track team. "You think the eligibility rule doesn't apply to you. Now you're finding out the hard way," his coach, Glenn Cothern, sadly told him.

That's when Oliver Lacy showed what he was made of. It wasn't easy, making up for lost time, but he buckled down during his sophomore and junior years and got his grades back up to the point where he was again eligible for the track team as he went into his senior year. "Are you sure your grades are going to allow you?" Cothern asked when Lacy showed up at the fieldhouse. "Coach, my grades are fine," Lacy told him. "I want to run."

When he couldn't get into Texas A & M after graduation, Lacy enrolled in a junior college in Chicago, and got a job working in a Loop clothing store. From time to time he stopped by the old high school to watch the younger guys run, and to talk with the coach. When he dropped by earlier in the year, before moving to Milwaukee, Cothern asked him to talk to some of the boys on the track team who were having attitude problems. Lacy did. He told them to get their acts together or they might miss their big chance in life, like he did.

"Oliver was a concerned person. He was a kind, nice person. He was understanding," his mother wept, after viewing the photos of his severed head.

Sadly, she returned to the yellow duplex with green trim that she had shared with her son, his twenty-three-year-old fiancee, and their two-year-old son. When Rose Colon learned that Oliver had been cut to pieces she went into shock, and had to be taken by ambulance to the Milwaukee County Medical Complex in Wauwatosa.

Once identification had been confirmed reporters started gathering in Catherine Lacy's yard, and piling into her small living room. Dozens of them, from all over, it seemed. Strobe lights flashed and the bright glare of television lights drove the shadows from every corner of the room.

"What about it, Mrs. Lacy? What can you tell us about your son?"

"He just wanted to get married—to have a home of his own," she wept.

Bail for Jeffrey Dahmer was set at $1 million cash

Wednesday, as police pressed their investigation into his troubled life. "We're not investigating a whodunit. This individual is in custody," Police Chief Arreola told the nagging press. "We're investigating why it was done, and to determine the extent of how it was done."

Arreola was lavish in his praise for Officers Rolf Mueller and Robert Rauth for their curiosity and thoroughness in following through on Monday night's incident of the would-be victim with handcuffs dangling from his arm. Had they simply unlocked the cuffs and set Tracy Edwards on his way, Dahmer would still be sitting safe at home contemplating his collection of human heads and bones.

The police chief did not rule out the possibility that more dismembered bodies might be found at other locations. Police set up a hot line, asking anyone with information about Dahmer's possible victims to contact them at 935-7379.

At the same time, Chicago detectives made the 100-mile drive to Milwaukee to hand over copies of reports on missing persons who could have been among the victims. Rumors that a serial killer was stalking gay nightclubs in Milwaukee and Chicago had been making the rounds for nearly a month. Chicago has approximately seventy-six gay bars, as opposed to only eight in Milwaukee, which would have made the Windy City a more productive hunting ground.

District Attorney E. Michael McCann, who vowed to prosecute Dahmer personally, said, "We're looking at at least eleven homicide counts."

Over at 924 North 25th Street the hoards of rubber-neckers from the previous day had dwindled considerably. Onlookers would pause in front of the building, stare awhile, and then move on, only to be replaced by a steady stream of newcomers. Late-arriving out-of-town news reporters were still driving by to get a look at the place where it all began, and Cable News Network led off its hourly reports with footage of what a local television station was hailing as "The Milwaukee Massacre."

One of Dahmer's neighbors, who had given dozens of interviews Tuesday afternoon, was feeling an attack of exasperation as reporters kept badgering her about the telltale odors.

"What about the stench of death? What did it smell like?" one Chicago newshawk persisted.

"It stunk," she said.

"How would you describe the stink?" the reporter pressed.

"You know how something smells when it stinks?" she asked. "That's how it smelled!"

Another of Dahmer's neighbors, Pamela Bass, had spent a fitful night, tossing restlessly in her bed. "What's the matter? Can't you sleep?" her husband asked.

"With the house all dark, I keep seeing him sitting at my table," she said.

"Maybe we ought to find another place to live," he suggested.

"He's gone," she said. "He can't hurt us now."

Once the building came to life with the light of day, however, she found some of the other tenants already packing their belongings. "After something like this happens, forget it," said Darrell Elliot, as he tossed his possessions into the back of a friend's car.

Another neighbor, Greg Filardo, who lived around the corner on Kilbourn Avenue, called the neighborhood "the armpit of hell." He'd been there fifteen years, and he'd had it. "If I could sell this house, I'd be out of here in a minute," he declared.

Meanwhile twenty-year-old Douglas Jackson, who lived downstairs from Dahmer, was counting his blessings. A week earlier Dahmer had invited him up for a beer, but he begged off after his girlfriend told him, "You're crazy to go into somebody's apartment you don't even know, especially that white guy's."

The white guy had been acting kind of weird, come to think of it.

"I'd always see him drinking a beer and standing near the trash container in the back yard," Jackson said. "And there'd be all these cats around him. I don't mean a couple, I mean a lot of cats, following him all over the place. And the guy didn't just go into his apartment, like most people open the door and go in. He squeezed in. He'd open the door just the littlest bit and squeeze through. He did that a lot.

"If I'd gone up there when he invited me, I'd be in one of those boxes they carried out of here yesterday."

Out on the street an undercover narcotics cop was gassing with a uniformed beatman. "You know, in a really sick way, it's kind of good that the neighborhood has heard about this. Down here, life is cheap. Hookers and drug dealers work the streets and there are drug houses everywhere. People get shot, and hardly anyone notices, even if it's in their apartment hallway. Maybe life won't seem so cheap after this. Well, maybe at least not for a few weeks."

Dahmer's father flew in from Ohio Wednesday to express his anguish for the families of the still unknown victims, and to tell his son that somebody still cared for him. Jeff's parents were divorced, and his father had remarried. He had not lived with his father for more than a dozen years, but the elder Dahmer had continued to be supportive of him.

"Jeff is hurting, and he's sorry, and he feels very bad that what has happened to him happened," said attorney Boyle, who spent forty-five minutes with his client Wednesday.

At a news conference afterward Boyle, a former prosecuting attorney, told the press, "The irony is that I prosecuted the first serial killer in Milwaukee, Michael Lee Herrington, and hopefully now I'm defending the last one."

Herrington, the son of a Kansas City police officer, had been convicted in the 1966 and 1967 stabbing deaths of a ten-year-old girl and an eighteen-year-old woman on the city's West Side, and the attempted murder of another young girl, who managed to get away from him.

Boyle described Dahmer as "a very sick young man who has many kinds of mental problems." He brought in a forensic psychologist, Ken Smail, to evaluate Dahmer's mental state. Smail met with the prisoner four times during the day, and advised the lawyer that he felt Dahmer was competent, and able to face the proceedings against him.

While feeling sorry for himself, Dahmer continued to cooperate with police. Once Oliver Lacy's remains had been identified, Dahmer recalled picking up the athletic black man who had gone to the ice cream stand at the Grand Avenue Mall. After talking him into coming to his apartment for a photo session, Dahmer said he gave Lacy a drugged drink and strangled him.

As Dahmer continued to enlighten authorities on his lifestyle, the unthinkable possibility emerged that he had practiced necrophilia as well as cannibalism. He told police that he had enjoyed sex with some of his victims before strangling them, and had performed a sexual act on at least one of them after he had been murdered—and then cut his heart out to eat.

In hopes of getting a better handle on Dahmer, prosecutors dug out the transcript of the two-year-old hearing in which he was sentenced for the 1989 sexual assault on missing Konerak Sinthasomphone's then thirteen-year-old brother.

At that time the prosecution had demanded a prison term for Dahmer. Gale Shelton, the assistant district attorney assigned to the case, told Judge William D. Gardner, "In my judgment, it is absolutely crystal clear that the prognosis for treatment of Mr. Dahmer within the community is extremely bleak . . . and is just plain not going to work. That's absolutely clear from every single professional who's looked at Mr. Dahmer; and the reality is that his track record exhibits that he is very likely to reoffend."

Prosecutor Shelton indeed appeared to have taken Dahmer's measure, right down to his socks.

Citing the serious nature of the offense, and Dahmer's "unwillingness to cooperate and his lack of motivation to do anything to change," she argued, "the only hope for treatment of Mr. Dahmer has to occur within a prison setting. His treatment needs to go far beyond his alcohol problem."

Dismissing Dahmer's contention that he would not have approached the Laotian youngster had he realized he was a minor, Shelton continued, "He preyed on the thirteen-year-old boy because he looked like a soft-spoken young man who could be easily victimized. Mr. Dahmer knew full well he was not dealing with a consenting adult."

In his own defense Dahmer had denied doping the boy, and claimed that any drugs that ended up in the youngster's body must have come from some residue left in a coffee cup. Shelton pooh-pooed this, pointing out, "The boy indicated that within a short time of drinking the coffee he immediately felt woozey. It's really a miracle that he made it out of there."

She termed Dahmer a "very manipulative" person who had only gone through the motions when ordered to undergo therapy for his earlier arrest for lewd and lascivious behavior. "He has deep-seated anger and deep-seated psychological problems that he's apparently completely unwilling or incapable of dealing with," Shelton asserted.

Dahmer asked permission to address the court before the sentence was handed down. Standing before the bench he told Judge Gardner, "The prosecution has raised some very serious charges against me. I've never been in this position before. Nothing this awful. This is a nightmare come true for me. If anything would shock me out of my past behavior patterns, it's this.

"All I can do is beg you to please spare my job to show that I can tread the straight and narrow and not get involved in a situation like this. I would not only ask, I beg you, please don't destroy my life."

Openly admitting his homosexual tendencies, Dahmer continued, "This enticing a child was the climax of my idiocy...I don't know what in the world I was thinking when I did it...I offer no defense.

"I realize I'm completely at your mercy. I do want to help. I want to turn my life around despite what the prosecution has told you. She doesn't know me like I know myself. This one incident has jolted me like nothing else has. I don't know what else to tell you. But other than I'm sorry."

Dahmer's eloquent plea obviously worked. Judge

Gardner sentenced him to eight years in prison, but stayed the sentence, placing him on five years probation instead.

"I thought the state's presentation was very persuasive, but I am going to opt to give you an opportunity in community," the judge remarked. "Now, the way I am going to do that is that I'm going to impose a punishment factor in there. I want to see to it that you get some treatment for the alcohol problem. But mainly I'm concerned about therapy, and I'm really concerned that we don't have a program in prison right now. I could send you to prison and you wouldn't get any treatment for the problem. You'd come out probably worse than you are right now.

"I want to make sure you are aware of the fact that protection of the community is extremely high in my mind and this is a very, very serious offense," he continued. "This is the kind of thing...that the prosecutor would just ask the judge to throw away the book, and the judge would say ten and ten consecutive and good-bye. But if there is an opportunity to salvage you, I want to make use of that opportunity."

As a term of the five years probation, Judge Gardner stipulated that Dahmer would spend one year in the House of Correction on a work-release program. This meant he could continue working at his job in the candy factory, returning to the correctional facility in Franklin to spend the nights.

Gerald Boyle, who represented Dahmer in that case as well as the current horror, had agreed with the judge that his client was a "sick man" who could not get the help he needed behind prison walls. He agreed to the five years probation, and said that if Dahmer faltered, he should be sent to jail.

Milwaukee reporters tried to pin down Gardner

Wednesday in view of what had happened since, but he declined to comment.

As the day wore on, and fiercely competing news reporters taxed their imaginations to come up with new angles in the fast-breaking case, it seemed that just about anybody who had anything to say was willing to get into the act.

How do parents cope with children who get spooked after watching news reports of the grisly happenings on television?

"These children are really terrified by these events," observed psychiatrist Bruce Axelrod in suburban Brown Deer. He urged parents to turn off the television when the news came on, and not to leave newspapers lying around for the kiddies to see.

Lois Gracz, a psychotherapist at a Milwaukee hospital, said, "Let them talk about their fears and take their fears seriously, seriously enough to say that I know you are scared, but you are safe here. You never want to blow off the fears of a child. You want a child to be able to discuss fears with you. I think parents can also be honest with their children, that some people do bad things and that they will protect their children from people who do bad things."

A family therapist at a Milwaukee psychiatric hospital, Steve Petri, said, "You've got to know your kids. If they are kids who keep things to themselves, I'd surely talk about what is going on with them, what's going on today. I'm not so sure I would directly say: 'Did you hear about the guy who is cutting people up?' That scares me. You don't want to cause alarm. You want to help them reduce their concern as much as possible."

They also stressed allowing children to sleep with

nightlights, and to review family rules about safety, and not talking to strangers.

So, how about tourism to America's Dairyland? Was the worldwide media attention directed at the deeds of Jeffrey Dahmer going to scare visitors off?

"Any time there's something with this kind of notoriety there's a negative perception of the place," suggested Dennis Frankenberry, a well-known advertising and public relations executive. "But I don't feel there will be any measurable damage done."

Cynthia Collyer, tourism director for the Greater Milwaukee Convention & Visitors Bureau, tended to agree. "Something like this does affect tourism, perhaps immediately. Remember, we're under a microscope now," she said. "We've made national news. When a story like this happens and makes bigger headlines because it's a ghastly situation, naturally people react. I don't think in the long term it will affect tourism at all."

The Dahmer affair also brought renewed demands for reinstitution of the death penalty in Wisconsin.

There had been only one legal execution in all of Wisconsin's history. That happened way back on August 21, 1851, when a man named John McCafferty was taken out to what was then the edge of town and hanged in Kenosha for throwing his wife, Bridget, down a well. It did not go smoothly, and the unfortunate episode aroused so much public revulsion that the state legislature abolished capital punishment two years later.

Now, after 138 years, State Representative Susan Vergeront declared that she would reintroduce death penalty legislation with a special provision that would allow capital punishment in homicide cases where mutilation was involved. "There are some crimes that are so horrific, so offensive to our common decency, that society should cry out for the ultimate penalty," she said.

Citing the Dahmer case and that of Joachim Dressler in neighboring Racine County, another female legislator also called for the ultimate punishment in cases involving dismemberment. "The people guilty of these crimes deserve a penalty no less severe than death," said State Senator Joanne Huelsman. "Imprisonment is neither a reasonable penalty nor sufficient protection for future victims of such crimes."

Even Dressler's defense lawyer got into the act. He subpoenaed some of Milwaukee's top police officials, along with all evidence in the Dahmer case, in an attempt to establish a link between the Dahmer and the dismemberment murder of James Madden, the environmental solicitor.

"It is our feeling that we have a duty to find out what we can about the Milwaukee case because it might exonerate our client," attorney James Mathie argued before Judge Gerald Ptacek. What he hoped to do was to plant in the jurors minds the suspicion that Dahmer, and not Dressler, might have killed Madden, in addition to the eleven victims in Milwaukee.

Judge Ptacek refused, however, to let Mathie introduce any of the Dahmer evidence into the Dressler trial.

As the third day of discovery drew to a close, Jeffrey Jentzen, the medical examiner, called in L. Thomas Johnson, a forensic dentistry specialist at Marquette University, and Kenneth Bennett, Wisconsin's only forensic anthropologist, to assist in identifying the remaining skeletons and body parts. Bennett, a professor of biological anthropology at the University of Wisconsin in Madison, was fresh off the Dressler case, where he had identified young Madden's dismembered body.

Shortly before nightfall police stopped by the Sintha-somphone home on Milwaukee's Northwest Side to ask members of the Laotian family to look at a picture. It was a Polaroid photograph of an Asian youngster that had been found in Dahmer's apartment.

It was fourteen-year-old Konerak, just standing there, looking at the camera. He was holding his hands above his head, and wearing briefs of some sort. It was the last picture taken of him, just before the attack.

# CHAPTER 7

---

# DAY IV
# JULY 25

The first charges in the case against Jeffrey L. Dahmer were filed on Thursday, July 25. Up to now police had been playing the case pretty close to the vest, not giving out any more information than they had to. Aware that the eyes of the world were on Milwaukee, they did not want to let anything slip out that might subsequently taint the prosecution.

In taking the matter into court, however, it was necessary to file an affidavit outlining the evidence they had amassed against the suspect, who was being charged with four counts of first-degree intentional homicide.

Conviction of intentional homicide in Wisconsin carries a mandatory sentence of life in prison. There was also a charge of being an habitual criminal, which could add ten years to each life term. In filing four counts of murder Prosecutor E. Michael McCann revealed, of course, that police and pathologists had positively identified three more of the victims, in addition to Oliver Lacy.

They were, as feared, twenty-three-year-old Jeremiah "Jeremy" Weinberger, who was last seen leaving a Chicago bar with a blond-haired white man on July 6; Matt Turner, twenty, also known as Donald Montrell, another Chicagoan, who was last seen in that city on June 30; and Joseph Bradehoft, a twenty- five-year-old Milwaukee man, whose family had not seen him since July 16.

Unlike most of Dahmer's other known victims, and contrary to earlier reports, Bradehoft was white, married, and the father of three children. Jeremy Weinberger was Puerto Rican, despite his misleading name.

Police were able to identify Weinberger through dental records. The names of the other three victims were ascertained through fingerprints on severed hands found in the apartment.

Police Chief Philip Arreola had assigned three teams of two detectives each to chat with Dahmer on a rotating basis since his stunning arrest Monday night. While one set of detectives was interviewing the suspect, the others were filing detailed reports for other investigators to follow up on the information Dahmer provided.

He claimed to have murdered Turner, Weinberger, Lacy and Bradehoft in a killing frenzy that covered less than three weeks. Turner was the first to find out that it did not pay to take up with strangers.

Dahmer had hopped a bus to Chicago to take in the Gay and Lesbian Pride Parade on Sunday, June 30, an event that provided a man of his tastes ample prospects to look over. That was the same day he reported to Chicago police that he'd lost his wallet. Afterward he encountered Turner at the Greyhound Bus depot in the Loop. He must have carried his wad in another pocket, because he offered his new friend money to ride back to Milwaukee with him, and to pose nude and view videos in his apartment. They took a bus to Milwaukee, and a cab to Dahmer's apartment.

Once he got Turner into his parlor, Dahmer said he slipped him a drugged drink. As soon as the drug took effect he looped a strap around his victim's neck and strangled him before submitting him to surgery.

Placing him in the bath tub, so as not to make a mess on the carpet, Dahmer took off Turner's head and put it in the freezer. He then dismembered the body and placed the parts in a fifty-seven-gallon barrel.

Dahmer did not remember his victim's name, but when detectives showed him a photograph of the missing man, provided by Chicago police, it was enough to jog his memory.

Police also showed him a photo that Chicago authorities had provided of the missing Weinberger. Yes, he had done him, too. Dahmer had enjoyed such good luck in Chicago that he was back there the following Friday night. He hit the gay bar circuit, and ended up in Carol's Speakeasy in Old Town. He and Weinberger struck up a friendship, and the twenty-three-year-old man agreed to return to Milwaukee with him to pose for photographs and to watch naughty videos.

"He stayed with me for two days, and had sex," according to Dahmer. Everything went fine until Weinberger suggested it was time to return to Chicago, on Sunday, or he'd lose his job. That settled it. It was time to slip him a sleeping potion.

As soon as the knockout drink took effect, Dahmer said, he strangled Jeremy with his bare hands. Then he laid him out for a postmortem photo session. After the picture taking Dahmer laid his Polaroid aside and picked up his tools. Off came his head, arms and legs. After he had his most recent lover in pieces, Dahmer related, he wiped off his hands, got out the Polaroid, and made a photographic record of his handiwork.

Then Weinberger's head joined Turner's in the freezer, and the rest of him was plunked into the formaldehyde drum.

It was eight days later that Dahmer was fortunate enough to run into Lacy, right there in the neighborhood. The transplanted Chicagoan was going down North 27th Street, just two blocks from Jeff's apartment, on his way home from the Grand Avenue mall, when Dahmer made him an offer he couldn't refuse. If he would come back to his apartment with him—right nearby—and sit for some pictures, he could make some easy money.

No harm in that. The skinny white dude wouldn't try to pull anything on the muscular onetime track star, would he? One thing about Lacy, he'd always been able to take care of himself.

Dahmer told the detectives that after Lacy stripped for the modeling session, he also disrobed, and the two gave each other body rubs. He then generously offered Lacy a drink before sending him on his way. Of course, Dahmer wasn't thinking of sending Lacy on his way home. What he had in mind was a shelf in the fridge.

The drink was spiked, and as soon as Lacy dozed off Dahmer went to work. First he strangled him, then he cut off his head. The head went on the bottom shelf in the refrigerator, next to the box of baking soda. It was Lacy's countenance that greeted the unsuspecting Officer Mueller when he opened the refrigerator door a week later. Dahmer told incredulous police officers he had anal sex with Lacy's dead body, after which he cut out Lacy's heart and "put it in the freezer to eat later." He also found room there for the heartless body.

Four days after Lacy's disappearance, on July 19, Joe Bradehoft was waiting for a Wisconsin Avenue bus near Marquette University, with a six-pack of beer under his arm, when Dahmer got off a bus headed the opposite direction and said, "Hi!"

Dahmer was a beer lover himself. The two men had something in common right off the bat. After a little more chit-chat Bradehoft allowed as to how he wouldn't mind making a little extra money by going home with Dahmer and posing for his camera.

Afterward, Dahmer told the detectives, he turned on the video, and once he'd gotten his guest aroused they had sex. "Then I offered him a drink with a sleeping potion, and strangled him with a strap while he slept," he said. Like the others, Bradehoft went into the bath tub, and was soon expertly carved into manageable pieces.

Dahmer placed his head in the freezer, alongside those of Turner and Weinberger, and the rest of him in the barrel along with the others.

It was now Thursday, just four days after Tracy Edwards had come flying out of that same apartment with one wrist shackled. Jeff Dahmer, freshly scrubbed and wearing a scruffy beard, blue-and-white striped shirt and black trousers, sat quietly and deliberately chewing gum in court beside his attorney as Prosecutor McCann reviewed the charges against him.

The courtroom was packed to capacity with spectators, craning their necks to get a firsthand glimpse at the onetime chocolate factory worker who had joined the ranks of America's most notorious serial killers. The jury box was jammed with reporters. A front row pew had been reserved for victims' families.

Everyone who entered the courtroom either had to be searched or go through a metal detector before being allowed to take a seat. More than eighty disappointed late arrivals were turned away because there was no more space.

Cameras whirred and clicked as Dahmer walked slowly into the room, where about a dozen sheriff's deputies stood guard. "That's him. That's him," were heard whispers from the crowd.

"Do you understand the nature of these charges?" asked Circuit Judge Frank T. Crivello, after explaining that, if convicted, Dahmer faced the rest of his life behind bars.

"I understand, your honor," the prisoner answered politely.

"And is it my understanding that you have agreed to waive the legal time limit before a preliminary hearing is held?"

"That's correct, your honor."

"All right. I am ordering that you be held for trial, and I'm continuing your bail, which has been set at one million dollars. There will be a preliminary hearing on August 22, and arraignment will be the week of August 26."

"The state anticipates filing more charges by August 6, your honor," McCann announced. "The investigation is not complete."

The entire hearing lasted only five minutes. As Dahmer left someone uttered, "Gee, he didn't look like a creep at all."

Chris Voss, who had waited three hours to get a seat, was also surprised at Dahmer's appearance. "You expect some sort of hideous monster to come out, but then, it's just a normal person."

McCann indicated afterward that police had uncovered information that Dahmer was responsible for as many as seventeen murders in the past decade—a dozen in his apartment and five more elsewhere, involving victims from Illinois, Wisconsin and Ohio.

Indeed, Chief Arreola had assigned a forty-one-member task force of detectives to investigate the skein of killings. They were turning up new information daily, not only in the Milwaukee area, but in cooperation with authorities in Illinois, where three of the known victims had come from, and in Dahmer's home state of Ohio.

In Summit County, Ohio, Sheriff's Sergeant Gene Scott advised his detectives to take a fresh look at a 1978 missing person case. The victim, a male about the same age as Dahmer, disappeared around the time Dahmer was living in the area.

And in Germany, authorities reopened the faded files on the unsolved mutilation murders of five women near the Baumholder Army base, where Dahmer served from July 13, 1979, to March 24, 1981.

They were also reviewing evidence in the murder of a twenty-two-year-old hitchhiker, Erika Hansthuh, found stabbed and strangled in a snowbank about fifty miles from Baumholder on November 30, 1980.

Back at the medical examiner's lab, Johnson and Bennett had established the identities of three more missing men and boys, including fourteen-year-old Konerak Sinthasomphone, whom the neighbor women had tried unsuccessfully to wrest from Dahmer's grasp in the early morning hours of May 27.

Letting the two police officers accompany him back to his apartment when they returned young Konerak to him as a "consenting adult" must have had Dahmer's adrenaline pumping faster than an Indy racer roaring down the homestretch. The cops didn't know it, and they didn't bother to look around—but behind the locked bedroom door lay the body of Dahmer's most recent victim, waiting to be disposed of.

And as soon as the cops left he killed the Laotian youngster as well. Clearly, to Dahmer's way of thinking, he had really put a good one over on the Milwaukee police department. He kept the boy's skull as a memento.

The other victims identified were thirty-one-year-old Tony Hughes, a visitor from Madison, who had not been seen since leaving a Milwaukee gay bar on the night of May 24, and Raymond Lamont Smith, a thirty-three-year-old Milwaukee man who also went by the name of Ricky Beeks. He had not been seen since May 29.

All of Dahmer's victims seemed to have been easy-going, outgoing people. Easy to meet. Easy to pick up.

Turner's family barely realized he was missing before his abused body was found. His stepfather, Wadell Fletcher of Flint, Michigan, started to worry on Wednesday when Western Union called to say Turner had failed to pick up $100 that had been wired to him in Chicago. Milwaukee police advised him the following day that Turner had been identified as one of Dahmer's unfortunate victims.

Turner had run away from home after dropping out of high school in his junior year. He spent a year and a half in the Job Corps before arriving homeless in Chicago. He spent two months in a halfway house for runaway young men on the South Side, before leaving at Christmas time. "He was basically a good kid," said Debbie Hinde, executive director of the Teen Living Program in Chicago, when she learned of his death. "He was bright and articulate. This whole thing is very sad."

By the time he left he had earned a high school

equivalency degree, and told friends he hoped to go on to junior college.

"It's a shock," his stepfather, a General Motors worker, declared. "I had to break the news to my wife, Rosa, the boy's mother. We just talked to him on the phone on July 1. He mentioned that he needed some money to buy something for the apartment, so we wired him $100. We had no idea he hadn't claimed it. He would call us every once in a while."

Turner had been in and out of Chicago, switching jobs frequently, and traveling to both coasts. For the last month and a half he'd been working as a counterman and busboy at the Chicago Style Pizza & Eatery, just outside the Loop on South Michigan Avenue.

"He was noticeable because he was really outgoing," Patti Schuldenfrei, owner of the pizzeria said. "He liked to go around to tables and schmooze. I had customers say to me, 'That guy's great. He's so enthusiastic. So upbeat.'"

He borrowed some money from his boss on June 26, which was his day off, explaining that he had some personal problems to deal with. He never came back again.

His parents said he visited Milwaukee regularly, because he had three aunts living there. That is probably where the slightly built Turner, who stood only five feet four inches tall and weighed around 135 pounds, was heading when Dahmer hooked up with him at the bus station and offered him money to sit for his camera.

"He loved to take pictures," Fletcher said. "He always wanted to be a model. He loved being in front of the camera. He used to enter those lip-syncing contests in the bars around Chicago, where he used the stage name of Donald Montrell. No one deserves to die like that."

Weinberger was a regular on Chicago's gay scene. His

former roommate, Tim Gideon, described him as a likeable chap. "He never was in a bad mood. I never saw him get mad about anything," he said. "He loved art and was very meticulous. His desk was always straight, and he knew where everything was. He always dressed nice and always worried about what he wore and how he looked. He took care of his hair."

He was also careful about who he hung around with. When he, Gideon, and two others shared a glitzy Gold Coast apartment on Chicago's Near North Side for a year, they had a rule that no one could bring home strangers.

Weinberger, whose father owned a coffeehouse, had two jobs. During the week he worked as a customer service rep at Images of the World, which was the video sales department of the Bijou, an adult theater in the Old Town area. On weekends he worked at the Bijou. "He was like a live wire. Very close to his family, a very honest and sincere person. You got a contact high just being around him," a former co-worker, Patrick Hughes, related. "Customers often asked for him specifically because they liked his manner."

Gideon talked at length with Weinberger and his newfound acquaintance, Jeff Dahmer, two weeks earlier at the Speakeasy, just down the block from the Bijou.

He and others distributed fliers around both Chicago and Milwaukee after he disappeared, asking anyone who had seen him to call a toll free number. "Jeremy wasn't the type of person who would just fly off on a whirlwind vacation," he said. "We never dreamed we'd find him like this."

Until he went off into the night with Dahmer, Weinberger lived with his father upstairs of the Caffe Pergolesi, which David Weinberger had owned for several years.

"Jeremy was just in the wrong place at the wrong

time," his father said, after learning of the young man's fate. "My son was hypnotized by a cobra. Unfortunately, he was bit. We can only hope that this cobra is caught and nobody else will be hurt."

Joe Bradehoft, the fourth of Dahmer's known victims with an Illinois connection, had lived in Greenville, a town of about 5,000 people, forty-five miles northeast of St. Louis, before coming to Milwaukee. He and his family moved in with his brother, Donald, thirty-four, and their sixty-four-year-old mother, Fern, while looking for work. He and his wife, Shari, had three children, ages seven, three and two. How ironic that Bradehoft's wife and Dahmer's stepmother shared the same first name.

Greenville Police Chief John King told Milwaukee detectives, "He was almost like a transient. He has no known relatives here. We know very little about him. There were two incidents involving him while he was here. In one, he was reported missing, but turned up two hours later. The second incident involved a report of a suspicious person at a restaurant, but we investigated and found no problem. I don't think he ever held a job here. He just took off one day and left Milwaukee as his forwarding address."

He was a native of St. Paul, Minnesota, where he also fathered a child. According to St. Paul police, Bradehoft was arrested in September of 1987 on a domestic assault charge for striking his twenty-five-year-old girlfriend.

"Our records indicate he came home drunk, threatened and punched Cheryl Ann Clark, grabbed a butcher knife, and left the house, threatening to slash the tires on her car," police spokesman Paul Adelmann told Milwaukee investigators.

Bradehoft had been living with his brother for about

a month when he left the house on Jaunary 16 for a job interview, and never returned.

"When Joe didn't come back, I began calling the bars where he used to hang out," Donald said. "Joe would always tell us that he could take care of himself, don't worry."

For Shirley Hughes, a Bible class teacher at a Milwaukee church, the discovery of her thirty-one-year-old son Tony's remains in Dahmer's apartment ended a two-month vigil of hope and fear.

"It's been a long, hard, two month wait," she wept when detectives broke the sorry news to her. "These aren't tears of sorrow or of disbelief or unfaithfulness. It's just prayers of hurt, tears of hurt," she said. "I feel relieved because now I know where my son is and we can take his remains and put it to rest. Because I had been praying and asking in the Lord Jesus Christ's name to let me know where my son was."

If Dahmer had menaced him, Tony Hughes could not have cried for help. He was deaf and unable to speak. He had lost his hearing after a bout with pneumonia when he was two weeks old. One of six children, he had graduated from the Delavan School for the Deaf.

Hughes had decided to leave Milwaukee and move to Madison, where it was safer, after the murder of his next door neighbor in July of 1990. On the day he was murdered he had come back to visit his family. Before leaving his mother's home to go to the Club 219 on the evening of May 24, he flashed signs to family members saying he loved them and would be back to spend the night. They never saw him again.

"After I found out that Tony knew Jeffrey Dahmer for quite awhile, and they started finding those bodies, I knew deep inside my heart that he would be one of them," she said. Shirley Hughes was one of those in court, curious about the man accused of doing those terrible things to the boy she had brought into the world.

"He didn't seem evil or anything," she said afterward. "Just to look at him, you wouldn't think he could do the type of things they said he'd done."

While Tony Hughes had come from a close-knit family that cared for him, police could find little of interest in probing into the background of thirty-three-year-old Raymond Lamont Smith, except that he also went by the name of Ricky Beeks. Relatives, who weren't too close to him, told police he had served some time in jail during 1990, but they didn't know what for. He had been living in Rockford, Illinois, with his ten-year-old daughter.

"It wasn't a bit unusual for Ricky to take off for long periods of time without contacting anyone," his half-sister, Donita Grace, thirty-six, explained. "I'm really surprised to learn his body was found in that house, because I had heard he was shot last year."

As near as police could tell, Beeks was the victim with which Dahmer initiated his new apartment on 25th Street. He was last seen on May 29, 1990. Dahmer told police he picked Beeks up in the gay bar at 219 South 2nd Street, and gave him some money to come home with him for a photo session. Afterward, Dahmer gave him a drugged drink, which put him to sleep. Once Beeks was unable to resist his advances, Dahmer said he strangled him, undressed him, and had oral sex with the dead body. Then he dismembered the body, boiled the flesh off the skull, and painted it.

But it was the discovery of young Konerak Sinthasomphone's tortured body in the house of horror that hurt the most, because, by all accounts, he should have been alive today. The tragedy was compounded by the fact that

Dahmer had victimized the family twice, having been convicted in court of sexually abusing Konerak's brother two years earlier.

The nightmare was something the Sinthasomphones never expected to encounter when they fled Communist Laos and came to the United States.

"We just swam across the river at nighttime," said the dead boy's twenty-seven-year-old brother, Anoukone, who made the break in 1977 and paved the way for the rest of the family. "The army or the soldier, if they see you . . . you could have got killed if they see you, shoot you when you escape, and take you away for good."

His mother, father, sister, and two brothers, of which Konerak was the baby, followed three years later, making the hazardous trip in a canoe the father had built. "It was in the morning. The whole town was having a party," said Keisone Phalphouvong, Konerak's twenty-two-year-old sister. "All the Communists and everyone else wouldn't pay so much attention to the river so we don't get shot." After being reunited in a refugee camp, they made their way to Milwaukee to start life anew. Now they were trying to comprehend what had happened.

So were Dahmer's stunned parents. They had suspected for some time that things weren't just right with Jeffrey. But nobody ever thought it would lead to this.

His parents were divorced, and his stepmother, Shari, had known him since she married his father in 1978, when the boy was eighteen. "Jeff came with my husband and the house," she said. There was also another son, David, who was eleven at the time.

"Because his father's a chemist, Jeff used to take animals and melt them down to the bone," she said. "It was always animals that were already dead, such as road-kills, and always with the supervision of his father, as far as I knew. I thought this fascination of his was a little strange, but his father didn't—he's a chemist.''

After Jeff got out of the Army he decided to live with his grandmother, Catherine, in the Milwaukee suburb of West Allis. ''He loved his grandmother, and she was a good influence in his life. She sent him money for holidays and birthdays,'' his stepmother recalled. ''He went to visit her in Milwaukee, and he liked it so much he wound up staying there.''

There he continued to pursue his interest in rendering animals, and God only knows what else.

''One time his grandmother went down to her basement and noticed just a foul smell in the air,'' Shari Dahmer told Ohio news reporters, who were pestering her for details about her stepson. ''Another time Jeff had concocted something in his grandmother's garage, and she called my husband. Lionel went to Milwaukee, and when he got there, whatever Jeff had melted down was gone. There was some slimy, viscous stuff left, but we had no idea what it was from. Jeff said he'd bought a couple of chickens from the grocery store and melted down the bones.''

Jeff often brought male friends home to his grandmother's house through a private entrance to the basement, she related. On one occasion he brought a friend home, and they were both drunk. His grandmother started down the stairs to say something, saw Jeff with his shirt off, and turned around and went back up.

''How would we know?'' his stepmother asked, fighting back tears as she spoke. ''If we had known, we'd have been up there and had him incarcerated.''

She and her husband last visited Dahmer at his Milwaukee apartment over the Thanksgiving holiday, and found nothing to cause them alarm. ''He wanted to show us the apartment. It was spotless, and it was bare. Obviously we didn't find anything," she said. Her only feeling at the time was that it was depressing for Jeff, having come from a spacious, comfortable home in Ohio, to be living in a tiny one-bedroom apartment. "But I guess that's not unusual for a single man."

The elder Dahmer had gone to Milwaukee to do what he could to cooperate in the investigation, and assure that his jailed son had the proper legal representation. He was staying with his eighty-seven-year-old mother at her West Allis home, where Jeff had once experimented with dead chickens.

"There's no doubt he's insane," he said, sadly. "I don't think I knew him at all. I've watched some of the reports on TV, and the agony of the relatives of the victims, the family and friends of the victims, I feel choked up. I don't know what to do."

He was so moved that he picked up the telephone and called a television talk show, "Smith & Company," that was doing a program on the rights of victims as he sat in his elderly mother's living room on Thursday night. It was his opportunity to share his sorrow with them, and to let Milwaukee area viewers know that Dahmer's own family members were victims of the horrible crime as well.

"I came here to be by my son, and I will always stand by him," he said.

"What will you say if they let you talk to Jeff?" the show's host, Joe Smith, inquired.

"I will say that I love him," the father replied. "I did not realize just how sick he was. I realize now that he is mentally ill, but I did not know the extent. And I will, as I always have, stand by him in my thoughts and prayers."

He asked viewers of the show, and the general public, to show some understanding, and to realize that the

Dahmer family was also going through the wringer. He said his elderly mother had been pestered unceasingly by news reporters, and plagued by crank calls late in the night.

"The feeling I have for the poor victims and their families is very deep. Prayer, that's all I can do."

He and his mother talked about what could have been, if they had only recognized the signs. "Jeff was never interested in forming a common bond. He wasn't that open. I just couldn't get things going with him," he said. "He would lie, and we'd catch him in lies. At other times he would be absolutely frank, and I'd check up and find he was telling the truth. You can't tell with a person like that, whether he's being honest with you or not."

On the night that Jeff was arrested his father had tried to call him, but couldn't get through. Jeff's grandmother was worried, because she hadn't heard from him recently, and had told her son in Ohio about her concern.

"We always had trouble getting a hold of him. I'd leave the phone ring and ring," he would recall later. "On Monday night I called from 9 p.m. to midnight. That was the night the man ran from the house into the road. Now I'm wondering, I have a feeling maybe that my phone call, the ringing, might have disrupted something that was going on."

On Tuesday when Dahmer called his son's apartment a detective answered. "Is Jeff there? This is his father in Ohio," Dahmer said. "Your son is alive and well. We're involved in an investigation, and the lieutenant will call you back," the voice replied.

Dahmer dialed his mother in West Allis. "I tried to call Jeff, and some policeman answered the phone. Do you have any idea what might be going on?"

"Good heavens, no. The police have been here, too."

Dahmer then called West Allis police, explained who he was, and asked if they could enlighten him. "This investigation—what is it about?" he asked.

"Homicide."

"What? What has that got to do with Jeff?"

"I really can't say at this point, except that we understand it involves the skulls of people."

That was when Dahmer called Gerald P. Doyle, a highly respected criminal defense lawyer, who had stood by his son earlier in the child molestation case. "You're the best, but I don't know what you can do to help Jeffrey," he said.

That was the big problem. Jeffrey Dahmer's bizarre clandestine activities had erupted with such shocking force that there seemed nothing that anybody could do— for Dahmer or any of the others involved. The question was, how had it ever been allowed to reach this point?

How about the overpowering stench coming from his apartment for days on end? Why didn't any of his neighbors get suspicious and notify authorities?

"Call police?" asked Pamela Bass. Foolish question. If you ask the people who live around 25th and State, they'll look at you like maybe you ought to go somewhere and have your head examined. They will remind you of the night Nicole Childress, Sandra Smith and Glenda Cleveland dialed 911 when Konerak Sinthasomphone ran naked and bloody out of Jeffrey Dahmer's apartment, and the cops told them to get lost.

Now, of course, with eleven bodies carted away from Dahmer's festering apartment in bits and pieces, the neighbors had the police department's undivided attention.

"We are deeply concerned about the allegations of the police inaction concerning the young man. A thorough investigation will be undertaken regarding this incident," Captain Dean J. Collins, the department's adjutant, assured the public on Thursday. "The Milwaukee Police Department is absolutely committed to providing the best possible service to *every* segment of the community."

That's not the way Johnnie Johnson, executive director of the Midtown Neighborhood Association saw it. "We are outraged with the lack of police responsiveness to African-Americans. We are terrorized because the criminals know the police are not responding."

Moreover, nobody in Dahmer's building really had an inkling of what was going on in his parlor behind closed doors. When Mrs. Bass called his attention to the sickening smell he apologized profusely and told her his refrigerator had gone on the blink and his meat had spoiled. "He was nice about it," she reflected. "He acted like a normal person. When I saw him, he always acted like a normal person."

Wasn't it a fact that, when neighbors called the police, Dahmer had used the same self-confident demeanor to sweet-talk the cops into believing that he and the Laotian boy were just having a lovers' spat?

And what would the busy, understaffed police have said if someone actually had called them and complained, "My neighbor's apartment smells?"

Are you nuts? They probably would have advised, "Hold your nose."

Art Heitzer, the forty-three-year-old president of the neighborhood association, suggested, "There is a perception, with justification, that the police are either not able or not willing to respond to complaints of residents in the area on many issues more serious than that of smell."

Dahmer chose his victims well. For the most part, police are not particularly sympathetic toward homosexuals, and if you're black to boot, it might be even more difficult to get them to give a rap if your regular seat at the local gay bar suddenly turns up empty.

Dahmer was reared with such a strong Christian fundamentalist view of society that he grew up feeling inwardly guilty about his own sexual drives. He had told others that he thought homosexuality had no redeeming social value, and AIDS was God's way of getting back at gays.

"Jeff hated homosexuals with a passion, particularly black queens," said Jean-Paul Ranieri, a street minister who spent six days a week circulating among Milwaukee's gay bars. Possibly something happened to Dahmer when he was in jail to instill such a hatred in him. "He found black queens disgusting."

Ranieri, a former drug addict and male prostitute who had become a lay brother in the Episcopal Church, encountered Dahmer twice in as many days in one of the city's gay bars, and had a long talk with him.

"You knew there was something peculiar about him, but you couldn't put your finger on it. He didn't look like the type of person capable of doing anything like this. He looked like a drunk yuppie," Ranieri recalled. Nevertheless, he put the word out among area gays—blacks in particular—to stay away from that guy. "I had no idea whether he was straight or gay. But in his own mind, it would seem, he used the platform of the gay bars to eliminate gay men," Ranieri surmised.

At the Ambrosia Chocolate factory, some of Dahmer's former co-workers were having trouble dealing with the fact that they had unwittingly worked side by side with the man who was becoming known as Wisconsin's greatest mass murderer. John Timson, the company's chief executive, brought a counselor into the shop to talk to them.

And another legislator, State Senator Joseph Andrea, a Kenosha Democrat, joined the two Republicans who had earlier announced they would seek legislation to reestablish the death penalty in Wisconsin. He frankly admitted, however, that he did not see much chance of the liberal Democrats ever letting such a bill get out of committee.

Ironically, print advertising for a new Paramount picture entitled Body Parts began arriving in Milwaukee on Thursday, to run in full page ads in the Sunday papers. Paramount yanked the ads, and also cancelled television promotions for the film. The theater chain that was to have shown the movie, beginning August 2, cancelled it because of a long standing company policy regarding sensitivity to community issues.

Sensitivity to community issues did not stop WLS Talk Radio 89 AM from sending a crew up from Chicago to do a live broadcast from the corridor of the murder building, outside Jeffrey Dahmer's apartment door.

"We wanted to give our listeners the humanity of the scene," a station spokesman explained.

# CHAPTER 8

![black bar divider]

# DAY V
# JULY 26

The Milwaukee Police Department, grossly embarrassed by the performance of three of its officers in handling the Konerak Sinthasomphone incident, which resulted in the Laotian boy's death, got a new jolt Friday when Chief Philip Arreola suspended the three men involved.

"I've confirmed that on May 27, 1991, members of the Milwaukee Police Department had contact with the accused, Jeff Dahmer, and the victim," a somber faced Arreola explained, in taking the action. "I have directed an immediate in-depth inquiry into this matter by the Internal Affairs Division. I intend to take whatever action is warranted just as soon as I have all the details."

The trio, identified as John A. Balcerzak, Joseph Gabrish and Richard Porubcan, were stripped of their badges and guns, but permitted to remain on the payroll pending the filing of internal charges against them.

"I can guarantee you that while their jobs are paramount in their minds, they're going through absolute hell because of their decision in the Dahmer case. That kid's dead because of their decision," a veteran detective, who worked with the uniformed men, said on learning of the suspensions. "Balzerzak and Gabrish aren't a couple of sluggos on the street—they're conscientious officers.

"They're decent with people, and do the job very well. They're thorough, and ambitious. If they've got a spare moment, they're going to be working on something."

The thirty-four-year-old Balcerzak was a six-year veteran of the force, and Gabrish, twenty-eight, started out as a police aide in 1983. Porubcan, twenty-five, joined the department in February of 1990. He had almost made it through the eighteen-months probationary period when the incident occurred.

"You can be assured that I will take whatever action is warranted as soon as I have all the details," the tense and visibly strained Chief Arreola promised. "There has been an urgency placed on this investigation. This incident has been a matter of grave concern to me and to the department. There is no doubt that I was taken aback by reports of what happened Monday night. As the chief of police, I must and I shall proceed meticulously to determine all of the circumstances of the contact between the officers, the victim and the accused."

The chief's action drew immediate fire from the Milwaukee Police Association. The organization's president, Bradley DeBraska, declared, "In his rush to find a scapegoat for the recent tragedies, the chief has suspended three Milwaukee police officers, knowing full well that the community would interpret the suspensions as his conclusion that they had failed to perform their duties. Even Jeffrey Dahmer gets a trial before he's convicted.''

He called for a vote of confidence on Arreola and added, ''If the membership returns a no-confidence vote, we will demand that the chief resign and be replaced by someone who can serve both the community and the department.''

The union demand, and DeBraska's comments, did not sit well with the powerful and respected *Milwaukee Journal*, which went to bat for the chief editorially.

''In suspending three officers who may have botched a chance to rescue a fourteen-year-old victim of suspected mass murderer Jeffrey Dahmer, Police Chief Philip Arreola acted reasonable. It's hard to understand—much less sympathize with—the police union's histrionic reaction to the suspensions,'' the *Journal* declared.

''Perhaps, once all the facts are known, it will be seen that the police officers acted appropriately. However, the hint of error is strong, making the suspensions reasonable. After all, had the officers acted, not only could the boy's life have been saved, but perhaps also the lives of others. The string of killings attributed to Dahmer might have been cut short.

''Many Milwaukeeans understand that if they mess up royally on the job, they might be suspended even before an investigation is concluded...DeBraska's contention that Dahmer was enjoying more rights than the suspended officers is nothing less than ridiculous. Dahmer was jailed before he was charged. The officers are suspended *with pay*, pending an investigation. The two cases really have no parallels.

''The conduct of the three officers—along with the reaction of the union—do argue ironically that the police officers could use better sensitivity training. Some officers defend their suspended colleagues by saying bizarre incidents are not uncommon in Dahmer's near West Side neighborhood. Perhaps more sensitive eyes could better distinguish danger in that area."

At the same time Milwaukee residents were reading the editorial, about sixty-five neighborhood residents held a protest march outside the 25th Street apartment building where the multiple murders took place. They were demanding that police show more accountability to people living in lower income areas.

The Reverend Le Havre Buck, one of the organizers of the rally, expressed outrage over the death of the young Laotian boy. "If that had been a black man, chasing a white boy down the alley and dragging him back, that would never have happened," he declared. "They would have investigated us and done everything to find out what's going on. This is crazy."

At a news conference announcing the suspensions of the three officers, Arreola was asked, "What about these charges, chief, about police being insensitive to complaints by blacks, and problems involving gays?"

"Obviously, those comments may be speculative at best. However, I am deeply concerned about any perception that any citizen of the community may have regarding the sensitivity of the Milwaukee Police Department," he answered.

"How does it feel to have had Jeffrey Dahmer slip through your fingers at a point in time when several of his victims were still alive?" another reporter asked, alluding to the fact at at least four of the killings took place on or after the night when police refused to intercede.

"I wish I could put that feeling into words for you today," Arreola said, uncomfortably.

"Could you try?"

"No, I cannot."

It was not one of Philip Arreola's better days.

Things were going better over at the medical examiner's office, where the busy pathologists had finally succeeded in identifying the last of the four bodies, or parts thereof, found in Jeff Dahmer's aromatic apartment.

They were Anthony Sears and Ernest Miller, both twenty-four, Curtis Straughter, eighteen, and Errol Lindsey, nineteen.

Sears, the last of the victims to be identified, was most likely the first of the eleven to accept the invitation to visit Jeff Dahmer. He was last seen on March 25, 1989, the day before Easter.

"He telephoned me the day before and said he was coming over for Easter dinner. I got everything ready, but he never showed up," his mother, Marilyn, told police when she belatedly reported him missing. "Tony's apt to run off with his friends at any moment, so I wasn't particularly worried at the time. But then I got to thinking. He just got promoted to manager at the Baker's Square restaurant over on Capitol Drive, and that's why he wanted to come over on Easter and celebrate. Now, I figure that it wouldn't make sense for him to leave town because he just got that promotion, and things were going so well. Now I'm beginning to get scared. I've just got that feeling that something is terribly wrong."

Police checked all of Sears' known hangouts, but nobody had seen him around either. Karolee Bulak, twenty-eight, his closest friend, said, "Something's got to be wrong. Otherwise, he surely would have called me."

Over the next two years Milwaukee police checked with Mrs. Sears no less than fifteen times, asking whether she or his girlfriend had heard anything, and bringing her up to date on their dead-end investigation.

Sadly, now, they had to drive over to her West Side apartment and tell her that the search was over. What was left of him had turned up in Dahmer's house of horrors.

"You don't want to think the worst, but I felt something was wrong," she said, resignedly. "Tony was a photo fanatic. He loved to have his picture taken. That's the only way I can figure it. He was a good lookin' boy, who had ideas about becoming a model.

"He was my only child, you know. He loved to talk to people. He was very sociable. He trusted everybody, and I'm sure that if this man invited him over to pose for pictures, he went right along with him."

You might say Sears was a "keeper." The story Dahmer told police was that he met Sears at La Cage Aux Folles, a gay bar on South Second Street. "I told him I was visiting from Chicago," Dahmer recalled. "Some friend of his gave the two of us a ride to West Allis, and we walked over to my grandmother's house."

This might have been the liaison his grandmother walked in on, when she discovered Dahmer partly undressed, turned around, and went back up the basement stairs. Dahmer told detectives he and Sears enjoyed sex, after which he slipped him a drink laced with sleeping pills. Once Tony had drifted off to Dreamland, Dahmer strangled him and dismembered his body, right there in his unsuspecting grandmother's house.

He explained to police that he boiled the head, to remove the skin. Once it had dried out he painted it gray, to make it look like plastic, so no one would ask any questions.

How Dahmer disposed of the rest of the body was not clear, but that might have been the smelly rendering experiment in the garage, that prompted Grandma to call Dahmer's father in Ohio.

When Dahmer moved out of his grandmother's house, he packed Tony's skull along with the rest of his belongings, and took it to his new apartment in Milwaukee.

Enter Ernest Miller. The last anyone had seen of Miller was on September 2, 1990, and he was dressed fit to kill.

"He was a nice person; never bothered nobody. He came up over Labor Day to get away from all that violence in Chicago," his aunt, Vivian Miller, told detectives who stopped off at her West Side home to deliver the bad news.

"We all went to the Golden Rule Church of God in Christ over on Hopkins Street Sunday morning. It was a day of celebration for Ernest. He had just won a scholarship to dancing school in Chicago, and he'd been free of drugs for one year—to the very day. After church we all went out together and ended up buying $500 worth of new clothes for him. Oh, he was a dresser, that boy was. He told us he was going out to get something to eat before going back to Chicago, but when he never came back to get the rest of his new clothes, we knew then that something was wrong."

What was wrong was this. Miller, all decked out in his new finery, was standing in front of a bookstore in the 800 block of North 27th Street, when Dahmer walked up and gave him the once over. "How'd you like to make some money?" Dahmer asked. The next thing you know, the two of them were in Jeff's apartment wrapped in a boy-boy entanglement.

After it was over Dahmer offered Miller a drink, and that was the last thing Ernie ever remembered. But this time, Dahmer decided to try something different. Instead of strangling his victim, as soon as he had dozed off, Dahmer said he took a knife and slit his throat.

Then he got out his Polaroid and recorded his handiwork to maybe put into a scrapbook some day. That done, he told police, he divided his houseguest into pieces and disposed of the flesh—all except for the biceps, which went into the freezer for when he got hungry.

Oh, yes. Dahmer said he also kept Miller's skull, which he painted and put on the shelf next to Tony Sears.

The pathologists had used dental records to put a name tag on the remains of Curtis Straughter, a strikingly handsome youth with full lips and high cheekbones, who called himself Demetra. It seemed that not much had gone right during his eighteen years of life, and he was trying to get things back together when his world ended in Dahmer's apartment.

He had problems coming to grip with his homosexuality, and felt estranged from some of his family members and friends. A high school dropout, who had recently lost his job as a nursing assistant at the Marina View Manor on Prospect Avenue, he had gone to live with his grandmother, Catherine Straughter. Neither she nor his friends had seen him since February 18.

"He felt that he was different," his best friend, seventeen-year-old Bernell Howard, would explain after Straughter's fate had been learned. "He had a lot of dreams. He planned to go to MATC (Milwaukee Area Technical College) and get his GED. He wanted to become a model and go to modeling school.

"It was nice out the last day I saw him. We spent the day baking cookies, talking, and walking along Lake Michigan. We were going to get together again the following week, but he never showed. I was a little puzzled, at first, but Demetra had been talking about moving to Philadelphia. I thought he'd gone there for a visit, and I'd hear from him when he got back."

How his best buddy ever ended up in Dahmer's apartment also puzzled Bernell Howard, since Straughter had a strong aversion to honkies. But he wanted desperately to become a model. If someone had offered him an opportunity to pose for the camera, he would have gone for it.

"Ever since I heard about Dahmer, I just got down on my knees and prayed that Demetra hadn't been in there. I didn't want to believe that he was in there," Howard said.

Believe it, Bernell. According to what Dahmer told police, he picked up Straughter at a bus stop near Marquette University, and offered him money to join him in his apartment. There Dahmer said he followed the usual procedure—a drugged drink, sex, and a leather strap around the neck. After Demetra was dead, Dahmer dismembered him and got out his camera. Then he added Straughter's skull to his collection.

Howard sadly told police that the man he knew as Demetra used to write lyrics for songs to reflect his inner pain.

Dental charts were also used to identify Errol Lindsey, whose family had been waiting for him to come home since April 7, when he went out to have a key made at a shop two blocks from Dahmer's address.

An easy going teen-ager, who was into rap music and weight-lifting, he didn't hang around bars, where Dahmer picked up some of his subjects. "Errol didn't even spend a night away from home. He was a mama's boy. He was real close to our mother," his thirty-one-year-old sister, Yohunna Barkley, told police.

He worked at a ceramic company where plastic molds were made, and had just gotten home from the Grand Avenue Mall when he ducked out to get the key. His family knew right off that something was wrong when he did not come back, because he was the type of person who always stayed in touch. Not long after he disappeared his family moved, but only around the corner from the old location.

"We figured in case somebody hit him on the head and he got amnesia, we'd move around the corner and stay in the same neighborhood just in case his memory came back and he'd come around to the house looking for us," his sister explained.

"My mama tried to get the police to go lookin' for Errol, but they told her that he was an adult."

Lindsey's sister, his brother, Reginald, and their fifty-six-year-old mother, Mildred, were in the crowd outside the 25th Street apartment that awful day when police finally discovered what had been going on inside. "Errol is up there in that house, Mama, I just know he is," Yohanna said, fearfully.

Mildred Lindsey, who had steadily lost weight since her son disappeared, brushed back a tear and said softly, "Yes. I believe he is."

How he got there was what puzzled his devoted family. When police broke the news to them, Lindsey's sister suggested, "He didn't have any money, except for that key, when he left home. If Dahmer offered him money, maybe that's how he got him into that house."

That's exactly what happened, Dahmer told police, in the rambling account of his bizarre sexual exploits. He claimed that he did not dismember Lindsey until after he had enjoyed oral sex with his dead body. Errol's was another of the skulls police found on Dahmer's display shelf —dental work and all.

Dahmer's apartment stood empty Friday, stripped of its furniture and contents by crime lab technicians who were going over everything the suspect owned. With the tenant gone, the building's owner sent in a cleaning task force. By the time they had finished their job, the lingering odor was gone, and his neighbors were able to breath easily for the first time in months.

Dahmer's arrest meant new work for police in the Town of Bath, Ohio, where the Summit County Sheriff's Department dusted off a 1978 missing person file after Dahmer told Milwaukee police he had killed a nineteen-year-old man there in that year and buried him near his parents' home.

Dahmer had lived in the Ohio community with his father and stepmother, after his parents were divorced.

Two detectives from Ohio flew to Milwaukee to question Dahmer Friday, to see what he could tell them about the incident in question. Dahmer, who would have been eighteen at the time, had just graduated from Revere High School. Based on what he told Milwaukee detectives, the Ohio killing was his introduction to murder.

The only missing person from that area who would have fit the description of the victim mentioned by Dahmer was nineteen-year-old Steven M. Hicks, who had lived in the Town of Coventry, about fifteen miles from the Dahmer family home. He had not been seen since June 18, 1978.

In his ongoing confession to Milwaukee authorities, Dahmer said he had met the other man in an Akron bar, invited him home, and had sex with him. After that he killed him and buried him in the yard.

"Potentially, we have a crime," Police Captain John Gardner of the Town of Bath agreed, after talking with Lieutenant Richard Munsey, who had interviewed Dahmer. "Until we can pinpoint the specific site, we're going to have to protect the whole area. As soon as word of this gets out, you'll have all kinds of people poking around there.''

The Dahmer family had long since moved from the 1.72-acre site in the affluent suburb of Akron, and the confessed killer's boyhood home was currently occupied by William Berger. The dark brown, three-bedroom contemporary ranch house was surrounded by trees.

Although they agreed to let Berger remain there while the investigation progressed, police ringed the entire property with yellow ''Police Line—Do Not Cross'' tape, to keep everyone else out.

''This is going to take a little time to find the burial site, if there is a body here like he says, because the incident would have occurred thirteen years ago,'' Chief Gardner surmised. He contacted the town highway department, and asked that barricades be put up to route traffic away from the area once the search began.

Ohio authorities weren't the only ones who went on the alert with Dahmer's arrest.

Kenosha County investigators huddled with Milwaukee police in an effort to determine whether a headless, limbless male torso found in Petrifying Springs Park west of town eight years earlier might be linked to Dahmer's activities. A hiker came upon the torso wrapped in a plastic bag on October 4, 1983. The victim was identified through X-rays as eighteen-year-old Eric R. Hansen of the Milwaukee suburb of St. Francis.

Hansen, a runaway and high school dropout, was a homosexual who earned money working as a male prostitute. He was well known in Milwaukee's gay community, and was a regular in the gay bars.

Recalling that Kenosha investigators had spent a good deal of time checking out leads in the case in Milwaukee's gay neighborhoods, Milwaukee police asked

Sheriff Allan Kehl to send them the files on the Hansen investigation, so they could see whether there was anything at all that might link Hansen to Dahmer. "We're trying to explore every lead that comes up in the Dahmer case, and wrap up any unsolved dismemberment homicides at the same time, if possible," Lieutenant Greg Bauer told the Kenosha County sheriff.

It was a long shot, that probably wouldn't hit any target. From what was known about Dahmer up to this point, he collected cadavers, he didn't leave them lying around in public parks to be shared with others.

An even longer shot was coming out of Fresno, California. Police Sergeant Rene Martin asked Milwaukee investigators if they could check to see whether there was any connection between Dahmer and the murder of a man in a California field four months earlier. Fresno police had little to go on. Somebody had found a tennis shoe in a vacant industrial lot on March 30, and inside the shoe was a severed left foot.

"We believe that Jeff Dahmer was out here visiting his mother, Joyce Flint, some time last year," Sergeant Martin advised Milwaukee authorities. "It's possible that he was in our area at the time of the homicide."

An investigation by Fresno Detective John Herrera indicated that the foot had once probably belonged to thirty-one-year-old Patrick Lawrence VanZant. His wife had told the detective, "Pat failed to come home on May 4, and I haven't seen him since. He phoned me three days after that and said he was all right, but that he was leaving me. That's the last I heard from him."

Police combed the lot where the foot was found, and came up with some blue jeans and a knife, but no additional body parts. And no corpse with a missing left foot had been reported anywhere else.

"What we have right now is a new lead in an open homicide investigation," Lieutenant Jerry Davis explained. "No one knows at this point whether Dahmer was even in Fresno at the time."

Once word got out that Dahmer's fifty-five-year-old mother lived in Fresno, reporters converged on her home. She refused to answer the door, and finally had her phone disconnected.

Back in West Allis, police had to shoo the press away from the home of Dahmer's ailing grandmother. "Some of them were even placing camcorders in the woman's windows, and that's rude," Police Chief John Butorac said. "We've had to send squads there to try to keep people away, just to give her some privacy."

Before the day was out Friday, Milwaukee police would also hear from detectives in Hollywood, Florida, who wanted Milwaukee investigators to question Dahmer about the 1981 abduction slaying of six-year-old Adam Walsh, whose murder became a national story.

Saturday, coincidentally, would be the tenth anniversary of the child's abduction. His severed head turned up in a canal 120 miles away two weeks later.

Florida authorities had established that Dahmer spent six months in the Miami area in 1981, and would have been only fifteen minutes away by freeway from the Hollywood shopping mall from which Adam Walsh was kidnapped.

It seemed like everybody was trying to clean up unsolved cases at Dahmer's expense. State police in Wakefield, Michigan, sent Milwaukee detectives the dental records of twenty-four-year-old Steven Tuomi, who disappeared in September 1987, after moving to Milwaukee from the Upper Peninsula town of Ontonagon.

Meanwhile Dahmer rambled on, amazing even the

most hardened cops with first-person tales of his ghoulish appetite for blood, sex, gore and human flesh. It was when he related what actually happened to young Konerak Sinthasomphone on the night of May 26 and early morning hours of May 27 that they found the courteous, soft-spoken man sitting before them most revolting.

Here sat Satan with blond hair, a friendly face and a pleasing voice.

Dahmer met Konerak at the Grand Avenue Mall, his favorite trolling ground, it would seem, and brought the unsuspecting boy back to his apartment for a modeling session. Konerak innocently posed for two photographs, after which Dahmer graciously offered him something to drink. The refreshment, of course, contained a liberal dosage of a sleeping potion.

After the fourteen-year-old had passed out, Dahmer said he engaged in oral sex with the unconscious youth. Once he had spent his passion, Dahmer discovered, to his consternation, that he was fresh out of beer.

Leaving the boy in what was supposed to have been a lasting stupor in his apartment, Dahmer edged out the door and hurried down the street to get another six-pack. He was returning to resume his ghastly night's work when, to his dismay, he spotted Konerak staggering naked out of the building and into the street.

If what happened next went down the way any number of neighbors said it did, they were witnessing what will be recorded as one of the sorriest moments in police department history. Police not only returned the injured boy to Dahmer, but two of them even accompanied them back into the apartment to make sure everything was OK. According to Dahmer's own account, no sooner had the police officers left than he strangled the boy whose brother he had once been jailed for molesting.

After Konerak was dead, Dahmer told police, he performed oral sex with the body, and then grabbed his Polaroid and snapped away to record what he had done. He then dismembered young Konerak and kept his skull as a reminder of what—for him—had no doubt been a romantic evening.

It was the preserved skull, with its dental work intact, that enabled the pathologists to positively identify the victim after relatives recognized him in one of the photographs Dahmer had taken.

The fact that they had, in a manner of speaking, lost two of their sons to Dahmer's insane boy-lust, only compounded the grief for the Laotian family that had come to America in search of a better life.

They were all too distressed to talk about it Friday, but the Reverend Peter Burns, a Catholic priest from Sheboygan who described himself as a family friend, met with members of the press outside the Sinthasomphone home in an effort to satisfy their story needs so they would go away.

Although it was now four days after Dahmer's arrest and the discovery of his dark secret, editors of the *Milwaukee Sentinel* had still not identified Konerak as one of his victims. While the public chewed on every word the papers churned out, the editors were agonizing over the moral issue of whether they should divulge the Laotian's name. Because if they did, they reasoned, they would be indirectly identifying his brother—still a minor—as having been the victim of a sexual assault.

Eventually they would go ahead and do it. They were in a box Dahmer had built for them, and there was no way out. Besides, every other paper was using the name and they were starting to look silly in the eyes of their own reporters.

On Friday, however, Konerak was still an Asian Anonymous, and reporters were trying to figure out how in the world they would write the story that was unfolding in the yard outside the Sinthasomphone home without mentioning any names.

"The family is deeply saddened and shocked by this senseless death. The ending of such a young life causes great pain," Burns told an elbowing mob of press people, some coming from as far away as Paris to hear his words. "Konerak certainly loved life. He was, like all teen-agers, full of energy, full of joy, of many hopes and dreams. He will certainly be missed."

Asked about the neighbors' claims that police failed to act when they could have saved Konerak from the killer's hands, he said, "The family is certainly distressed by that story. The Police Department has expressed their sympathy, but . . ."

"Have the police apologized, Father?"

"No, they have not apologized."

"Why didn't the family tell police about the molestation case involving Dahmer when the youngest boy disappeared?" Burns was asked.

"Because they simply did not suspect a connection."

The family had lived about a mile from Dahmer's apartment at the time of the assault, but they had moved into the new neighborhood, much farther away, in the spring.

"The family appreciates the prayers and support from the people of the community, and I would like to extend the family's sympathy to all of the others who have been hurt as they have," Burns concluded.

Corinne Giesa, a neighbor who had known Konerak, turned to a reporter on the fringe of the crowd and said,

"It makes me very angry. Too many boys have been sacrificed since May, when police had a chance to stop it."

It wasn't as though Dahmer didn't know things weren't right in that head of his. He had once tried to get help, police learned Friday, but walked out of a mental health center after fifteen minutes of waiting for someone to notice him.

Jefferson Aiken, a spokesman for the Department of Health and Human Services, said records indicated Dahmer had visited the Milwaukee County Mental Health Complex in Wauwatosa on October 4 at approximately 10:00 a.m., but left at 10:15.

"Dahmer has never received treatment of any kind at the Mental Health Complex and has never been an outpatient or an inpatient," he stressed.

In examining records kept by Donna Chester, who had been Dahmer's probation agent, authorities determined that his mind had been on a downhill roller coaster for more than a year, a fact she duly recorded.

While Chester had gotten herself excused from paying housecalls on Dahmer, which was required as part of her job, she was still seeing him at her office. On three separate occasions, according to probation department files, Dahmer had talked to her of suicide.

The first was on July 9, 1990, when he complained to her that he was undergoing serious financial problems. "The client looks rough and tired," Chester wrote in her report of the interview.

At their next meeting, on August 13, Dahmer told Chester he was being inundated by bills, and had just learned he was being sued by West Allis Memorial Hospital for failing to pay a medical bill. "The only way I can see a way out is to jump from a tall building," Dahmer told her.

"I think what you should do, Jeff, is hire an attorney and possibly file for bankruptcy," she advised him.

There were more signs on August 27—the September meeting held several days early—when Dahmer moaned, "about how miserable life is . . . how hard life is for him," she wrote in her report.

During their October 23 session Dahmer showed signs of anger. He was mad about people who made more money than he did, and who did not have his financial problems. "Why are they so lucky?" he asked her.

The holiday season was in full swing when Dahmer had his last meeting of the year with Chester December 17. His father and younger brother were coming from Ohio to visit him and his grandmother for Christmas, but it was not going to be a joyous event to his way of thinking. "I'm uncomfortable being around my family because my father is so controlling," he told Chester. "And I've got nothing in common with my brother, Dave. He's in college." He also said he was embarrassed in the presence of family members over that sexual assault matter involving the boy whose family had come over from Laos. Chester wrote it all down.

In May 1991, there were serious problems in the new apartment building he had moved into on 25th Street in Milwaukee. One of the tenants, a man who lived there, had been strangled, Dahmer told his probation officer on May 13. "A detective came around and asked me and other people in the building whether we'd seen or heard anything."

"Had you?"

"No, I didn't know anything about it."

Dahmer was approaching the brink on July 8, when he told Chester he was in danger of losing his job at the chocolate factory. "I'm getting close to being fired, because of lateness and missing work," he explained.

"Well, Jeff, that could lead to serious complications —losing your job," she told him.

"If I lost my job, that would be a good reason to commit suicide," he replied.

Chester wrote it down.

Dahmer did lose his job, on Monday, July 15, when he didn't show up once too often. Three days later he was back in Chester's office, to tell her he was going to be kicked out of his apartment because he had no money to pay the rent.

This was the apartment Chester had chosen not to visit. The apartment that reeked to high heaven of decaying human flesh at that very moment. The apartment that had a human head in the refrigerator, a barrel full of torsos in the bedroom, one man's heart and another man's biceps in the freezer, a potfull of hands and some genitals in the closet, and human skulls on every shelf in the place.

Whatever was Jeffrey Dahmer going to do?

"The client has dirty clothes, is unshaven, and during the interviews was yawning as if having problems staying awake," the probation agent attested in her report. "The client is in severe financial difficulty. He will lose his apartment the 1st of August. He talks of suicide."

In four more days Tracy Edwards would come flying out of that apartment with a handcuff dangling from his wrist, and Officers Mueller and Rauth would go in and discover—better late than never—why Jeffrey Dahmer dearly didn't want to leave.

# CHAPTER 9

**━━━━━━━━━━━━━━━━━━━━━━━━**

# DAY VI
# JULY 27

In Northampton, Massachusetts, a town of 30,000 about eighty-five miles west of Boston, thirty-one-year-old David Rodriguez stared in disbelief at the television screen, which was giving daytime viewers a close-up of the man currently being hailed as America's most grotesque monster.

"Well, I'll be dipped. . . ."

Turning to a co-worker at the Veterans Administration Hospital, where he was a psychiatric nursing assistant, he shook his head slowly from side to side and declared, "No way! This is too hard to believe."

"No way what?"

"That guy on TV. He's nothing but a gin-swilling wimp. I was in the Army with him."

"You actually know him, Dave?"

"Shit yes! We were in the same medical unit at

STEP INTO MY PARLOR

Baumholder Air Force Base in Germany. We took the first-aid course together, six weeks, but I didn't think he ever took much of an interest in anatomy.''

Which proves how wrong some people can be. Where else could Jeff Dahmer have picked up the surgical skills that got him where he was today?

"There were eight of us, shared a room for nearly a year in 1979,'' Rodriguez said. "He was a wimp. He was big and goofy. Jeff would drink his gin—he used to drink Beefeater gin—he spent most of his weekends getting drunk and passing out on gin.

"This stuff in Milwaukee...it didn't seem like he was capable of anything like that.''

He was, of course. You have Jeff Dahmer's own word on that.

Prosecuting an individual who did anything as heinous as this, as far outside the bounds of moral decency as the human mind can imagine, would be a new experience for Milwaukee County District Attorney E. Michael McCann. He decided to go to a man who had been there, for advice. He put in a call to an old friend who had once taught with him at the National College of District Attorneys in Houston, Texas. Bill Kunkle was now in private practice in Chicago.

The beefy, forty-nine-year-old Kunkle had been a prosecutor in Cook County for thirteen years. He was the man who put John Wayne Gacy away for the homosexual slayings of thirty-three young men and boys a decade and a half earlier. Gacy was given twelve separate death sentences and twenty-one sentences of life in prison without parole. He is now on Death Row in the Menard Correctional Center at Chester, Illinois, going through the never-ending appeal process.

"I don't know enough about your case to talk about

the similarity of the people involved, Mike, but obviously they're multiple homicides," Kunkle told McCann during a brain-picking session that lasted most of the day. "They are situations where there may be unidentified remains. These things are exact similarities, of course."

"Everybody's going to be watching this one. We want to be prepared for some of the motions that will certainly be filed, so we know how to respond to them, you know, how you responded to these things."

Gacy's court-appointed lawyers, Robert Motta and Sam Amirante, had tried to show he was insane, while Kunkle and his co-prosecutor, Terry Sullivan, introduced the jury to no less than seventy-nine witnesses, including seven psychiatrists and psychologists, who testified that Gacy knew exactly what he was up to.

It seemed a safe bet, early on, that Dahmer's lawyers would have to chart the same course.

"What I can do, Mike, is get you some of the transcripts from the Gacy case, some of the motions that were filed and what our responses were, and some of the legal research that's been done before on the same questions that you're going to be presented with," Kunkle agreed. "There's something else that you should be concerned with, and that's the media coverage. By overstressing the homosexual aspect here, they could scare away possible new leads. I feel, even today, that that's what happened in the Gacy case."

While Dahmer kept all or part of most of his victims close at hand in his festering apartment, Gacy laboriously buried twenty-nine of his people in the crawl space beneath his suburban home. Four others were found in nearby rivers, where he had tossed them when he ran short of ground.

Police, prosecutors and the press could not help but

notice that, while Dahmer seemed to be gut-wrenchingly frank in discussing his bizarre lifestyle and the grisly murders that were a part of his day-to-day activities, he was careful to talk about homicides that took place only in states that do not have the death penalty, or where it doesn't apply. He only killed in Ohio and Wisconsin, he insisted.

To make sure his client was being properly understood, attorney Gerald Boyle released a statement Saturday, quoting Dahmer as saying, "I have told police everything I know." Boyle added that Dahmer denied involvement in slayings in Florida, Illinois, California, or anywhere else in the United States except the bundle in Wisconsin, and what he called the "incident" of the nineteen-year-old he had picked up in an Akron bar in Ohio thirteen years earlier.

Meeting briefly with the press after huddling with Dahmer, Boyle read a statement from his celebrated client:

"I have told the police everything I have done relative to these homicides. I have not committed any such crimes anywhere in the world other than this state, except I have admitted an incident in Ohio. I have not committed any homicides in any foreign country or in any other state. I have been totally cooperative and would have admitted other crimes if I did them. I did not. Hopefully this will serve to put rumors at rest."

In the Summit County suburb of Bath, ten miles northwest of downtown Akron, Ohio, authorities were preparing to dig up the yard around Dahmer's boyhood home first thing Monday, to see whether they could find any evidence to substantiate his version of the so-called "incident."

And in Milwaukee, Jeff Dahmer played host to the first visitor, except for cops and his lawyer, that he had received since his arrest. His father, Lionel, who had flown in from his present home in Medina, Ohio, to offer what moral support he could under the circumstances, was finally permitted to spend about twenty minutes with his son at the Milwaukee County jail. Earlier Lionel Dahmer had to resort to calling in to a radio talk show to get word to Jeffrey that he loved him and was standing by him.

Every father wants to be proud of his son, and hopes to live long enough to see him carry on the family name. It is a crushing blow for some to discover that a son is not of the sexual persuasion that will keep the lineage flowing. Some fathers, and mothers, too, disown and deny their sons when they discover to their horror what direction their lives are taking. Others, like Lionel Dahmer, show their true mettle in time of crisis. He might not have devoted all the time he should have to Jeff during the boy's formative years when Dad was too busy trying to give his family the finer things in life, but he was there now when Jeff really needed somebody who would not look upon him in disgust.

It was something the Dahmer family would have to learn to live with. For the rest of his life whenever the elder Dahmer registers at a hotel, or lays down his credit card, there will always be someone who will look up in surprise and blurt out, "Are you.....?"

He would have to find a way to cope with that. The families of some of our more celebrated criminals often end up in court, changing their names, because that seems to be the only way out.

Boyle stood by during the entire meeting, since it would also be necessary to discuss some of the legal strategy that the elder Dahmer was footing the bill for.

Due to Dahmer's ongoing confessions to three sets of detectives, there seemed little doubt that Boyle would ever be able to get him off. The only question appeared to be whether Dahmer would spend the rest of his life in a state prison or a mental facility.

There are those who suggested that the reason Dahmer killed was because he harbored an abiding fear of being left alone. He didn't want his apartment guests to leave him, ever.

He had no fear of loneliness now as he paced his eight-by-twelve-foot cell at the county jail. He couldn't even sit on the toilet without someone watching him. Although he wasn't going anywhere, he was literally under twenty-four-hour-a-day surveillance. Authorities feared that if Dahmer were allowed to mingle with the other 440 inmates, his life might not be worth two cents, especially if a couple of the black prisoners got their hands on him. If left to his own devices, on the other hand, there was a genuine fear that he might carry out the threats he had made to his probation officer and do the Dutch act.

"We want to make sure that nothing happens to this inmate. We are taking extra precautions," Sheriff's Lieutenant John Lagowski explained.

Over in the wood-paneled precinct house on West Vliet Street, which the three suspended officers had worked out of, you'd almost have to scrape the morale off the floor, it was so low. The order of the day seemed to alternate between gloom and doom.

One detective, ignoring Chief Philip Arreola's admonition not to discuss the case with the media, couldn't speak highly enough about Balcerzak and Gabrish, both of whom had been field training officers, known as FTOs, since February 1989.

"The FTOs act as mentors to the rookies. They help the new, young officers learn what procedures are, like writing reports, conducting investigations, what's involved in becoming a police officer," the detective said. "They take the new officer under their wings, and show them the ropes."

FTOs are all veteran officers who volunteer for the assignment, for which they receive no extra pay. In being examined and rated by their superiors for FTO positions, the highest score an applicant can achieve is twenty-five. Both Balcerzak and Gabrish had attained perfect scores, he said.

"When something like this happens, it hurts inside," he said, the pain showing on his own face. "It's bothering me terribly. Everybody takes it personally. It's not just them—it's all of us."

Other colleagues of the suspended trio argued that the full story had yet to be told. "There's no way a cop would see someone bleeding and not do anything about it," one of them insisted.

When other cops on the overnight shift asked Balcerzak, Gabrish and Porubcan what in the world had gone wrong, they related that Dahmer was already trying to calm the naked boy down when they drove up. "The women were yelling at us, and he seemed calm. He appeared like an intelligent person...didn't act goofy or anything like that.

"You have what appears to be a domestic situation. You have one party who's drunk and whose speech is impaired. Then you have another party who calmly tells you this guy is your house guest and he had a little too much to drink and got crazy. You can't explain this to people. You had to be there. A lot of bizarre things happen in that part of town all the time. People have been known to run naked down the street."

As far as why they hadn't bothered to run a check on Dahmer, which would have shown he was a convicted sex offender, such checks are time consuming. They regularly take a half hour to forty-five minutes, and rarely produce results.

Four police officers actually responded to the women's 911 call. One of them, a rookie just out of the Police Academy, stayed in the squad car while Balcerzak, Gabrish and Porubcan dealt with the problem. The rookie was not suspended because he hadn't done anything wrong. He hadn't done anything.

"It's easy to Monday morning quarterback with the police," a supervising officer said. "We're the ones out there. We're the ones who have to get an immediate perception and decide at the moment what to do.

"Here you have this incoherent person who can barely speak English, and then this other guy walks up calm and cool and tells the cops the guy is his houseguest who had too much to drink. Then, the Laotian guy walks away with Dahmer without a struggle. What are the cops supposed to think—'Gee, I wonder if he's going to go back and kill the kid?'"

Another cop, in arguing how the incident was rubbing off onto all of them, said, "I went out to answer a burglar alarm last night and the woman at the house sez, 'You're not one of those crazy cops that let that little boy get killed, are you?' Jeez. Sometimes I think I'd rather be a street sweeper."

If the unfortunate incident had cast a pall over the police department, the scene in the city's gay community was no less disheartening.

"It's like this guy has been in a frenzy for a month. Why didn't somebody do something?" questioned Mitch Eichman, the night manager of a downtown hotel. "I know of three other gay fellows who are missing, and I fear for their safety. Who do you trust now?"

In Chicago's gay community, where Dahmer traveled to find some of his victims, the wariness and worriedness was just as deep.

"What happened up in Milwaukee has put the fear of God in me—or the fear of the Devil," a thirty-three-year-old man who called himself Jeff was telling the bartender at the AA Meat Market on North Lincoln Avenue. "Every time you meet somebody, the news flashes before your eyes. Since I heard about Dahmer, it's definitely in the forefront of my mind.

"With all the things I have to think of—AIDS, half a dozen sexual diseases, now all of a sudden I've also got to think, 'Oh, by the way, the guy I'm talking to might be an ax murderer.'"

"That Milwaukee thing is all anyone's talking about," said Rick, a thirty-three-year-old musician at Little Jim's. He wasn't sure how lucky he was to be talking about it himself.

"Awhile back several of my friends introduced me to a fellow who invited me up to Milwaukee to spend the weekend. I had the time and the inclination to go, but for some reason I didn't."

Was the Milwaukee guy Jeff Dahmer? Rick never got his name.

The Dahmer affair also brought the rank opportunists out of the woodwork. Among them was Alderman Michael McGee, a black activist who in the past had drawn attention to himself by blowing a whistle to disrupt City Council meetings.

"A blind man can see this is a race crime. The majority of Dahmer's victims were black," McGee bleated. "He hates black people, period."

At a Saturday news conference in his Black Panther Militia headquarters, McGee demanded the resignation of

Mayor John Norquist, Police Chief Arreola, and just about any other white city or county official whose name popped into his mind. "What we know so far is just the tip of the iceberg. What's been swept completely under the rug is the racist nature of this thing."

McGee suggested that Dahmer might not have acted alone, saying the murder spree could have been motivated by a neo-Nazi group.

State Representative Gwen Moore also held a news conference Saturday. Poised outside Dahmer's murder factory on 25th Street, she announced her intention to ask the state attorney general's office to evaluate the entire Milwaukee Police Department. "They should step in and investigate the training, policy and procedures which may have contributed to a diminished police response to victims of this particular crime," she said. "I believe only an independent agency can assist us toward mending the many wounds which perceived lack of police support has wrought."

Milwaukee County Circuit Judge Russell Stamper, who participated in the media event, publicly questioned why Dahmer had been allowed to make his initial court appearance wearing street clothes.

"It's unusual the way this prisoner was treated in comparison to the orange suits and shackles that most brothers that I see wear," he observed.

Judge Stamper was shooting from the hip, and he missed his target by a mile. Authorities quickly pointed out that Dahmer was still an inmate of the City Jail when he first went to court. It is County Jail prisoners who are generally shackled and wear bright orange jumpsuits, and Dahmer would be so attired when he next went before a judge.

By week's end, what had happened in Milwaukee

was clearly the number one news story in America. Two movie/television producers and one author were already trying to nail down exclusive rights to Jeff Dahmer's own story, and probably half a dozen reporters were already beginning to pound out books, or were in various stages of planning them.

Dahmer's family wasn't saying no thanks. The right deal would certainly help pay legal fees. But such talk was still a little premature.

"A book on Dahmer will sell because he appears to be educated and middleclass—not the usual profile of a multiple murderer," one New York publisher proclaimed. "Mass murders are a very hot topic right now. Just look at the success of the movie *Silence of the Lambs*. Well, here we have a real life 'Silence of the Lambs.'"

# CHAPTER 10

# DAY VII
# JULY 28

A bone was produced Sunday on the grounds of Jeff Dahmer's boyhood home in the tiny town of Bath, Ohio. Dahmer earlier had told authorities that this was where he made his first kill, more than thirteen years ago, right after he got out of high school.

Milwaukee police got on the horn and told Summit County Sheriff David W. Troutman about Dahmer's claim just as soon as he confided in them that Wisconsin was not the only place where young men had died at his hands.

Summit County Detectives John T. Karabatsos and Town of Bath Lieutenant Richard Munsey flew to Milwaukee where they interviewed Dahmer for some three hours over the weekend, getting him to fill in some of the blanks.

"He was more than willing to talk with us," they told

Sheriff Troutman upon their return to Ohio. "He was re-
laxed, and quite open." Dennis Murphy, one of the Milwaukee detectives leading the investigation, and
Dahmer's lawyer, Boyle, sat in on the interview.

Earlier, Ohio authorities had suspected that the victim was probably nineteen-year-old Steven Hicks, who
had been missing from his home in the Coventry Township since June 1978. Karabatsos and Munsey showed
Dahmer a photograph of Hicks, a smiling white teen-ager
who wore his dark hair down to his shoulders. The picture jogged Dahmer's memory, and he recalled his first
victim's name.

"Yes, sir, that's the guy," he said politely.

Earlier recollections were a bit fuzzy. Where were
you on the night of June 18, 1978? Dahmer, who was eighteen at the time, first told authorities that he had met the
young man in an Akron bar and brought him to his parent's home.

Now, on studying the photograph of Hicks' smiling
face, it all came back to him. He had actually picked up
Hicks right in front of the Bath Police Department, of all
places, about a mile from his house. He'd been feeling
down in the dumps because his mother and father were in
the midst of a bitter divorce action that had been dragging
on for nine months, and he was looking for company.

Hicks, who said he was hitchhiking to a rock concert, decided to accompany Dahmer to his comfortable
three-bedroom home instead. There the two of them spent
the evening drinking beer. Dahmer had earlier told police
he and the Ohio victim had engaged in sex. Now that his
memory was more in focus, it might not have happened
exactly that way. But as the evening wore on, it was the
same chapter as later-day visitors to Dahmer's living quar-
ters. "He wanted to leave," Dahmer said. "I picked up a

barbell and hit him in the back of the head with it. Then I strangled him with the barbell.''

How does a novice killer dispose of a body that is suddenly taking up floor space in his parents home?

"I dismembered him," Dahmer explained. "I smashed the bones with a sledgehammer and buried them in the yard. Then I washed the blood off the bedroom floor."

Hicks' family waited patiently for him to come home. When he did not turn up after six days they filed a missing person report.

In doing so, they unwittingly set police to looking for him in the wrong direction. The last anyone in his family had talked to him, he told them he was going to a festival in the town of Chippewa. How he ended up standing in front of the Bath police station, a good fifteen miles from his announced destination, was one of the mysteries police faced more than a decade later. Another was why his parents waited nearly a week to report their son missing.

That Dahmer had indeed encountered Hicks, there was little doubt. He described some of Hicks' personal belongings that the investigators had never known about. They checked with the youth's father, Richard, who verified Dahmer's information Sunday.

The burial of young Hicks was all done rather on the spur of the moment. Later, when Dahmer was again home alone, he told Karabatsos and Munsey, "I dug up the body and buried it in a better spot."

The more he thought about it as time wore on, the more he felt that planting Hicks in a single grave wasn't too good of an idea. So he dug him up a second time, he said, and reburied the body parts in a number of different locations about the place.

Karabatsos and Munsey showed Dahmer aerial photos taken of the heavily wooded property. After studying the pictures Dahmer pointed to several locations where he said parts of Hicks would be found.

Sheriff Troutman and Bath Police Captain John Gardner went over Dahmer's story with Karabatsos and Munsey, trying to pin a motive on the killing—if indeed there was one. In the end they were convinced that sex was not the reason.

"We don't believe that at any time Steven Hicks went to the Dahmer residence was there any type of homosexual activity that was going to take place," the white haired Troutman said Sunday, in answer to calls from Cleveland and Akron newspapers.

Bath Police Chief William Gravis had ordered the property placed under a twenty-four-hour police guard, to insure that nothing would be disturbed until the search for Hicks' remains began on Monday. A search warrant was obtained for the spacious yard as a matter of formality, although the current, William Berger, was cooperating fully in the investigation.

"We want to do this right. We don't want anything to come back at us after we're done," Chief Gravis told his men.

Meanwhile Berger had been thinking, ever since investigators had posted a guard and strung yellow "Police Line—Do Not Cross" tape around his property. "You know, I remember finding a bone about a year ago, when I was doing some landscaping," he told sheriff's detectives. "I threw it in the trash heap, and as far as I know it's still there."

Sure enough, he was able to recover the bone from a pile of discarded brush. He presented it to the lawmen as the first solid clue in their investigation. Sheriff Troutman turned it over to the Summit County coroner's office.

Now comes the interesting part. One source close to the investigation quoted Thomas Marshall of the coroner's office as confirming the bone was human. It had come from an upper right arm, he said. But another source, just as close to the investigation, said that Joseph Orlando, also from the coroner's office, told him it was part of a femur—a thigh bone.

Sheriff Troutman decided to pass the clue on to Owen Lovejoy, an anthropologist at Kent State University, to get a third opinion.

"If a body was discovered on the former Dahmer property, and Dahmer was convicted of killing Hicks, he would face a maximum of life in prison," Summit County Prosecutor Lynn C. Slaby said. "As far as bringing him to trial in Ohio, we will most likely wait until after they're through with him in Wisconsin. "This could take anywhere from one to two years."

The apparent strategy of Dahmer's defense lawyer, in letting him rattle on to his heart's content about murders in Wisconsin and Ohio, was beginning to become clear. Legal experts pointed out that a man who has been convicted of a crime in one state cannot begin serving a sentence for a crime in another state until the first state's sentence has been served.

Even if authorities in a state that has capital punishment turn up enough evidence to convict Dahmer for a homicide he hasn't owned up to, they would be unable to carry out the sentence unless they were able to try him first. The mandatory sentence for first degree murder in Wisconsin is life in prison, and once Dahmer began serving that term, no other state could execute him.

Ironically, a "mandatory life in prison" sentence in Wisconsin means a convicted killer could become eligible for parole after spending less than fourteen years behind bars. If Dahmer somehow gets out on parole, through one of the many miracles of the modern legal system, Ohio at the moment has next dibs on him, and he can't be put to death there, either, even though Ohio is a death penalty state.

Ohio reinstated capital punishment in 1981, but it does not apply to a murder that took place in 1978. There are currently about 100 convicted killers on Ohio's death row, but the state's electric chair hasn't been called into service since 1962.

While Ohio authorities got their tools together and prepared to dig for Steven Hicks, another name surfaced as a possible Dahmer victim back in Milwaukee.

Richard Guerrero, twenty-one, had left his parents' North Side home with only $3 in his pocket on March 24, 1988, and hadn't been seen since. He clearly fell into the Dahmer time frame.

Even though all eleven victims, or parts thereof, found in Dahmer's apartment had been identified, authorities found it unlikely that he did not engage in any fatal activities between the time he left Ohio and when he set up housekeeping on 25th Street.

More than one long-neglected missing person file was being dusted off, and Guerrero's was one of them. He was a slightly built man, five feet six inches tall and weighing 130 pounds. He fit Dahmer's pattern.

On the day Guerrero left home he told his mother, Irene, that he was going over to a friend's house. Because he had so little money, he didn't ever bother to take his wallet. The friend was the first person his family called when he failed to come home. ''No, I haven't seen him,'' the friend said. ''I was waiting for him to come by, but he never did.''

His family reported him missing to police, and they

gave it their usual shot, but could find no trace of him. Four months later the Guerreros hired a private investigator.

The detective gave it his best shot, too, but finally called off the search. "I'm sorry, but I'm running into nothing but dead ends," he told the family. "It doesn't make any sense for me to stay on this case any longer."

The missing man's family refused to give up. His desperate mother went downtown to the newspapers with Richard's picture, and had them run stories. The family also printed hundreds of flyers bearing his photo and description, which they distributed around the North Side. On weekends a number of his friends joined family members in combing the banks of the Milwaukee River.

Every couple of months for the next three years Guerrero's brother, Pablo, or their sister, Janie Hagen, pestered police about how they were doing the case. "Your brother's not the only one who's missing," one cop told the sister. Twice the family was told that the file had been closed, but they kept right on pestering.

"My brother was real close to our family," Hagen told police. "He took my mom shopping whenever she had to go anywhere. He ran errands for her. He wouldn't just up and leave without telling anyone. That's not his calling. Something like that just isn't in him.

"The only thing we can think of is, maybe he has amnesia and he doesn't know where he is."

When police couldn't find him the family wrote to the "Unsolved Mysteries" television show, and consulted a psychic. But not even the psychic had the mystic powers to see behind the plain wooden door of apartment 213 on 25th Street.

When the horrendous Dahmer story hit the headlines, Janie Hagen raced right down to police headquarters to make sure police hadn't forgotten about her missing brother.

She didn't have to. They had already pulled his file, and were right on top of the situation. In fact, they got right to the point. "Did your brother ever mention the name of Jeffrey Dahmer as one of his friends?" the cops asked.

"It says in the papers how this man offered young men money to come to his apartment and pose for photos, and things like that," Pablo Guerrero said, in kicking the matter around with his sister. "Rich only had $3 when he left home. Suppose he stopped off for a beer somewhere, and was running short of money. And this other guy was in the bar buys him a beer, and says he'll give him some money to come home with him."

"I pray to God that's not what happened, I pray it isn't so," the missing man's sister said. But in her heart she feared it could be.

"The cops are working as hard as they can on it," Pablo said encouragingly.

"I know," she said. "But how come it took an apartment full of bodies to get them going?"

Richard Guerrero was not the only missing male in Milwaukee, to be sure. Some of them weren't even known by name, but there was suddenly genuine concern that they wouldn't be seen around anymore.

E.C. Fitzpatrick, a cabdriver, wheeled his City Veterans Taxicab up to police headquarters on Sunday and went in to relate an incident that had just popped back into his mind.

"About two months ago I pick up this black guy and a white guy at the Club 219, a gay bar over on Second Street. I never saw the white guy before, but I knew the black fellow. I don't know his name, but he's been in my cab quite a few times," he said.

"Do you remember where you took these two people?"

"That's the point," Fitzpatrick said. "I didn't think any more about it until I see this Dahmer guy's face on television. He's the white guy that was in my cab. Then I went back and checked my logs. The place I took them was 924 North 25th Street."

"Dahmer's address," the cop noted.

"Right," Fitzpatrick. "And the black guy? I haven't seen him since."

Fitzpatrick was the second Milwaukee cabdriver who had provided police with information in the ongoing investigation. Everett N. Gieskieng explained to authorities how Dahmer was able to get that forty-seven-gallon barrel, in which he marinated his guests' torsos, into his apartment.

"It was July 12," the sixty-nine-year-old cabdriver reported, consulting his trip sheets. "It came to me when I was watching police carrying the barrel out of the guy's house on television. I was the one who gave him a ride home with it. He had this big blue barrel. He put it in the trunk of the cab.

"I thought it was kind of odd, you know, why some guy would want a barrel of acid. I was thinking about asking him, but I don't get too nosey. I do remember asking him what the barrel cost. It was either $53 or $56. He didn't have much to say. Kind of quiet the whole trip. Nice, polite gentleman, I remember that."

The Milwaukee investigators also heard from two other law enforcement agencies on Sunday—Chicago and Kansas City, Missouri.

Two Chicago detectives who had worked on the John

Wayne Gacy case were dispatched to Milwaukee to lend their expertise in assisting Wisconsin police in the Dahmer probe.

Authorities in Kansas City were simply touching base, as a matter of procedure, since they were involved in an almost identical case. In fact, the similarities were startling.

Albert Riederer, the Jackson County prosecutor, sent District Attorney E. Michael McCann in Milwaukee a court file and a bundle of newspaper clippings about a series of killings in Kansas City by forty-two-year-old Bob Berdella.

"I frankly don't believe there is any connection between the two cases, but you will see that there are many similarities," Riederer pointed out to McCann.

Berdella had pled guilty in 1988 to torturing, killing and mutilating six men in the basement of his middle-class home in Kansas City. His guilty plea enabled him to avoid the death penalty, and he was sentenced to life in prison without parole.

Like Dahmer, Berdella had grown up around Akron, Ohio. And like Dahmer, his victims were young homosexual males whom he picked up and brought to his home, where they were drugged. In Dahmer's apartment police uncovered photographs he had studiously taken of the dismembered bodies of his victims. Police in Berdella's case found photographs of his victims, along with copious torture logs.

Furthermore, both men fell into the hands of the law after an intended victim escaped and fled to police. The fortunate man who fled from Berdella's murder house was wearing only a dog collar at the time. Tracy Edwards, who alerted police to Dahmer, had a handcuff affixed to one of his wrists.

In Fresno, on this day, Jeff Dahmer's mother, Joyce A. Flint, who works as an AIDS victim counselor, went into seclusion and hired a lawyer to help keep the clamoring press off her back. "Mrs. Flint doesn't have anything to say to anybody. You can imagine her state of mind," Fresno attorney Patience Milrod, told reporters.

Criticism of the initial police handling of the Dahmer case continued to rumble through Milwaukee's black and gay communities.

Leonard Wells, president of the League of Martin, an organization of black police officers who named their group after Martin Luther King, Jr., called for more sensitivity training to help do away with harmful stereotypes and enable police to better understand varying lifestyles and cultures.

"The sensitivity training stinks," he said of the sixteen hours of coaching he and fellow officers were given during their twenty-week program at the police training academy.

"In terms of the effects of it and the seriousness of it, if you put it on a scale of one to ten, I would rate racism and homophobia as an eight. It goes directly to how you interact with people of color and people of different interests and values than your own," he said.

M. Nicol Padway, Milwaukee's fire and police commissioner, responded that the commission had been analyzing the police department's cultural awareness and civility training for several months.

"I know there are problems out there," he acknowledged. "This is a 2,000-person force, and it's just filled with many diligent, talented concerned officers. It is also a force comprised of a broad mix of personalities, philosophies and personnel. There is no guarantee there will always be the level of sensitivity that you would like."

It was definitely not up to the level that the gay community wanted to see.

"Many gays simply do not trust police, even though their attitudes toward us have improved over the last five years," said Christopher Lubus, a member of an anti-discrimination group that called itself the Queer Nation.

"I've been treated badly by cops because I was gay. A lot of the younger cops are more oriented to working within the community and working together because that's the way the department is teaching."

Lubus knew four of Dahmer's victims. He and other gays had become disturbed when their friends began disappearing, and had set up a program to make sure one another got safe rides home from gay bars.

"Tony Hughes hit particularly close to home. I've known Tony for two years," he said. "When you miss someone you see all the time, it hurts."

He pointed out that intolerance toward homosexuals made them particularly susceptible to crimes of violence. "Gay men who don't have supportive families are more likely to take unannounced trips, which makes it harder for their true friends to find out if something has happened to them," he said. "What do they have holding them here? The family isn't there for them, so what do they care? That's why it's so important that we stick together, or else we'll fall through the cracks."

The Sunday issue of the *Milwaukee Journal* featured a two-column ad placed by the city of Milwaukee, as the first step to try to narrow the rift between blacks, gays and law enforcement authorities:

# PUBLIC NOTICE

The City of Milwaukee Fire and Police Commission seeks citizen input relative to its citizen complaint process. Citizens are invited to attend a meeting at West Division High School, 2300 W. Highland Avenue, on Wednesday, July 31, 1991, at 6:30 P.M.

The purpose of the meeting is to solicit citizen input on how to effectively modify the present complaint process in order to better serve the needs of the community. Citizens who are unable to attend the meeting but who wish to communicate with the Commission on this subject may write to the Fire and Police Commission, 749 W. State Street, Room 706, Milwaukee, Wisconsin 53233.

City of Milwaukee

Michael L. Morgan
Executive Director

# CHAPTER 11

# DAY VIII
# JULY 29

Oops! That wasn't a human bone that William Berger raked up after all on the former Dahmer property north of Akron, where he now made his home. Despite being identified earlier by the Summit County Coroner's office as (a) a bone from an upper right arm or (b) a thigh bone, the Kent State anthropologist advised Sheriff David Troutman that it had come from some kind of an animal.

It could still have been the work of Jeffrey Dahmer, however. He had told Milwaukee police that before he graduated to working with humans, he had beheaded animals, and boiled the skin off their bones.

He once told a fellow patron he struck up a conversation with in a gay bar that he liked to kill animals and collect their skulls.

"I said, 'Are you telling me you go around killing people's pets?' He said, 'No, no. I just find them dead,'" the man later told police. "I asked him what kind of animals he found dead. He grew evasive and said, 'Just animals.'"

A former neighbor of Dahmer's in Bath, Ohio, told authorities he once found a dog beheaded and its carcass "crucified" in woods behind the Dahmer home.

"It scared the heck out of us." said thirty-three-year-old Jim Klippel, in recounting the discovery made by his girlfriend and now wife, Renee, and his kid brother, Paul, about seventeen years earlier. "The dog was skinned, gutted, and it was beheaded."

Paul Klippel, now twenty, said he remembered getting a glimpse of the animal before his brother hurried him away. The carcass was hung on two large tree limbs that formed a crude cross standing about three feet tall.

Summit County Common Pleas Court Judge Glen B. Morgan issued a search warrant Monday, authorizing the sheriff's men to go over the grounds to see what else might have been discarded there. The warrant, based on information Dahmer had passed on to Detective John Karabatsos, specifically listed bones, trash bag remnants, clothing bits and jewelry that might have belonged to the long missing Mark Hicks.

Dahmer told the detectives that after caving in Hicks' head with a barbell, he dragged him from the bedroom into a crawl space under the house. There he dismembered the body and stored the pieces in garbage bags.

After several days, however, it became quite evident to anybody with a nose that worked that something was rotten under the house. "I got the plastic bags and carried them out to my car when no one was around," Dahmer said. "I was going to take them somewhere and dump them, but then I changed my mind. Somebody might find them. So I took them back home and buried them in the yard."

After disinterring Hicks, reburying him, and digging his body parts up the second time, Dahmer said he cleaned the remaining flesh off the bones and smashed them into as many pieces as he could before strewing them about the yard.

As the sheriff's men prepared to see how much of Dahmer's do-it-yourself project they could recover, prosecutor Lynn Slaby advised them, "If we find anything at all it's going to be near the surface. I think that the majority of what we recover will be gotten by raking." "Do you think this guy was nuts, Lynn?" Sheriff Troutman asked. "Is he gonna plead insanity and get off the hook?"

"That's probably what his lawyers will claim, Dave, but I don't think they can pull it off. The acts of committing the crime and the attempts to hide the body and destroy the evidence clearly show that he knew his actions were wrong. All we have to show is that the defendant knew right from wrong, and is able to cooperate with his attorney."

"Well, we sure have our work cut out for us, thanks to him. From the size of this lot, I figure it'll take us about two days to do this job right," Troutman speculated. "There's quit a bit of poison ivy in the weeds and brush, and the men are going to have to be pretty careful."

In addition to an array of rakes, some of the sheriff's crew of fifteen were armed with metal detectors, hoping to find evidence of teeth with fillings in them, as they went over the ground for bits of Hicks' smashed skull.

"Pay particular attention to the general areas which he marked on the map, fellows," Troutman urged. "When we get done out here, we'll see what we can find in the crawl space under the house."

STEP INTO MY PARLOR

Somebody else's body parts, meanwhile, were being mulled over in California. Hard on the heels of the request by Fresno authorities to ask Dahmer about the foot found in the tennis shoe, Los Angeles police asked Milwaukee detectives if they would query him about a pair of feet and a head.

"A transient found the human head and feet in Hollywood while rummaging through a dumpster looking for food last October," L.A. Police Lieutenant Dave Lampkin advised Milwaukee investigators. "It took us awhile, but now we've I.D.'d the subject as one William Newton, twenty-five. He came out here from Wisconsin. That's the connection. Try to find out, if you will, whether Dahmer was in Hollywood on or about October 29."

Milwaukee said they'd run it past Dahmer, although it wasn't likely he was going to readily admit to doing anything that might cost him his life.

Elsewhere Monday, Milwaukee and West Allis police removed a number of items from the home of Dahmer's elderly grandmother, where he said he had done some of his earliest work.

"We certainly don't expect to find the remains of any of his victims, because of the method he said he used to dispose of the bodies," said Deputy Chief Robert Due. "What we are looking for is something that might confirm that one or more persons had been killed here.

Among the items police confiscated were a sewer grate, a sledgehammer, a hatchet and some prescription pill bottles. All fit into Dahmer's way of doing business. He had told police in the past that he used pills to drug his victims; the ax could have been used in the dismemberment process; the sledgehammer for breaking up what bones he didn't care to keep; and the sewer for washing down the mess.

152

Meanwhile, police working downtown came up with the identification of another of the quiet man's victims. That brought the total known victim count to fifteen, however authorities were certain the number would climb higher.

Based on lengthy interviews with Dahmer, they determined that one of the men he did away with had to have been twenty-eight-year-old Eddie Smith. Smith, who was black, was reported missing June 14, 1990. His remains were never found.

His sister, Caroline, thirty-seven, with whom he lived, filed a missing person report. When asked to provide a description, she said, "Eddie is a gorgeous-looking guy. He wants to become a professional model. He's the kind of person that, if you were in a crowd of 300, you'd notice him. He's a totally down-to-earth person, close to his family."

How many times had Milwaukee police heard that before in going over reports of young men whose families reported that they seem to have disappeared off the face of the earth? "...quiet and unassuming...good looking ...down to earth...close to his family..." He was also gay.

Smith had intended to attend the Gay Pride parade in Milwaukee the day after he was last seen, but never showed up along the line of march.

Nine months later, in March 1991, his sister received a curious telephone call. A male voice told Caroline, "Don't even bother looking for your brother any more."

"Why not?" she asked, incredulously.

"Because he's dead."

"How do you know that?"

"Because I killed him."

A chill came over the woman's body as she hung up

the phone and the conversation kept repeating itself in her head. She reached for the phone again and dialed police.

"I'm sorry ma'am, but we have no record of anyone by the name of Eddie Smith being reported missing," the officer who took the call told her.

"Of course you have," she insisted. "I filed the report myself, last June."

"Well, we either lost it, or there never was one," he retorted.

There was one, of course. Police took no action then, but after Dahmer's arrest detectives began to pore over scores of missing person reports, pulling out those of young black men in particular, who had been reported missing in the last year and a half. The report on Eddie Smith was among them.

The report was passed on to the teams of detectives who were questioning Dahmer. Did he remember this one? Dahmer looked at the missing man's photo, and the date he was last seen alive.

Yes, Smith was one of his.

Yes, he was the person who made the anonymous phone call to his sister.

A homicide detective drove over to Caroline Smith's home on North 11th Street to ask for her brother's dental records. These were turned over to Jeffrey Jentzen, the medical examiner. He checked them against the teeth from the heads and skulls in Dahmer's gruesome collection, and verified that Eddie Smith was not among them.

The homicide detective drove back to the Smith home Monday to break the news to her. "Your brother's case is different, but I don't think this is the time to go into details," he told her.

"What do you mean, different?"

"It's so disgusting—the gruesome details—but it's different than the others. There are no remains. He disposed of the body."

Now things started to come together. Once the identification was made, friends of her brother told Caroline that Eddie had met Jeffrey Dahmer about two months before he disappeared, at the Club 219.

"Eddie liked to go to 219," she said. "He always figured it was safe there."

Caroline Smith was the second relative of a victim who had received a telephone call from Dahmer. He had also phoned the Laotian family. Police checked with families of other known victims.

Yes, shortly after her grandson, Ernest Miller, disappeared on September 2, Corrine Miller said her husband took a phone call from an unidentified man who kept chanting, "Help me! Help me! Help me!"

"Not long after that I got a call myself, from a man who just made gagging and choking sounds, and when I asked who he was, he hung up," she recalled. "Then, a little while after that, he called again, and made groaning noises, as if he was in pain."

Did Jeffrey Dahmer go about his grim chores alone, or did he have help? And if so, where can you get that kind of help?

The question of whether Dahmer worked solo was raised Monday when lawyers for the *Milwaukee Journal*, the *Milwaukee Sentinel* and the *Racine Journal-Times* went into court in an effort to find out why Detective David Kane, who was working on the Dahmer case, along with two Milwaukee County prosecutors, had gone to see Judge Gerald Ptacek, who was presiding over the Joachim Dressler dismemberment trial in Racine.

Dressler's lawyers had tried to interject the Dahmer

case into the trial, but Ptacek barred them from bringing the matter before the jury. The jurist then held a closed session of his court in chambers to hear testimony from the detective and the two prosecutors, so he could determine for himself whether there was any connection between the two cases. He decided there was not.

He had barred the media from the closed meeting, however, because he wanted nothing to appear in the press that might influence the jury sitting in his court. The newspapers had challenged the judge's action on general principles, arguing that anything that transpires in court is a matter of public record.

The Dahmer case also figured strongly in the daily work of Medical Examiner Jentzen. He declared a financial emergency Monday, and asked the County Board for more funds to cover the cost of the eleven post mortem examinations and other work in trying to identify the many victims.

"No problem," County Executive David F. Schultz told him. "We can take corrective action on any costs not covered in your budget."

Police still trying to tie up loose ends in the case asked for a blood sample from Dahmer. "There was blood all over his apartment. We want to know whose blood was there. It's just part of the investigation. As the investigation at police headquarters continued in an effort to determine why young Konerak Sinthasomphone was given back to Dahmer after he had escaped from the apartment, police and firemen began pointing fingers at each other.

The three suspended police officers told Chief Arreola that Fire Department personnel were already on hand when they rolled up to the scene, and had the Laotian boy wrapped in a blanket. The youngster did not need medical attention, they surmised, because the Fire

Department crew left the scene. The officers also insisted that Konerak gave them a name, different than his own, and told them that he was nineteen years old.

Fire Chief August G. Erdmann disputed the police version. "The police officers, not Fire Department personnel, were at the scene when the emergency medical technicians arrived," he said.

Public outrage over who was at fault continued to mount as some 200 people gathered in front of Dahmer's abattoir at 924 West 25th Street. "The city is a time bomb, a time bomb getting ready to explode," asserted the Rev. Cleveland Eden of the Clothed in Christ Ministries. He called for a march from the slaughter house to police headquarters, and declared, "Folks are going to take the situation in their own hands. When they see something go wrong, they are not going to call police anymore."

An astrologer also got into the act Monday, asking authorities for the birth dates of each of the victims, as well as the exact time of Dahmer's birth on May 21, 1960. "He has been making negative use of the Saturn Aspect, also known as the Grim Reaper," she explained. "We all have it, but that doesn't mean that we all use it."

In Chicago, *Sun-Times* gossip columnist Michael Sneed led off her daily column with: "Gagsville...Milwaukee—Rumors are circulating that admitted serial killer Jeffrey Dahmer may have performed amputations on at least one drugged victim before he died! (Is that why police are describing Dahmer's activities as 'torture'?)"

That was news to anyone in Milwaukee.

# CHAPTER 12

---

# DAY IX
# JULY 30

Two more of Jeffrey Dahmer's victims were identified Tuesday. Pulling old missing-person files was beginning to pay off for Milwaukee police.

It now appeared that they had all the bodies, bones or pieces they were going to get. From here on out they would have to rely heavily on Dahmer's own memory of his unspeakable adventures into the bizarre.

Richard Guerrero was one of the victims whose identity was nailed down Tuesday. He was the man whose family had searched diligently for him for three years after he walked out of his house on March 24, 1988, with only $3 in his pocket, and never returned. Guerrero was one of two Hispanic men Dahmer told police he lured to the basement of his grandmother's neat colonial home in West Allis, killed and disposed of their remains.

The other man identified Tuesday was David C.

STEP INTO MY PARLOR

Thomas, twenty-three, of 6432 West Birch Street, Milwaukee. No one had seen hide nor hair of him since September 24, 1990, when his girlfriend, Chandra Beanland, reported him missing.

Police and pathologists now had the names of fifteen of the seventeen men and boys Dahmer admitted to having slain.

The gray-painted skull of Anthony Sears was the only memento Dahmer kept of the three he said came home to grandma's house with him. "The other bodies I totally destroyed," he told detectives.

The twenty-five-year-old Guerrero was identified through a family photograph. As soon as Dahmer saw the picture he recognized it as one of his earliest subjects. "I met him in a gay bar, and he went with me to my grandmother's house," he told police.

Guerrero's family had been apprehensive ever since the Dahmer case broke, and police started carrying body parts out of his apartment.

"My brother was not a homosexual. He was a mama's boy," his sister, Janie Hagen, insisted on learning that Dahmer had named him as one of his victims. "He liked to drink and he liked to get high. He was very trustful of people. If somebody offered him free beer and a good time, he might well have accepted."

Guerrero's mother, Irene, fainted when police told her that Dahmer had recognized a photo of her son as one of his early victims.

"At least now we know what happened to him," Guerrero's sister said. We're relieved, in a way. Now we'd like to give him a decent burial."

If what Dahmer told detectives was true, however, there was nothing left to bury.

Dahmer told police that two months after he killed

Dahmer's 1978 high school yearbook photo. He had already started killing people.

Jeffrey Dahmer (right) in this early 1980s portrait with his father, Lionel, and younger brother, David.

Jeffrey Dahmer's grandmother's home in West Allis, a suburb of Milwaukee, was the scene of three of Dahmer's murders, according to his confession.

Masked investigators in Ohio search for traces of blood in home of boyhood friend of Jeffrey Dahmer. Dahmer has said he killed first in Ohio.

Bones believed to be those of Dahmer murder victim Steven Hicks are marked and bagged by police searchers. Scene is backyard of Dahmer's family home in Bath, Ohio.

Investigators take samples from the crawl space under the house where Jeffrey Dahmer lived in Bath, Ohio. The investigators sought evidence to implicate Jeff Dahmer in an unsolved 13-year-old slaying case. (Photo courtesy of the *Cleveland Plain Dealer*)

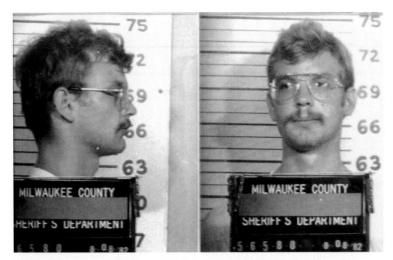

Milwaukee County Sheriff's Department mug shots of Jeffrey L. Dahmer taken August 8, 1982. He was arrested August 7 by State Fair Police for disturbing the peace. He was later convicted and fined $50. (Photo courtesy of Milwaukee County Sheriff's Department)

Glenda Cleveland complained to police that Dahmer was abusing a 14-year-old boy, but she was told the child was a "consenting adult."

12-10-89

Dear Judge Gardner,

My name is Jeff Dahmer. On Sept. 20, 1988 I was arrested in Milwaukee WI. for taking pictures of a 13 yr. old minor. On Sept. 27, 1988 I was released on bail from the Mil. Co. jail. On May 24, 1989 after having entered a plea of guilty in your court, I received my sentence. It was as follows, One year on work release at CCC, and five years of probation. I have, as of this date, served six months and four days of my sentence. Sir, I have always believed that a man should be willing to assume responsibility for the mistakes that he makes in life. That is why I entered a plea of "guilty" to the crime of which I was charged. During my stay at CCC, I have had a chance to look at my life from an angle that was never presented to me before. What I did was deplorable. The world has enough misery in it without my adding more to it. Sir, I can assure you that it will never happen again. This is why, Judge Gardner, I am requesting from you, a sentence modification. So that I may be allowed to continue my life as a productive member of our society.

Respectfully Yours,
Jeff Dahmer

Jeffrey Dahmer's letter to Judge Gardner asked for a break on his jail sentence, imposed in 1989, for abusing a minor boy. Dahmer wrote that he could be a "productive member" of society.

**The Grand Avenue shopping mall.** This is where Dahmer met
Konerak Sinthasomphone and David Thomas. (Photo by Jeffrey
Phelps)

**Milwaukee Greyhound Station.** Jeffrey Dahmer arrived here with
Matt Turner after meeting Turner at the Gay Pride Parade in Chicago.
(Photo by Mark Bloom)

**The Phoenix Bar** on Second Street in Milwaukee. Here Jeffrey Dahmer met Eddie Smith and Richard Guerrero. Next door is C'est La Vie, another Gay bar that Dahmer frequented in his quest for victims. (Photo by Mark Bloom)

**Club 219,** just down the street from the Phoenix Bar and C'est La Vie, is where Dahmer picked up Raymond Smith and Tony Hughes. Dahmer also picked up 14-year-old James E. Doxtator, who was waiting outside the club for a bus. (Photo by Mark Bloom)

**La Cage Aux Folles.** A gay bar on Second Street where Jeffrey Dahmer hung out. (Photo by Mark Bloom)

Dahmer's closest neighbor, Pamela Bass. She told him, "Jeff, your place stinks."

Door to Dahmer's Milwaukee apartment, sealed to preserve the scene of horror for evidence technicians.

Police found human heads in the refrigerator of Jeffrey Dahmer's apartment, dismembered bodies in a barrel in the bedroom, a bucket full of human hands in the closet, and skulls on the shelves. (Floor plan by Sheryl O'Brien)

LIVING ROOM

BEDROOM

DINING AREA

# JEFFREY DAHMER RESIDENCE

Crowds gathered outside the Milwaukee apartment building in which Jeffrey Dahmer confessed to committing a series of murders of young men and boys.

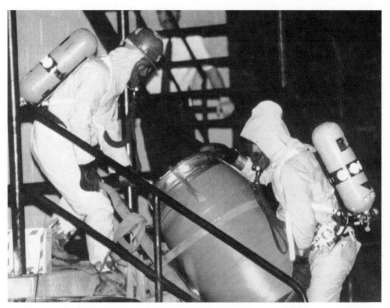

Taking no health chances, this two-member team in chemical suits removes a barrel containing body parts in acid from Jeffrey Dahmer's apartment.

As a resident watches intently from upstairs, police remove human body parts from the apartment of confessed serial slayer Jeffrey Dahmer in Milwaukee.

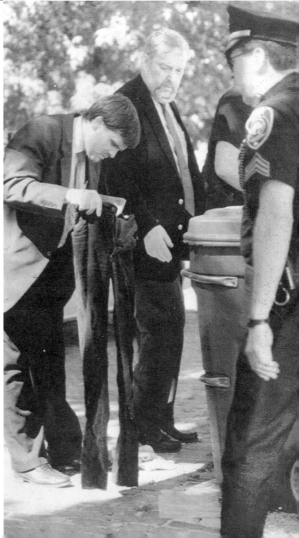

Everything found in Jeffrey Dahmer's stench-ridden apartment was viewed with suspicion, including this bloodstained pair of men's trousers.

Jeffrey Dahmer, accompanied by his lawyers, Gerald Boyle and
Wendy Patrickus, makes his initial appearance on multiple murder
charges.

# THE DAHMER VICTIMS

The 17 known victims of Jeffrey Dahmer in the order he said they were killed.

1. **Steven Mark Hicks,** 19, white, of Coventry Township, Ohio. Last seen June 18, 1978. His shattered bone fragments were found scattered around the yard of Dahmer's boyhood home in Bath Township.

2. **Steven W. Tuomi,** 28, white, of Otonagon, Michigan. Last seen September 15, 1987, when he left his job in a Milwaukee restaurant. His remains were never found.

3. **James "Jamie" Doxtator,** 14, American Indian, last seen in Milwaukee in January 1988, was the last of Dahmer's victims to be identified.

4. **Richard Guerrero,** 25, Hispanic, disappeared in Milwaukee in March of 1988. His remains were never found.

5. **Anthony Sears,** 24, black, last seen March 25, 1989, in Milwaukee. His remains were found in Dahmer's Milwaukee apartment.

**6. Raymond Lamont Smith,** aka Ricky Beeks, 33, black, of Rockford. Last seen in Milwaukee on May 29, 1990. Remains found in Dahmer's apartment.

**7. Edward W. Smith,** 28, black, disappeared in Milwaukee in June of 1990. His remains were never found.

**8. Ernest Miller,** 24, black, last seen September 2, 1990, in Milwaukee. Remains found in Dahmer's apartment.

**9. David Thomas,** 23, black, of Milwaukee. He was last seen March 7, 1991. His remains have not been found.

**10. Curtis Straughter,** 18, black, last seen in Milwaukee on February 18, 1991. His remains were found in Dahmer's apartment.

**11. Errol Lindsey,** 19, black, last seen in Milwaukee on April 7, 1991. Remains found in Dahmer's apartment.

12. **Anthony Hughes,** 31, black, of Madison, last seen in Milwaukee May 24, 1991. His remains were found in Dahmer's apartment.

13. **Konerak Sinthasomphone,** 14, Laotian, last seen outside Dahmer's apartment May 27, 1991. His remains were found in the apartment.

14. **Matt Turner,** 20, black, of Chicago, last seen June 30, 1991. His remains were found in Dahmer's apartment.

15. **Jeremiah "Jeremy" Weinberger,** 23, Puerto Rican, of Chicago. He was last seen with Dahmer on July 6, 1991. His remains were found in Dahmer's apartment.

16. **Oliver Lacey,** 23, black, of Milwaukee. He was last seen July 12, 1991. His remains were found in Dahmer's apartment.

17. **Joseph Bradehoft,** 25, white, of Milwaukee. He was last seen July 19, 1991. His remains were found in Dahmer's apartment.

Tracy Edwards escaped with his life from Dahmer's chamber of horrors and, at last, led police to Dahmer.

Guerrero he picked up another Hispanic man in a Milwaukee bar, enticed him into his grandmother's basement, and killed him, too. His body was also destroyed.
Unfortunately, Dahmer could not recall the man's name.
"He never even told me where he lived," he told detectives.

Unlike most of Dahmer's victims, Thomas, the father
of two, was not a "keeper." Dahmer did hang on to some
pictures of him, for the record, which ultimately led to his
identification.

"All right, Jeff, tell us about this guy, now," police
urged, showing Dahmer one of the pictures found in his
25th Street apartment.

"That guy I met last fall, around Second Street and
Wisconsin Avenue," Dahmer recalled. "I offered him
some money to come to my apartment. When we got there
we drank, and talked, but we didn't have sex."

"You say you did not have sex with this man, Jeff?"

"That's right."

"How come? You had sex with the other ones."

"After we got to my place, I decided that this man
just wasn't my type."

"So, what did you do, then?"

"I gave him a sleeping potion, and he passed out."

"If this guy wasn't your type, and you didn't have sex
with him, why did you kill him?"

"I was afraid he would wake up and be angry."

After killing Thomas, Dahmer told the interrogating
officers that he methodically dismembered his body, just
like the others, recording each step along the way with his
trusty Polaroid. The nice thing about an instant camera is
that you don't have to send the film out to be developed.
In Dahmer's case, it could have been disastrous.

In not being Dahmer's "type," Thomas had a

girlfriend and two children, and apparently didn't qualify as a switch-hitter. Because Thomas hadn't been Dahmer's type, there was nothing about him that he wanted to keep. He told the detectives matter-of-factly, "I disposed of the whole body."

After Dahmer told the investigators about his non-affair with Thomas, Detective Brian O'Keefe took a portion of a photograph, showing only the dead man's head and face, that Dahmer had snapped during the dismemberment orgy. He drove out to the Thomas home on Birch Street and showed the picture to Thomas' sister, Leslie.

"Do you recognize the man in this photo, Miss Thomas?" he asked her.

"Oh, my Lord, that's David!" she gasped. "Is he dead?"

"I'm afraid so. Are you sure it's your brother?"

"Yeah. In fact, we took a picture of David when he was sleeping, once, and this one looks almost like it."

At the detective's request, she got the sleeping picture of her brother out of the family album and showed it to him. "You're right," O'Keefe agreed. "It looks like the same person in both photos, all right."

"What happened to my brother?" she asked. O'Keefe explained it to her, leaving out all the lurid details.

Thomas's girlfriend, Chandra Beanland, agonized over how she would tell her three-year-old daughter, Courtia, what happened to her father. "How do you tell a three-year-old her father is dead?" she asked. "That's all she talks about now, her daddy. She keeps saying the policemen are going to bring her daddy back and take her shopping."

The detective asked her, "Was David a homosexual? Would he have let Dahmer take his picture?"

"No way," she insisted. "That's not David."

Ending up under Dahmer's buzz saw was the one thing Thomas' family hadn't suspected of him. They, too, agreed that he was not Dahmer's type. Dahmer had somehow misread him, an error in judgment that cost Thomas his life. Thomas, of course, had made a fatal error, too. He had gone home with a man he didn't know. You can't trust new friends, sometimes.

Police learned that some of Dahmer's victims, or at least the parts of those he didn't want, apparently ended up in the garbage, to be hauled away to landfill sites. George Finch, Jr., a city worker assigned to the pick-up route in the alley behind Dahmer's apartment, recalled Tuesday, "Sometimes there was a real peculiar smell coming from the Dumpster. The garbage area is overrun with rats, cats and squirrels, so we didn't think too much of it. But the peculiar thing about the smell was it stood out from all the other smells."

There was another time, he remembered, when a large bag from Dahmer's building broke after it was thrown onto the truck. "There was a large amount of blood mixed with water. We saw the bag, and the bag was busting, and there was bloody water running out of it."

"Didn't you report this to anyone?"

"Naw. We didn't pay too much attention. You see all kinds of stuff in the back of a truck."

While police managed to identify two more of Dahmer's victims Tuesday, the medical examiner's pathologists struck out in the laboratory. The dental charts of the missing Finlander from Michigan, twenty-four-year-old Steven Tuomi, did not match either of the victims that remained unidentified.

"Well, I guess that puts us right back where we started," Michigan Trooper Greg Wardman said in Wakefield, when notified of the doctors' findings. "We don't have a thing to go on. Looks like the guy just disappeared."

Four hundred miles away, meanwhile, the dig was showing positive results in the Town of Bath, Ohio. Sheriff David Troutman's men had unearthed about fifty bone fragments in the wooded area behind the former home of Dahmer's parents, where he said he had scattered what was left of Steven Hicks.

"From the looks of it, Dave, I'd say sixty to seventy percent of these fragments are human," Coroner William Cox told Troutman. "We've got what looks like pieces of a rib, a vertebra, and the top portion of a human skull. Of course, it's going to take some DNA testing before we can be a dead sure, and that could take four to six weeks."

"How are you gonna do DNA, Bill?"

"We got lucky. We've got a hair sample from the Hicks boy, that his parents saved from when he was a baby."

In the dirt-floored crawl space beneath the home the sheriff's men found a substantial amount of blood, using chemicals to bring it out of the soil. This was where Dahmer had said he dismembered Hicks, after killing him with the weight lifting barbell. Crime lab technicians also found a bloody hand print on the cinder-block wall.

Jeffrey Dahmer had the spacious house all to himself at the time of the murder, in June 1978, right after his high school graduation. His parents were locked in a bitter divorce battle. His father, Lionel, had moved out of the home, and his mother, Joyce, had taken Jeff's little brother, David, and gone to Chippewa Falls, Wisconsin.

"My guys have found what looks like scars and chips from a sledgehammer on a rock slab back there behind the house," Troutman told the coroner. "I guess that's where he tried to pulverize the bones. So far everything's right where he said it would be found.''

Sheriff Troutman had doubled his work force to thirty Tuesday, as half a hundred news reporters and photographers lined a neighbor's driveway bordering the roped-off Dahmer lot. Spectators' cars were parked along either side of Bath Road for a distance of half a mile.

Two enterprising teen-agers circulated among the crowd, selling coffee and lemonade. Who said crime doesn't pay?

The first echelon of an eight-member crisis team began arriving in Milwaukee, at the behest of Mayor John Norquist, to help residents cope with the tragedy. Calling the killings ''the most heinous crime committed in the history of Milwaukee,'' Norquist asked members of the Washington-based National Organization for Victim Assistance to work with families of victims, residents of the neighborhood where the murders took place, and government employees involved in the case.

And other communities, still trying to clean up unsolved homicides, were sending more files to Milwaukee police to run by Dahmer. The latest came from DuPage County, Illinois, where Chief Deputy Sheriff Robert Soucek was still trying to put a handle on who killed twenty-five-year-old Patrick Denesevich, whose nude body was found in a frozen pond near Willow Springs on New Year's Eve.

Denesevich, a third-year medical student, had been strangled with his own shirt.

Robert Soucek, chief of the Cook County Sheriff's patrol division, sent Milwaukee investigators a summery of the case file, along with a photo of the victim, who had been missing since October 6.

''We see no real similarities in this murder and those

in Milwaukee, but we don't want to leave any stone unturned," he said. "Denesevich appears to have been bisexual, and he was last seen in an adult book store in Downers Grove. Why not check it out?"

Dahmer told detectives that he had no idea the young Laotian boy he killed was the brother of the teen-ager whom he had sexually assaulted three years earlier. Konerak Sinthasomphone was strictly someone he picked up at the downtown mall, and smooth-talked into coming home with him to pose for pictures, he said.

The horrendous incident involving the Laotian boy was going to live in infamy along with Pearl Harbor if Alderman Michael R. McGee had anything to say about it. The Milwaukee alderman, who favors Fidel Castro-type attire, denounced police handling of the affair in a live appearance on CNN's "Crossfire" program.

"The only reason this happened was because of the racial attitude of the Milwaukee Police Department," he huffed. Spouting Jesse Jackson-style slogans, he hooted, "In Milwaukee, if you're white, you're right. If you're black, stay back."

Another panel member on the CNN show, Joseph Morris of the Lincoln Legal Foundation of Chicago, argued that what had happened in Milwaukee was a failure of the justice system, and had nothing to do with racism. "If the Hindenburg burned in Milwaukee, Alderman McGee would claim that's a racial incident," he said, not too inaccurately.

Elsewhere in Milwaukee, services were held for the first of Dahmer's victims to be released by the medical examiner. More than 200 mourners, many speaking in sign language, crowded into the Golden Gate Funeral Home to pay their last respects to Tony Hughes, the deaf mute, who would not have heard Dahmer if he crept up behind him.

"That guy had to have taken Tony by surprise," surmised one of his friends, who said his name was Rufus. "He did not take Tony face-to-face. Tony would have struggled for his life. That man destroyed eight of my friends. I hope they didn't suffer. That's the worst pain inside me."

Downtown, at the Police Administration Building, Chief Philip Arreola played tapes of radio communications between officers on the night of the Konerak Sinthasomphone incident for thirty-five of his inspectors, district captains and other supervising officers.

As the words "boy-boy trouble" and talk of returning to headquarters for "delousing" crackled from the speakers, remarks such as "unprofessional" and "doesn't sound too favorable" were heard among the audience.

Arreola played the tapes without comment. He wanted other department leaders to form their own opinions as to why three of the officers who handed the 911 emergency call that ended in a boy's death were under investigation.

As far as innuendos emanating from the Joachim Dressler dismemberment trial that Dahmer had to have had help in such an ambitious undertaking, Arreola said, "The evidence is pointing more and more to Mr. Dahmer acting alone."

In an effort to try to restore harmony on the department, Arreola issued a memo to all members of the force explaining why the three officers had been suspended. It read in part:

> On July 25, 1991, information was developed from numerous sources which indicated that the department had prior contact with the suspect and one of the victims on May 27, 1991 . . . The fact that this victim was thirteen years of age and reported by citizens

STEP INTO MY PARLOR

as being at the time threatened and assaulted by the suspect Dahmer lent an urgency to the immediate follow-up investigation. (Records showed the victim was actually fourteen.) Witnesses were interviewed, reports examined and to his credit, one officer brought this contact to the attention of investigating detectives...The allegations were so serious as to demand an immediate and separate investigation by the Internal Affairs Division.

The police chief stressed that the suspension of the three officers did not presuppose guilt. He said the decision to relieve the trio of their duties was not an easy one, and that he had shared it with Bradley DeBraska, president of the police union, before he made the announcement. His memo continued:

This is a serious matter, a matter which reflects upon the integrity and honor of the entire Milwaukee Police Department and its members. I am duty bound, as we are all by our sworn oath, to take whatever action is warranted. The results of this investigation will be shared with the department immediately upon completion.

He ended with a plea for "mutual support in these trying times."

At the same time Arreola's cops were reading his memo, they were receiving ballots from their union asking for a vote of confidence, or no confidence, in their chief.

The questionnaires, which union members would answer anonymously, contained three questions:

1. How would you rate Chief of Police Philip Arreola's performance since his appointment? ___ Very Good ___ Acceptable ___ Below Acceptable ___ Poor.

2. Do you have confidence in Chief of Police Arreola's ability to run the Milwaukee Police department? ___ Yes ___ No.

3. Do you feel the Chief of Police should have suspended the police officers prior to a complete investigation? ___ Yes ___ No.

President Thomas P. Donegan and seven members of the Common Council shot off a letter to DeBraska, the union president, calling his action "ill advised." They urged him to recall the ballots and "take more seriously our roles as public servants."

That night more than 350 community residents and politicians packed a steaming hot Fellowship Missionary Baptist Church on the Northwest Side to condemn police actions surrounding Dahmer's arrest.

There were impromptu shouts of "Tell it!" and "Dahmer's nothing but a devil!" as Alderman McGee worked the audience to a fever pitch, calling for another rally at City Hall Thursday night. "We've got to show that this isn't us coming together to blow off some steam," he said.

Others called out "Fire them! Fire them!" when County Supervisor Terrence L. Pits declared that the three officers, suspended with pay by Chief Arreola, were getting "free paid vacations." "The wrath of Jeffrey Dahmer and the non-attentiveness of the Milwaukee Police Department are only symptoms of the problems that confront black, brown, red and yellow people," declared another speaker, State Representative Marcia Coggs.

And back where it all began, for the first time since Dahmer's murder factory was discovered, police took down the barricades blocking traffic from the street in front of the apartment building.

The 900 block of 25th Street, between State and Kilbourn, filled up with cars as though someone had opened the floodgates. Occupants of vehicles of every description hung out the windows and gawked, pointed at the murder sight, and snapped pictures as other motorists beeped their horns and yelled at them to move on. There was one cheerful bit of news that emerged from the Dahmer furor Tuesday. Geraldo Rivera, the straight man for that embarrassing "Capone's Vault" television show out of Chicago, announced that he did not foresee doing an on-the-scene program from Dahmer's now-vacant apartment.

Jeff Erdel, a spokesman for Rivera, said, "This is not for us. We have no desire to exploit this story or create a television program around such a devastating tragedy for the sake of a couple of rating points."

As the score now stood, Dahmer's victims appeared to includ ten black men, Anthony Sears, Raymond "Ricky Beeks" Smith, Eddie Smith, Ernest Miller, David Thomas, Curtis Straughter, Errol Lindsey, Tony Hughes, Matt Turner and Oliver Lacy; two whites, Steven Hicks and Joseph Bradehoft; two Hispanics, Richard Guerrero and Jeremiah Weinberger, the Puerto Rican; and the Laotian youngster, Konerak Sinthasomphone. He also claimed to have killed another Hispanic, and a seventeenth man, about whom very little was known at this point except that he was white.

The scorecard belied those hysterical claims that Dahmer's killing spree was strictly racist in nature. Although he obviously favored black homosexuals, he had proved by his very deeds that he was an equal-opportunity body surgeon.

Still no sign of Jesse Jackson.

# CHAPTER 13

# DAY X
# JULY 31

It is an axiom in the newspaper business that you can't keep a running story alive more than nine days. Any sockdolager of a yarn that can stretch out that long is called a "nine-day wonder." Despite the most aggressive reporting and around-the-clock digging for new angles, even the best of stories peter out 99 per cent of the time as every possible fact becomes old news, and the jaded public wearily turns the page to something else.

The Jeffrey Lionel Dahmer homosexual, necrophiliac, cannibal, dismemberment serial murder story was one of those rare exceptions. It had something to disgust everyone, and there was no end in sight. Small children, who were watching it on the six o'clock news, were afraid to go to sleep at night. Sick Dahmer jokes winged their way across the country as fast as Fax machines could spit them out.

The conservative *New York Times* and the celebrity fawning *People* magazine sent in their heavy hitters to bring the story back to fact-hungry readers. "Once, he told the police in Milwaukee, he fried a victim's bicep in vegetable shortening and ate it," the staid *Times* would confide to them on page one.

"Police reports. . . said Mr. Dahmer met his first victim in Milwaukee at the 219 Club, a bar frequented by homosexuals. They went to the Ambassador Hotel, where a room for two costs $43.88 a night, plus a refundable $10 key deposit. In the police report he did not say he had killed the man; he just talked about how the two of them got drunk and passed out. 'When we woke up, the guy was dead and had blood coming from his mouth,' the report said of Mr. Dahmer." (The *New York Times* calls everybody mister, even the President.)

"He told the police he left the body in the room while he went to a mall, bought a suitcase, returned to the hotel, put the body inside, called a taxi and took it to his grandmother's house. . . dismembered the body and disposed of it."

*People* noted that there was no food in Dahmer's apartment, only condiments. "Inside the freezer were packed lungs, intestines, a kidney, a liver a heart—the latter, he said, had been saved 'to eat later.'" CNN Correspondent Margaret Lowrie explained, "What has kept us here are the shoes that continue to drop."

Elsewhere in Milwaukee, as Jeff Dahmer moped in his jail cell under an around-the-clock suicide watch, new angles were coming from every angle.

The story had become a nine-day wonder, and then some. Ever since Day One newspaper circulation drivers were having a hell of a time keeping their curbside vending boxes stocked.

The *Journal* flushed out a fifteen-year-old Hispanic boy who told reporters he'd been assaulted by Dahmer in the now famous 25th Street apartment a year earlier, but got away with his head and shoulders intact by out-talking his host.

The youngster, too young to drink legally, said he was loitering outside a gay bar on July 8, 1990, when a man he then knew only as Jeffrey offered him $200 to go back to his apartment with him and pose for nude photographs.

This fifteen-year-old kid would do almost anything for $200, and the boy said, "It's a deal." Jeffrey flagged down a taxi, and they rode to the man's apartment in style.

After the photo session, as he was preparing to leave, the boy said Jeffrey told him, "I don't want you to go," whacked him on the back of the head with a rubber mallet and commenced strangling him. The kid must have been one fast talker. He said he convinced Jeffrey he wouldn't tell anybody about the incident, and Jeffrey took his hands from around his neck and called him a taxi. "He told me he would kill me before I could call the cops," he said.

The boy was so visibly rattled at the unsettling experience by the time he got home, he said, that his foster mother insisted he tell her what was the matter. "I told her I was assaulted, but I didn't go into detail," the boy said. "She doesn't know I'm gay."

The youth's foster mother notified the social worker, who called police. They questioned him, but the boy was either unable or unwilling to give investigating officers enough information to follow up on the assault. The young victim was taken to Sinai Samaritan Medical Center, where he was treated for bruises and sent back home.

Police kept a file on the incident, however, and when

the Dahmer case broke a detective went back out to the home and talked to the boy. The cop pulled a few more facts out of him, and only then did the boy realize that the man he knew only as Jeffrey was undoubtedly that Dahmer fellow everybody was suddenly talking about.

Had his host not been using a rubber mallet at the time, they might be holding his funeral today instead of Errol Lindsey's.

The mortician had reassembled Errol as best he could, and what was left of Lindsey reposed in a gray casket adorned with red and blue flowers in Greater Spring Hill Missionary Baptist Church, where he sang in the choir.

His mother, Mildred, broke down sobbing, "Oh, my baby. Oh, my baby," as a woman seated near her in the front pew reached over and handed her a Kleenex.

"Errol was very faithful—and a good drummer," the Rev. Robert T. Wilson told the mourners. "He was that type of jolly person. I always called him 'Cool Breeze.'" After the service Lindsey's remains were shipped to Michigan City, Indiana, to be laid to rest in Greenwood Cemetery.

Over at Konerak Sinthasomphone's home, where the air weighed heavy with the pale smoke of incense, there was no corpse to mourn for. Flickering candles cast a soft glow on the Laotian boy's eighth-grade picture, propped up on a coffee table behind a tray of food and drink for his spirit's journey to Heaven.

The tray featured a colorful arrangement of the youngster's favorite snack, sliced apples and spice sauce, along with a glass of orange juice, and traditional Laotian staples such as beef, pork and rice.

It is a Buddhist custom to set out food for the deceased until his soul can be put to rest. Such a memorial would be maintained for two or three days under normal circumstances. But in this home the candles had been burning ever since the family learned that their youngest member had fallen into the clutches of a mad man. They would continue to burn, and his mother and father and brothers and sisters would pray for his spirit each day in front of his colored photograph until his young body could be returned to them for cremation. This would have to wait until the Sinthasomphone phase of the pathologists' investigation was over and the medical examiner's office released his remains.

"It has been a week, and we don't know how long we have to do this. Maybe another week, two weeks," his older brother, Anoukone told visitors and well-wishers. "That man—it's unbelievable that he would get two of my brothers. The feeling inside is very hard to explain. Police officials told us they were going to put him away for good. We never thought he was going to get out."

For weeks after Konerak, who had lived all but three of his fourteen years in Milwaukee, failed to return home from his soccer game his family had searched for him in vain. Their quest took them all over Wisconsin and down into Illinois, to Michigan, Minnesota and even into Ohio —every place that Konerak had ever talked about one day wanting to see. And all the while they prayed for his return. Today they prayed for his spirit.

The boy's parents had fled Laos with their eight children more than a decade earlier to escape the violence, and had suddenly slammed head-on into it in the Midwestern city famed for its *gemutlichkeit*, circus parades and beer. It hurt, but they did not blame Milwaukee.

"The truth, inside our heart, inside our mind, is that Milwaukee, or America here, is just like our homeland," Anoukone told a visitor amid the flickering candles.

"Milwaukee is the first city that we came to since we left our country. This is our home. A bad thing can happen anywhere, no matter where you go, no matter what country." No one realized at the time what a prophetic statement that would be.

Meanwhile a picture of Jeffrey Dahmer, the man, was slowly emerging as police, press, lawyers and probationers all dug into his past to try to find out what had gone wrong.

In some ways he was a very responsible individual. On November 4, 1988, he had run up a $324 hospital bill for injuries he said he suffered in a mugging incident. He balked at paying the hospital costs on grounds that it wasn't his fault he'd been mugged.

West Allis Memorial Hospital finally took him to court, and Dahmer agreed to pay the full amount, plus $51.50 in court costs—$100 down and $25 a week until the debt was clear. From August 20, 1990, until November 5, he showed up once a week at the hospital lawyer's office on Wisconsin Avenue, cash in hand. Once the debt had been erased he told Amy Dropik, a legal assistant in the office of attorney Gerald S. Boisits, "I just want you to know for your benefit that the bill occurred because I was mugged. I don't think it was fair."

Even after he had satisfied his debt, Dahmer continued to stop by the lawyer's office almost weekly to say hello. "I just want to make sure everything's square," he told Dropik, as though he didn't want to get a bad name. Of course, the lawyer's office was hardly out of Dahmer's way. It was on the same street as the Grand Avenue mall, where we now know he had other interests.

Don't be misled by the name, Grand Avenue. The trendy tri-level shopping center, in the old Plankington

Arcade building, is right downtown on Wisconsin Avenue, Milwaukee's "Main Street."

Looking back, police figure the reason Dahmer caved in so easily and agreed to pay the disputed bill was because he didn't want any trouble with the legal system. He was living in the Oxford Apartments on 25th Street by that time, and certainly didn't need anyone coming around asking questions.

Another clue as to what made Dahmer tick might have been found in the records of Donna Chester, his probation agent. A resourceful *Sentinel* reporter got hold of one of the reports, in which Lionel Dahmer wondered whether his son's sexual problems could be traced to the fact that he'd been sexually abused by a neighbor boy in Ohio when he was eight years old.

Dahmer flatly denied ever having been messed around with by a neighbor kid when Milwaukee police asked him about it. Ohio authorities tried to find a record of the alleged assault when the wire services picked up the copyrighted *Sentinel* story, but couldn't come up with anything. Finally Bath Township Police Captain John Gardner got on the phone and asked the Milwaukee detectives if they'd mind asking Dahmer about it.

The confessed serial killer, who was admitting to just about every horrendous act the human mind can conjure, said the story his father had told the probation agent was not true. "I was not physically or sexually abused, as a child, by anyone," he insisted.

It was almost as if he wanted to make sure nobody suddenly got the idea that he wasn't normal.

Somebody else who had been probing into Dahmer's lifestyle also made a disclosure Wednesday. Judge Gerald P. Ptacek, who was hearing the Joachim Dressler dismemberment case in neighboring Racine County, said he was satisfied that there was no possible link between the two accused mutilation murderers.

In secret meetings he'd been having in chambers with Milwaukee detectives, prosecutors, and Dr. Jeffrey Jentzen, the medical examiner, Judge Ptacek had them lay their cards on the table so he could decide whether to allow Dressler's lawyers to put the Dahmer investigators on the witness stand in Dressler's defense. Furthermore, he had sent the detectives back to Milwaukee to specifically ask Dahmer whether he knew anything about Dressler or James Madden, the young dismemberment victim.

"The information obtained from those interviews is that there is no connection between Jeffrey Dahmer and James Madden," the judge revealed. "Any attempt to link these cases would have a misleading effect on the jury. As far as I'm concerned, this matter is concluded and done with."

Concluded and done with is what they also were over at the medical examiner's office. John Teggatz, the deputy medical examiner, said pathologists had finished their post mortem examinations on the last of the eleven victims—or parts thereof—found in Dahmer's apartment. Whether Dahmer had actually eaten any of his houseguests was a matter of conjecture, but Teggatz stressed that the doctors found no bite marks on the parts that were left over.

In Dahmer's old neighborhood that evening, some fifty residents met in a nearby high school auditorium with National Organization for Victims Assistance (NOVA) counselors, who were helping them cope with the fallout of their fellow tenant's nocturnal activities.

One man, who lived across the hall, told of being awakened by the buzz saw going in the middle of the night. When the whirring stopped he heard Dahmer scream, "Motherf---er! I told, you, goddamn it!" In retrospect, he realized that his neighbor had just finished cutting up another caller.

"Anger, sadness, guilt, resentment are all emotions we are encountering here," said Dennis Davis, a clinical psychologist who headed the NOVA task force to Milwaukee. "The community is very traumatized. We have to help them realize that Dahmer did this to the community, not the Police Department or the probation office."

While the counseling session went on in the school, another forty people rallied outside the murder apartment, chanting, singing, and venting their outrage against the the police department.

The Rev. LeHavre Buck then led them in a march to the Police Administration Building, where they voiced their support for Chief Arreola, and urged him to stand by his decision to suspend the officers involved in the Laotian boy incident.

And in Bath, Ohio, where the dig continued, Sheriff David Troutman's posse of amateur archeologists ended their day with six more bones unearthed from the yard and crawl space of the former Dahmer estate. Four of them were identified as human.

# CHAPTER 14

**THE CHIEF TAKES ACTION**

It was not until August 1, as the "nine-day wonder" moved into its eleventh day, that *Sentinel* policy makers solved their inner struggle between morals, ethics and just plain logic. Until this day, *Sentinel* readers knew only that "a fourteen-year-old Laotian lad" had been the vortex of the Dahmer storm.

Of course, if they listened to the radio, watched television, talked to their neighbors or read any other paper—just about anywhere—they knew that the boy was Konerak Sinthasomphone. By the time the paper finally got around to using his name the competition reporters had memorized how to spell it, and the TV anchor faces were reading it off their teleprompters as if they actually knew what they were talking about. Nevertheless, before the *Sentinel* went ahead and printed his name, a reporter was sent over to the dead boy's house to get his befuddled parents' blessing.

Downtown a grim-faced Philip Arreola filed formal disciplinary charges against the three officers who had unwittingly returned the boy to Jeffrey Dahmer and to certain death. The chief talked slowly, taking deep breaths, as he briefed the media on the worst crisis to face the department in the two years since he took over as its head.

"The investigation has concluded," Arreola said grimly, "that the Police Department individuals who responded failed to conduct a basic proper police investigation into the matter. Basic law enforcement practices were not followed."

The chief said he saw the incident as a challenge to rebuild confidence and bridge the gap between police and the community.

"This has been an extremely trying time for the Police Department, the city of Milwaukee, and obviously, all of its citizens. There is no way we can change what has occurred."

Union officials admitted publicly, for the first time, that the officers had actually accompanied Dahmer and Konerak back into the apartment, but said they saw nothing amiss, and "didn't smell anything terribly unusual."

With the filing of charges, the department released the damning tapes of the 911 emergency call, in which one of the cops could be heard joking about the "intoxicated Asian naked male," and saying his partner would "get deloused at the station" before heading for their next assignment.

This set off a new firestorm of protest. More than 200 black activists rallied that evening at City Hall, under the direction of Alderman Michael McGee, to give the city a triple-whammy. They demanded the resignation of Mayor

John O. Norquist, called for the outright firing of the three suspended policemen, and asked for a federal investigation into the manner police handle complaints from blacks and other minorities.

They prepared a list of fourteen demands, including one that Governor Tommy G. Thompson declare the Oxford Apartments building where Dahmer lived a disaster area, and tear it down.

Over on 25th Street Glenda Cleveland was particularly distressed when she heard the police officer's taped laughter on the night she was so upset about the bleeding youth. "They thought it was a joke when I called because I said he was buck naked," the thirty-seven-year-old woman said. "I really sympathize with the boy's family, to see how they took this boy's life so lightly."

And at the downtown Zeidler Park an estimated 150 members of the Southeast Asian community congregated to hear their leaders condemn police handling of the unfortunate incident.

"The fact that the boy was Laotian is not the issue. The fact that he was a fourteen-year-old child in need of help who did not get it is the issue. Was this poor judgment, racism or what?" asked Shoua Nao Xiong, a community spokesman. "There is a lot of looking the other way by police when Southeast Asians are in trouble. I have seen this type of looking the other way, this odd kind of quietness, many times before. It is a veil of silence."

Everywhere in the minority neighborhoods people were talking about Jeffrey Dahmer, and the murders many felt could have been prevented. "It's high time people do something about this city!" Clearly, Milwaukee was a town on tenterhooks.

# CHAPTER 15

**HE IS COMING**

This just in: The Reverend Jesse Jackson is coming to Milwaukee. He will go into the neighborhood where the unspeakable tragedy took place, and address a Wednesday night rally in St. Luke's Emanuel Baptist Church on Highland Boulevard. The rally will be free and open to the public.

*     *     *

More than a thousand people crammed into the church as Jackson, surrounded by Alderman Michael McGee's Black Panther Militia, marched down the aisle in all his finery. Addressing the throng, he likened what had happened in Milwaukee to the police crisis in Los Angeles, where cops had mercilessly beaten a black motorist while being recorded on videotape.

Speaking softly at times, his voice ringing from the rafters at others, Jackson said, "This is an opportunity as well as a challenge, while America is watching, to maybe address America from Milwaukee. There is a lot of brokenness in the community, broken hearts, broken dreams and broken relationships. Yet in all of this brokenness the leadership will have to pick up the pieces and turn to each other and rely on each other."

Jackson termed the Police Association's no-confidence vote on Arreola a "public mutiny." He urged a thorough investigation of police handling of the Konerak incident, which he called a "sin of omission," and he called for community-wide understanding of Jeffrey Dahmer's neighbors in the 25th Street apartment building.

"The people in the building should be loved, embraced, understood. They're the victims of these horrible crimes. They're being attacked and blamed. You must help these children survive this nightmare."

By the time he left the church, the collection plates were piled high with $5,000 in donations to help bury Dahmer's victims.

Earlier in the day Jackson met with Mayor Norquist and other elected officials in City Hall, and then held a news conference, telling the press that he was calling for state and federal investigations of the handling of the tragedy.

He also met privately with the families of Dahmer's victims, and visited the murder factory to see for himself where their sons and brothers died. He talked to Glenda Cleveland, the neighbor who tried to get involved, but got quickly uninvolved by responding officers. "The police chose the word of a killer over an innocent woman. That leaves everyone vulnerable," he sympathized.

"I just want to get back to normal," the slender, soft-spoken woman said. She had been pestered by reporters from as far away as France, talk show hosts from all over the country, and well-wishers who wouldn't let her phone stop ringing. "Just give me a pole, some water and bait, and I'm fine," she said.

By the time Jesse Jackson got to her, it seemed like she had told her story to just about everyone, except maybe a few isolated polar bears on an ice floe somewhere in the Antarctic. Even as she talked with Jackson, her phone kept ringing. The limelight was a role she wasn't really used to.

An unwed mother, Cleveland had come to Milwaukee from Carthage, Mississippi, in 1973 as a girl of nineteen, with her baby in her arms. She quickly found work, learned data processing at a trade school, and now worked as a data entry clerk and typesetter at Milwaukee's C.P. Gauger Co.

"My daughter, Sandra, is my main concern right now," she said, trying to wish off all the attention she was getting. "I want her to finish school and get an education. That's a must. I'm not saying I'm poor, but then again, I'm not rich. But I think Sandra wants a little bit more out of life."

Sandra, too, had become pregnant unexpectedly, and now had a seven-months-old son. "She would have graduated from high school, but she had to drop out when the baby came."

From Cleveland's balcony she could see the window of Jeffrey Dahmer's now vacant apartment—the one bedroom apartment that turned her world upside-down. "I can't do anything about what happened," she mused. "When it comes to the Dahmer situation, there could be a Dahmer anywhere."

When it happened she got on the phone and told her parents in Carthage what she had done.

"My dad is a truth freak. The truth. The truth. My daddy does a lot of reading. He keeps up to date on things. When I called my folks about this thing, they just said they believed that I did the right thing, and that they were proud of me . . . and that they love me."

After his visit with Mrs. Cleveland, Jackson prayed with neighborhood residents, and led a march to the church, with McGee's militia at his side. "We Shall Overcome," they sang. "We Shall Overcome." Before going in he paused to register voters in the mostly black crowd of 2,000 milling outside, hoping to catch a glimpse of him or shake the hand of the man who wants to be President.

Police Chief Philip Arreola was there, too. The crowd gave the chief a standing ovation, and Jackson gave him a vote of confidence, as he stepped up to the podium. "I think you're doing a great job, chief," yelled a voice from the crowd.

Arreola acknowledged the applause, and assured the assemblage that he has no intention of stepping down from the job, despite demands from his policemen that he resign after suspending three of their colleagues.

"I am not—nor am I even thinking of—resigning or stepping down. We—you and I—have too much to do, and we need to do it together," he told the partisan throng.

He promised his complete cooperation with State Attorney General Jim Doyle, who disclosed that the Wisconsin Justice Department was stepping into the case at the request of District Attorney E. Michael McCann.

Then Jackson was off to Connecticut, where he was needed to lead a march from Bridgeport to Hartford, the capital, fifty-four miles away, to draw attention to government apathy. "He was cheered by a crowd of blacks, whites and Hispanics," the ever-present press reported.

While Jackson was busy saving Connecticut, Mayor Norquist acted to calm the troubled waters in Milwaukee. He announced plans to form a citizen commission on police-community relations.

"A vicious, cold-blooded, calculating killer has preyed upon our citizens. He has caused incomprehensible grief to the families of the victims. He has also preyed on the minds and hearts of the entire community," he asserted. "The Dahmer case has raised many questions about the ability of 'the system' to cope with the problems of our city. We have some of the answers. I am committed to getting the rest."

Working with the Fire and Police Commission, the mayor said he would include law enforcement representatives, community leaders and experts in the field of police-community relations on his proposed panel. He would ask members to conduct an overview of police performance, responsiveness and sensitivity to the community, as well as to examine police training courses, and a means of improving the citizen complaint process.

"I expect the panel to include some critics of the department, and I do not expect them to pull any punches," he stressed. "I will ask them to report back to me in sixty days."

There were immediate calls from both the gay-lesbian and Asian communities, asking to be represented on the panel.

As each new development was announced, the shoes continued to drop for Jeffrey Dahmer.

The operator of a gay bathhouse told police he kicked Dahmer out in 1986 for drugging other customers. Bradley Babush, who ran the now defunct Club Bath Milwaukee on Wisconsin Avenue, said he had to call the paramedics to revive one of Dahmer's victims.

"The complaints were all the same. He got them drunk and drugged them. They just got sick, and nobody ever wanted to press charges. Police followed right up afterward. They talked to Jeffrey, they talked to employees, and they didn't think anything was serious enough, so they didn't investigate any further," he recalled. "I kicked him out that same night. I didn't want to deal with him anymore."

One customer who remembered the incident said, "It was a pick-up place, you know. Everybody walked around wearing nothing but a towel. Jeffrey caught my eye because he was fairly good looking—blond, about six feet tall. I went to his room—it was about 1 or 2 a.m. He offered me something to drink. Even as I said 'no' he was already pouring it. He insisted that I was tense, that I needed to relax and have a drink.

"I thought I'd take a couple sips to make the guy happy and get on with it. The next thing I remember, I was out in the common area, fully clothed, and somebody told me he had drugged me and I had gotten sick all over the place. His interest in me didn't seem to be sexual. It seemed to be to get me to drink. Maybe he was experimenting with me to see what it would take to put someone out."

Not long after the incident the City Health Department put the place out of business. It was about that time, police figured, that Dahmer started working out of his home. Now that Dahmer was out of the 25th Street building, and his neighbors finally realized what he'd been up to all those months, they wanted out, too.

"I can't sleep. I've lost ten pounds," John Batchelor, complained as the unending caravan of rubberneckers continued to drive by the Oxford Apartments in their cars, vans, station wagons and pickup trucks. "Look at them. Jeez. I can't afford it—this stress. You have people driving around here like it's a museum, like it's a zoo. Everyone comes to look at the animals in Oxford. I just gotta get away from here."

I can't stand it, either," said another tenant, a woman who was half way through her pregnancy. "I haven't gained nary a pound since the night they took Dahmer away. I can't sleep at night. I have nightmares."

Later that day, when she went for her check-up, she complained to Lisa Monagle, the supervisor of obstetrics and gynecology at St. Mary's Hospital. "People are sleeping on the floor in the lobby, with the lights on. They don't want to stay in their apartments. Some went to motels."

"Why don't you move? It's not doing you any good, staying in that hell house," Monagle told her. "Takes money to move," she said. "Everybody wants out, but it ain't that easy."

"You can move," Monagle told her. "This is affecting your pregnancy, and we can't have that. Just wait here." Monagle left the room and came back a short time later with $200 from the hospital's charity fund, and gave it to the grateful woman and her husband. "If this isn't a deserving charity, I don't know what is."

Help for other residents of the murder building came from the American Red Cross. Although the apartment did not qualify by definition as a disaster, Jay Wallace, director of Red Cross disaster services, said he had been authorized by state and county officials to provide funds to help residents of the building move out.

"They want out right now, but that's practically impossible," Public Works Commissioner John Bolden said.

"State aid is available for people wishing to relocate, and we'll try to expedite the process. Certainly they should be out by the end of the month."

The apartment building owner, Metropolitan Associates, was more than sympathetic to tenants' apprehensions about continuing to live in a building where so many men had died. Metropolitan agreed to break leases of anyone who wanted out, and to return their security deposits. As an incentive to encourage residents to stay, Metro offered to reduce their rent from $307 to $250 a month.

When operators of the Indian Health Center, two blocks away on North 27th Street, heard about the plight of the Oxford tenants, they went into action. With help from an anonymous donor, the center moved thirty-six residents of the 25th Street building into a Milwaukee hotel. "These people are our neighbors, and we want to do what we can for them," said Jackie Schellinger, executive director of the Indian Health Board. "They're as much victims as anyone else."

While other people wanted to get out of the building, one person wanted in. Catherine Lacy, whose son, Oliver, had died there, wanted to be a part of her son's last moments. Finding her way to Dahmer's floor, she went up to the sealed-off room 213, and placed her hand on the door. It was as if to let her son know, somehow, that she was there.

On the Ohio front, new evidence against Dahmer was being unearthed daily, as Sheriff David Troutman speculated the digging would be finished by the end of the week.

"Thursday was our largest find—parts of fifty bones and three teeth. It equaled more than the other days combined. Most of what we found was one to two inches below the topsoil, but we're retracing our steps and digging deeper in some places."

In all, the sheriff's men had recovered more than 100 skeletal fragments of somebody, and the discovery of the teeth meant they might be able to prove it had been Steven Hicks.

Prosecutor Lynn Slaby said he hoped to bring the case before the Summit County grand jury within a month. "In my opinion, based on the information we have, combined with what has been found, we have enough for an indictment on first-degree murder," he said.

For Richard and Martha Hicks, the discovery of the bits and pieces of what had once been their son brought only bewilderment and belated grieving. For thirteen long years they had wondered what happened to Steve after he left home to attend a rock concert and never returned.

"Steve had qualities that would make any parent proud. He also had problems not uncommon to youth of that time: drinking, smoking, traffic tickets and occasional rowdiness of youth," his mother said. "Now we just want to be left alone to grieve in private."

Richard Guerrero's family had no body to mourn either, as they gathered with friends in St. Francis Parish on West Brown Street in Milwaukee. His was one of the bodies Dahmer told police he had "destroyed" three years earlier.

"We still don't have evidence of a body. I've been so confused. There could be a mistake," his mother, Irene, told a friend who stopped by to comfort her. At the same time his sister, Janie Hagen, was telling a friend, "I said to the police, 'How do you know he's telling the truth?' We're really back to square one."

Of the seventeen people Dahmer had admitted killing, dismembering, and distributing in garbage cans or around the countryside what parts he didn't want to keep, two still remained unidentified, but Milwaukee pathologists were working on it.

# CHAPTER 16

# THE ONE WHO GOT AWAY

Tracy Edwards, the Dahmer fish that got away, was wallowing in the fifteen minutes of fame that Andy Worhol said every man is entitled to once in his lifetime. He was probably so glad to have gotten away with all his parts intact that he plumb forgot to shift that brain of his into gear. From the moment he'd come tearing out of Jeffrey Dahmer's apartment with that handcuff on one wrist, the thirty-two-year-old Edwards had been an instant celebrity.

The *Milwaukee Journal* interviewed him. The *Milwaukee Sentinel* interviewed him. The Chicago papers sent their reporters up to talk to him. The radio and television lemmings were poking microphones and waving cameras in his face.

Edwards was more than agreeable. He'd tell anyone who would listen about the lucky night of July 22, when he woke up having a real life nightmare and ran for his life.

"I feel like I'm still living in a dream," he said, standing there in that familiar Georgetown baseball cap that everybody had seen on television.

It was raining that night, and Edwards had run into Dahmer at the Grand Avenue Mall. He recognized him as a guy he'd seen around the neighborhood. They even said "Hi" when they passed on the street. Edwards wanted to stop by the apartment of his twin brother, who lived near Dahmer, so the two of them shared a cab.

When they got there Edwards discovered, to his dismay, that his brother wasn't home. He'd gone all that way for nothing. "Hey, you don't have to sit there and watch the rain," Dahmer said pleasantly. "Come on in and have a brew."

The stench in the building was enough to wilt a skunk, but Dahmer quickly apologized that he'd been having sewer problems. It was always worse when it rained, naturally.

"Everything else seemed normal," Edwards told his interviewers. "I saw a couple of guys on a poster. There were no nude ones. But the stinking apartment. It wasn't the apartment itself. It was the building. I don't see how the people stayed there. You just open the door on the second floor and it would knock you down."

While Edwards was acclimating himself to the aroma, good host Dahmer made him a rum and Coke. He also gave him a beer. "I was getting ready to leave, and he kept saying, 'Finish your rum and coke,' but I only took a sip." He didn't realize that Dahmer had laced the cocktail with knockout powder.

"Didn't you suspect anything?" a reporter asked penetratingly.

"No. It seemed normal to me. Nice furniture, black lacquer lamp, beautiful aquarium. That's how he got me off guard. He was talking about the catfish, and how they clean the bottom of the tank. A split second later he throws a handcuff on one arm and sticks a big-ass military knife right below my rib cage—right below my heart.''

What happened next, said Edwards, a tall thin man with a pencil-mustache, was a scene right out of *Psycho*. He's sitting on the couch, trying to push himself as far back into the upholstery as possible, pleading and wheedling, "What's goin' on, man?'' And the wild-eyed Dahmer has straddled him, trying frantically to slap the handcuff on the other wrist.

They tumble onto the floor, rolling around. Edwards is trying to distract his host, as Dahmer keeps insisting, "I want to listen to your heartbeat. I'm going to eat your heart.'' "It was sickening,'' Edwards told his audience. "This guy was serious. I feel he would have eaten my heart. I believed everything he was telling me.''

Dahmer somehow got him to his feet, and forced him at knifepoint into the bedroom, where various body parts were stored, and there were "disgusting'' pictures on the wall, and a television set on which Dahmer had the movie *The Exorcist* playing. They watched the film for fifteen minutes—Edwards not by his own choosing. Dahmer still had the knife in his ribs. He kept babbling about the people he had killed. Luxuriating in the fact that he had someone in his power.

"That turned him on more than anything,'' Edwards related. "He didn't say anything against blacks or gays or anything like that. All I could follow, my understanding of this was . . . he didn't want people to leave him. In my opinion, that's why he kept the bodies around him.''

At this point, getting the hell out of there was the

foremost thought in Edwards' mind. The idea of becoming one of Dahmer's household decorations did not appeal to him. "I was trying to placate him, you know, trying to distract him, and he's saying, 'You're good.' I was pretending I was really interested in being handcuffed and photographed, you know, and all of a sudden he was making these funny motions, like bobbing his head like a snake.

"I had my eye on the doorknob, and a split second later I moved. If I hadn't turned that deadbolt the right way, I wouldn't be here today."

Edwards said Dahmer was remarkably strong, and exceptionally slick. "He worked out at Vic Tanny. If he conned me, he was good. Like he had practiced before, because I'm not easily fooled."

Edwards was a good interview. Smooth. Articulate. The networks picked it up and ran it on the ten o'clock news. He was a national celebrity.

Down in Tupelo, Mississippi, where the TV was blaring away in the police station, a detective turned to Deputy Police Chief Jerry Crocker and said, "Hey, Jer. Ain't that the guy we took to the grand jury in November? What the hell is he doing in Milwaukee?"

"Beats the shit outta me. Surprise, surprise!" The cops ran a quick check.

Sure enough, ol' Trace was wanted on a fugitive warrant for jumping bond on a rape charge. It would seem that the night he was Dahmer's prisoner was not the first time he'd been in handcuffs, which might explain his aversion to having them clamped onto both wrists at once.

He'd been arrested in Tupelo on September 7, 1990, on a charge of sexually assaulting his girlfriend's fourteen-year-old daughter. He was originally charged with capital rape, which carries a death penalty in Mississippi. The Lee County grand jury indicted him on the lesser charge of sexual battery, however, because police were unable to determine whether the assault came before or after the girl's fourteenth birthday.

Milwaukee police had checked Edwards' background when he was questioned in the Dahmer case. Mississippi police had not entered his name in the national computer network of fugitives, however.

As soon as police in Tupelo saw their man on the TV screen they alerted Milwaukee, and Edwards was taken into custody. He was arraigned before Court Commissioner Frank J. Liska, Jr., on a charge of being a fugitive from justice, and ordered held without bond for Mississippi authorities.

Later, when Milwaukee prosecutors learned that the charge against Edwards had been reduced to sexual battery, he was brought back into court, and Liska set bail at $1,000. Unable to come up with bail, the prisoner was escorted back to Milwaukee County Jail, where Dahmer was also being held.

It was not a cozy situation for Edwards. Dahmer had told other prisoners, ''This is all Tracy Edwards' fault. If it weren't for him, none of this would have happened.''

Edwards must have done something right in his lifetime, because good fortune suddenly came his way in the person of Syed A. Salat, a lawyer from Baton Rouge, Louisiana. Salat appeared with $1,000 in cash and got Edwards out on bail. How Salat got involved in the case from such a distance added another touch of mystery to the Dahmer affair. Dahmer, meanwhile, had become somewhat of a celebrity, much to the consternation of other inmates, who called him the ''Chop Chop Man'' and hurled homosexual insults when they passed him. They complained that he got special meals, was allowed to smoke while others were not, and that he had so many visitors—between his lawyers, his family, local police, visiting detectives, shrinks—that it interfered with their own visiting privileges.

Fellow prisoners also complained about Dahmer's language, which included liberal use of the word "nigger." From their cells they could hear him ask the guard, who was reading the paper to him, "Why is that nigger watching me?"

Dahmer obviously enjoyed making other inmates uncomfortable. On one occasion when the jail had quieted down for the night, they heard him call out, "I love it!"

Two of the patrol officers who had been assigned to watch Dahmer while he was under twenty-four-hour surveillance in the City Jail subsequently fell under investigation themselves, when it was learned that they had obtained the prisoner's autograph.

"Maybe they're too young and naive to realize how this looks. Ninety-nine out of a hundred people wouldn't want the guy's autograph," a police spokesman said.

Or, maybe they weren't so dumb. An autograph expert said Dahmer's signature could probably be auctioned off for about $1,000. It would be infinitely more valuable if it were affixed to a confession, he said.

Meanwhile an investigation was under way to determine how the *New York Times* obtained Dahmer's confession. It was the prestigious *Times* that revealed that Dahmer fried one of his victims' biceps in vegetable oil and ate it, while the Milwaukee press was still trying to get the grisly details of what Dahmer did when he was alone with his guests.

The finger of suspicion eventually pointed to twenty-nine-year-old Stephen Sessions, a Safety Building janitor. Under questioning by police, Sessions admitted that he lifted confidential material from the desk of a deputy district attorney, while cleaning his office, copied it, and passed it on to *Times* reporters. Whether Sessions did so for financial gain, or out of the goodness of his heart, was the question.

He was suspended from his $8.30-an-hour job while the incident was being investigated by the District Attorney's office, Milwaukee Police, and the Public Works Department, for whom Sessions worked. "We are pursuing the matter," District Attorney McCann assured the bescooped local press.

Where Dahmer got the "sleeping potion" with which he knocked out most of his victims before strangling them or slicing their throats became apparent when authorities discovered he had been under the care of William J. Crowley, a psychiatrist who worked as an $85-an-hour consultant for the State Division of Probation and Parole.

Police found Crowley's name on prescription forms in Dahmer's apartment for lorazepam, an anti-anxiety drug that could be used as a sleeping pill, and doxepin, an anti-depressant. A controlled substance under federal law, lorazepam depresses the central nervous system. One investigator said, "You crush it up and put it in a drink—it'll knock you out."

# CHAPTER 17

# TWO MORE WHO DIDN'T GET AWAY

By mid-August police and pathologists had come up with the identities of the last two known victims of Dahmer's lust. One of them was the Finlander, Steven W. Tuomi, who had come to Milwaukee from Michigan's Upper Peninsula to seek his fortune. The other was an American Indian, fourteen-year-old James "Jamie" Doxtator.

The twenty-eight-year-old Tuomi had earlier been tentatively ruled out as one of Dahmer's kills, when his dental records did not match any of the skulls police found in the murder apartment. Information provided by Dahmer, however, who seemed to enjoy working with police, indicated that Tuomi had indeed been included in his collection.

The Michigan man had last been heard of on September 15, 1987, when he left his job as a restaurant worker on Wells Street. His father, Walter, reported him missing to Milwaukee police in December of that year. Police told him at the time that there was nothing they could do, since there was no hint that Tuomi had been a victim of foul play.

Like many of the other men or boys who disappeared into Dahmer's hands, he had been a quiet, unassuming individual.

"There are few of us who remember him. He was very quiet and very artistic. Nobody seems to know what Steve did after he left here," Lou Gregory, the superintendent of Ontonagon High School from which Tuomi was graduated in 1981, would recall.

One of his classmates added, "Steven never made any waves, but he always fit in. He didn't say too much. He hung out with girls. He was quiet. He was into graphic art and that stuff. He was pretty much kind of a loner type."

The other victim, Jamie Doxtator, was identified by West Allis police on August 16. His body was one of those Dahmer cut and broke into pieces and disposed of in the garbage after killing the youth at his grandmother's house.

Dahmer must have looked young Doxtator over pretty well while dismembering him, because his identification of the victim was based partly on an appendix scar on Doxtator's abdomen, and other scars on his chest, chin and face.

The information about the scars, and a photograph of the fourteen-year-old, were provided by his mother, Debbie Vega, who now lives in a trailer park near Tampa, Florida.

Doxtator was last seen near his Milwaukee home at South 10th Street and West National Avenue in January of 1988. His mother reported him missing on January 16. "I believe he ran away from home," she told police at the time.

Dahmer told West Allis police he met the boy at a bus stop on the corner of South 2nd Street and West National Avenue, and brought him to his grandmother's house.

"When I first heard about Dahmer, I considered the possibility that Jamie might have been a victim," his mother said. "But when I heard that the victims were black, Hispanic and Laotian, I thought I didn't have to worry. James was part Stockbridge Indian and part Oneida."

After learning of her son's death, Mrs. Vega expressed her bitterness to Milwaukee police. "One of my son's favorite sayings from the Bible was 'Forgive them, for they know not what they do.' But I will never feel that way about Dahmer. He sits there so calmly and explains all the things he did. He knew what he was doing," she said.

"One day, when all this is forgotten eight or ten years from now, some parole board along the line is going to let him walk again and he's gonna be out there taking victims all over again."

West Allis Detective Lieutenant Ken Risse, who talked to Dahmer about the boy's murder, described it as a particularly unique experience.

"It was different. I have never worked on anything of this magnitude and had such cooperation. It was hard to believe. He was so open. He talked about everything in a very matter-of-fact way."

Authorities now had identified all seventeen of Jeffrey Dahmer's known victims, and were ready to firm up additional murder charges. This could get a little tricky, since only parts of some of their bodies had been found. In other cases, where victims' remains never were, and never will be, found, police and prosecutors had only Dahmer's word to go on.

The final score was revised to show ten blacks, Sears, Beeks, Smith, Miller, Thomas, Straughter, Lindsey, Hughes, Turner and Lacy; three whites, Hicks, Bradehoft and Tuomi; two Hispanics, Guerrero and Weinberger; the Laotian youngster and the American Indian boy.

# CHAPTER 18

# THE PROMISED LAND

Jeffrey Dahmer's nightmarish murder spree led straight to the Promised Land for the legal profession.

Police still had not identified all of Dahmer's victims when the mother of one of them, Catherine Lacy, filed a civil rights suit in U.S. District Court in Milwaukee seeking $3 million for the death of her son, Oliver. The suit was filed in Federal Court because Mrs. Lacy was charging racial discrimination on the part of Milwaukee police in failing to prevent her son's homicide.

Mrs. Lacy's lawyer, Davied E. Wittenberg, said police should have arrested Dahmer in May, but did not act because of the officers' "discriminatory practice of inadequately responding to requests for protection by minority complainants."

The suit alleged that twenty-three-year-old Oliver was killed on or about July 14, more than six weeks after three police officers were inside Dahmer's apartment, at which time they allowed Konerak Sinthasomphone to remain in Dahmer's custody, despite witnesses' reports that the Laotian youth had been molested and was in mortal danger.

"There was racial animus," Wittenberg declared. "If this boy had been white there is a high probability there would have been a more thorough investigation and Mr. Dahmer would have been taken off the streets, not left out there to sacrifice people."

The suit named as defendants the city of Milwaukee, and the three police officers who had been on the scene the night of Konerak's murder.

"Our client died after police delivered the boy to Dahmer on a platter," Wittengerg charged.

The parents of another of Dahmer's victims, Matt Turner, filed a $4.5 million claim with the Milwaukee City Clerk's office, alleging that police failed to halt the murders and mutilations.

Turner's mother and stepfather, Rosa and Waddell Fletcher of Flint, Michigan, argued in their claim that if police had determined on May 27 that Dahmer was on probation as a convicted child molester, they could have prevented the "wrongful kidnapping and death of Matt Turner," according to Madison attorney Charles W. Giesen.

The families of Curtis Darrell Straughter and Ernest Miller thought even more of their loved ones. They each filed suit for $3 billion.

"The billion is really meant to quantify the horror and the loss to the family. The money tells people how bad the harm is," said attorney Thomas M. Jacobson, who filed suit in behalf of Catherine Straughter over the death of her grandson, Curtis.

Jacobson also represented the family of Ernest Miller, in the other $3 billion suit. Judgments won through the suits would entitle the families to any money Dahmer might be paid for the rights to his story by publishers or movie producers, he explained.

Suits filed by the first four families totaled 6 billion, 7.5 million dollars. Lawyers generally receive one-third of any such amounts won in litigation.

Attorneys who had been approached by families of some of the other thirteen victims were not overly optimistic. They pointed out that recent U.S. Supreme Court treating of landmark civil rights decisions of the 1960s and 1970s made their chances in court difficult at best.

A parallel to the Dahmer case was that of a four-year-old boy, Joshua De Shaney, who suffered permanent brain damage at the hands of his father, shortly after being returned to the father's home by the Winnebago County Department of Social Services. The court ruled in that case that the social workers were not at fault in returning the boy to his father, even though they were aware that he had repeatedly abused the youngster in the past.

"To succeed in a civil rights claim, you have to show more than just negligence," explained attorney Curry First, who handled the DeShaney case. "You have to show intentionality or deliberate indifference."

Another lawyer publicly warned families of victims against lawyers who might promise multimillion-dollar verdicts.

Several attorneys pointed out that, even if such a case got past a judge, it might not set well with a jury in a conservative community like Milwaukee, where people tend to side with the police.

# CHAPTER 19

## THE CRUELEST THIEF

It seemed as though nothing more could happen to the Sinthasomphone family. Since fleeing Communist Laos for the relative safety of America, two of their sons had been victimized by the same creature, Jeffrey Dahmer—who left one of them mutilated and dead.

But they were about to get one more lesson on the American way of life.

About 250 mourners attended a traditional Laotian funeral service for Konerak in a West Side mortuary, where Buddhist monks and Buddhist women in flowing white robes symbolically led the youthful victim's spirit to Heaven before his body was cremated.

"Today we unite everybody to help bless his soul or spirit to go to Heaven," intoned Bouathong Souvan-marath, a monk from Milwaukee's Lao Buddhist Temple, through an interpreter. Each mourner, including news reporters and funeral home employees, symbolically "gave Konerak the way to go to Heaven" by placing bundles of candles tied to incense and flowers inside a basket next to the casket, which they then sprayed with perfume.

His parents, brothers and sisters and the women in white knelt on white cotton sheets beside the casket containing the boy's remains as the monks chanted prayers while holding a long cord of multi-threaded cotton, tied to one of the coffin's handles.

A tray of food and drink had been placed beside the casket throughout the week to nourish Konerak's spirit while it remained earthbound, awaiting the cremation rite. From the mortuary the procession went to the cemetery, where the cotton cord attached to the casket was tied around the officiating monk's waist as he led family members and other monks into the chapel.

As part of the service, the monk read the story of Konerak's life, and details of his untimely death.

But the Sinthasomphone family's bad luck did not end with the cremation of their son. It continued into the night, while the Sinthasomphone family slept. Someone, a thief of the lowest possible repute, either crept into their home or reached through an open bedroom window, and lifted a purse containing $6,000 in cash and checks that had been donated by friends, relatives and well-wishers from throughout the country to help pay for the boy's funeral and other expenses.

It was an extra hurt the Sinthasomphones didn't need.

To help spare the family from another form of heartache, Alderman Paul Henningsen asked the city to tear down the Oxford Apartments where Konerak and the other Dahmer victims lost their lives.

The forty-nine-unit apartment, built in 1962, had attracted thousands of curiosity seekers since the slayings.

"We should do everything possible to prevent the building from becoming a morbid tourist attraction," he said. "I would say that the community consensus is that this should be taken down. We don't want it to be a source of pain."

Minor Vandermade, executive director of a neighborhood association, proposed that a memorial be erected on the building's site, bearing the names of Dahmer's victims. "It would be nice if that place could become a park, or a small garden, or something else," he said.

As Dahmer sat in the Milwaukee County Jail awaiting trial, things were winding up for the area's other dismemberment slayer, Joachim Dressler, in neighboring Racine County.

A jury deliberated just two hours before finding him guilty of first-degree intentional homicide in the death of James Madden, the twenty-four-year-old Whitefish Bay man, who had been going from house to house soliciting funds for a program to enrich the environment.

The forty-three-year-old elevator mechanic showed no emotion as the verdict was read, but his wife, Kathleen, sitting a few feet behind him, burst into tears. Conviction for first-degree intentional homicide carries a mandatory sentence of life in prison in Wisconsin.

Some day, perhaps, Dressler and Dahmer might even end up as cellmates. Stranger things have happened. And, Heaven knows, they would have a lot in common to talk about.

# CHAPTER 20

---

# MAN OR MONSTER?

On an autumn day more than a dozen years ago, sixteen-year-old Jim Klippel was cutting through the woods behind a neighbor's home in Bath Township, Ohio, when he stumbled across something that made his blood run cold. It was the severed head of a dog, its toothy mouth agape, impaled on a sharp stick next to a wooden cross near circles of scorched earth. The mutilated animal's carcass, skinned and gutted, had been nailed to a nearby tree.

Right then and there folks should have started wondering seriously about the boy who lived in that house, Jeffrey Lionel Dahmer.

Who is this painfully shy candy factory worker who, as a boy, liked to skin dead animals and, in his adulthood, graduated to human beings? As far back as high school, his friends thought he was a bit strange or, as one former classmate put it, "one weird dude."

He had a rather distinctive way of walking to the high school bus stop that guaranteed no one would fail to notice him—four steps forward, two steps back, four steps forward, one step back. Picture the rather handsome six-foot tall, 150-pound youth with long blond hair and glasses, studiously marching toward the bus, four steps forward, two steps back, four steps forward, one step back. It was a bizarre dance routine that never varied, as long as school was in session.

Looking back now, it is easy to see that Jeffrey Dahmer was a lonely person, crying out for recognition. He would try anything, just to be noticed.

Though Milwaukee has disowned him—claimed he "isn't even a native"—the fact remains that he was indeed born there, in Evangelical Deaconess Hospital, on May 21, 1960, while his father was studying at Marquette University.

Two years later, after Lionel Dahmer received his electrical engineering degree from Marquette, the family moved to Ames, Iowa, so he could attend graduate school.

In October 1966, the Dahmers moved to Doylestown, Ohio, near Akron, where Lionel Dahmer took a job with PPG Industries in suburban Barberton. The family rented half a duplex, and enrolled Jeffrey in first grade. His brother, David, was born two months later. In 1968, with Lionel Dahmer prospering, the family moved into the three-bedroom home in affluent Bath Township.

According to his father, Jeffrey was sexually abused by a neighborhood boy at the age of eight, an incident which left him traumatized. Dahmer today denies it ever happened.

Jeffrey went to Bath Elementary School, Revere Middle School, and on to the prestigious Revere High School in Richfield. He also began drinking heavily, often downing several beers for breakfast before heading for class. "It's my medicine," he told a fellow student, who saw him swigging from a bottle of Scotch as he sat at his desk.

He seemed preoccupied with torture and death, and kept the skulls of chipmunks and other small animals in his back yard clubhouse. He enjoyed working with a chemistry set, given to him by his father when he was ten, experimenting with acid to scrape the meat off dead animals. "He kept chipmunk skeletons and squirrel skeletons in that shed, and he had an animal burial ground, with graves and little crosses," says Eric Tyson, whose home was across the street.

Jim Klippel, who came upon the dog's head mounted on a stick in 1975, recalls today, "It scared me to death." Other neighbors would encounter dead cats or frogs similarly impaled, or staked to trees.

It was a side of Jeffrey Dahmer that he did not display at school. "The kid minded his own," recalls Bill Mulrooney, who conducted the intra-mural tennis program in which Jeffrey participated. "He always seemed to be alone," recalls the Dahmer's next door neighbor, Georgia Scharenberg.

It was Jeff's mother, Joyce, whom Scharenberg remembers as a strange one. The two of them had quite a run-in over a pond that straddled both their property lines. "She was just crying and carrying on about it when she learned the pond wasn't entirely on her property," Scharenberg says. "She was so upset I suggested filling in a portion of the pond so it would be all on their property. She seemed like a very hyper person."

In addition to participating in the tennis program, Jeff played the clarinet in the school band. He was considered a bright student, but he failed to apply himself, and his grades ran the gamut from A to F.

He would rather be the class buffoon.

"He had a bizarre sense of humor. He bleated like a sheep in class, had fake epileptic seizures in the hallways," says a onetime classmate, John Backderf. "I don't remember having a normal conversation with him."

His distinctive sense of humor prompted him to crash the Honor Society photo session for his school year book. It was not until after the class picture was developed that the other forty-four students, lined up shoulder to shoulder and beaming at the camera, discovered the face that had no place among them. There was nothing to do but blacken it into a silhouette with a marking pen, and send the book off to the printer.

When the rest of the students look at that picture today, marred by the blackened image like the Grim Reaper in their midst, they do not think well of Jeff Dahmer. Little does he care. He got their attention, didn't he?

He was a smooth talker when he wanted to be. On a class trip to Washington, D.C., he conned his way into Vice President Walter Mondale's suite, and columnist Art Buchwald's private office.

"Whatever had gone on in Jeff's life, he couldn't talk about it," recalls a long-ago classmate, Martha Schmidt. "But it seemed so clear all along that it was someone saying, 'Pay attention to me.'"

Another former classmate, Greg Rogerson, says Jeff liked to imitate less fortunate people who had physical deformities. "He would run through one of the malls and act like he was mentally retarded."

He also liked to draw outlines of nonexistent bodies on floors, as though there had been a homicide. After awhile, outrageous, stupid behavior by anyone in Revere High became known among the student body as "doing a Dahmer."

Jeff wanted to take sixteen-year-old Bridget Geiger to the senior prom, but was so shy he prevailed upon one of his friends to ask her in his behalf. Bridget bought a powder-blue dress for the occasion, but the unpredictable Dahmer, not deigning to rent a tuxedo like his classmates, showed up in a brown suit. Geiger, now twenty-nine, recalls, "It wasn't what you'd really call a date. I went more out of friendship. He was so nervous my mom had to pin on my corsage, because Jeff was afraid he might stick me. And he didn't say two words to me all evening."

In fact, Dahmer vanished for a half hour, leaving his date sitting alone in the Akron dance hall. When he wandered back she asked, "Where did you go, Jeff?" "Oh, I ran over to McDonald's because I didn't get enough to eat," he explained.

Geiger will never forget being taken home after the prom, which is considered the biggest night in any teenage girl's social life. "He didn't even kiss me good night! He shook my hand. At that age, most guys are wolves and prom night is supposed to be the biggest hanky-panky night of the year. He shook my hand."

By the time Jeffrey was graduated from high school in June 1978, his parents were locked in a bitter divorce action, each charging the other with "extreme cruelty and neglect of duty."

Jeff's father, Lionel, moved into a different part of the house to put as much distance between him and his wife as possible. He even jerry-rigged a crude alarm, a string pulled across the room with keys hanging from it that would jangle if she tried to slip in while he slept. He finally moved into a motel, and Mrs. Dahmer took eleven-year-old David and moved to Chippewa Falls, Wisconsin.

And Jeff, the "loner," was left with the stately three-bedroom house all to himself, with a broken refrigerator, no food, and no money.

Not long afterward Jeff invited his prom date, Bridget Geiger, to a party in the big empty house. When she arrived she discovered he and a group of friends were holding a seance. She didn't hang around for the results, and never went out with him again.

She believes Dahmer was intimidated by women, because he had no control over them.

"We always saw Jeff as the type who might commit suicide—but not harm somebody else," she says.

It was right around this time that the lonesome Dahmer ran into nineteen-year-old Steven Hicks, and brought him home with him, nevermore to leave. It was his first kill.

Later that year Lionel Dahmer took a new wife, Shari, and moved back into the house in Bath. Only then did Dahmer learn, to his dismay, that Jeffrey suffered from an acute drinking problem. Thinking military service might straighten him out, he prevailed on his son, who had dropped out of Ohio State University after one semester, to join the Army.

It didn't work. Jeff enlisted right after Christmas. After basic training at Fort McClellan, Alabama, he signed up for the Military Police, but dropped out before completing the course. He was then transferred to Fort Sam Houston, Texas, for training as an Army medic. In July 1979, he arrived at the Army base at Baumholder, West Germany, where booze continued to be his master.

"Sometimes he would lie on his bunk all weekend, with earphones on his head, listening to heavy-metal music and drinking martinis until he passed out," one of his bunk mates recalls.

Another, Billy Capshaw, remembers, "He talked

about his dad a lot. He wanted to please his dad. We thought he was an only child. He never said anything about having a brother."

His Army room commander, Michael Masters, says, "If you were to test his IQ, I'm sure it would be 145 or above. He did a lot of reading, but when he drank he became very obnoxious, and he had a passion for being a racist."

The military service had no need for alcoholics, and in March of 1981 the Army handed Pfc. Dahmer a discharge and sent him home.

He lived briefly in Miami Beach, where he worked in a sandwich shop, but he couldn't hold onto that job, either. He ended up sleeping on the beach.

Learning of his plight, his stepmother talked him into coming back to his father's house in Ohio. The elder Dahmer met his son's plane in Cleveland. He barely recognized the slender six-footer with thinning blond hair, blue eyes, pockmarked cheeks and a thin, scruffy beard.

"It was evident he was in bad shape, physically and financially. He was lit up."

Jeff confided to friends that he planned to become an FBI agent. It didn't seem to register to him that a snowball has a better chance of freezing in Hell than a college dropout who had been drummed out of the Army would of being accepted into the FBI.

On October 7, 1981, he also acquired a police record. In his first recorded brush with the law, police in Bath charged him with disorderly conduct, having an open container of liquor, and resisting arrest after he refused to leave the local Ramada Inn. Dahmer was a gentle person, but when he'd had a few drinks, it took four policemen to hold him down. On the way to the stationhouse he begged the cops, "Please, stop the car and beat me up."

It was the same drinking problem as before, Lionel Dahmer says. ''The same sort of things started happening. He'd be in a bar and get in trouble, and I'd have to go find him. This was probably very wrong to do, but I didn't have the wisdom to do anything differently.''

Later that same year, with his father's encouragement, Jeff made his way back to the area of his birth, and moved in with his elderly grandmother, Catherine Dahmer, in the Milwaukee suburb of West Allis. ''It's a new scene,'' his father encouraged. ''You two loved each other. You can mow the lawn and help her with the chores.''

Jeff worked for a downtown blood bank for a time, before landing a stock clerk's job at the Ambrosia Chocolate factory in 1985. He appeared fascinated by horror flicks, such as Friday the 13th and Nightmare on Elm Street, and continued his chemistry experiments in his grandmother's garage and basement.

When the mysterious concoctions seemed to be getting out of hand, Grandma Dahmer phoned her son, Lionel, in Akron, to complain about the foul odors. He flew to Milwaukee to see what he could do.

''I looked around, the house, the garage, the yard, and I found nothing but a little, slimy, black viscous residue in the garage. It wasn't real thick, but thick enough. The bad smell was gone, the garbage men had come and taken it. I asked Jeff what on earth his grandmother was talking about. He was reluctant at first to say anything.

''When I pressed him he said he was embarrassed. I asked him why, and he said, 'I just had too much time on my hands and I just wanted to see what chemicals would decompose the chicken I bought.' ''

At the chocolate factory in Milwaukee Dahmer was known among his co-workers as an angry young man.

"He hated his job and he hated the welfare system," one of them remembers. "He didn't see why the taxpayers had to foot the bill for people on welfare who were too lazy to work. He was angry about things like that."

Dahmer occasionally showed up for work too broke to buy a pack of cigarettes. When asked what he did with his money, he'd explain, "I spent the weekend in Chicago, where I spent it all having a good time."

During his time on the work-release program at Milwaukee's House of Correction, where he was serving time for the sexual assault on Konerak Sinthasomphone's brother, Dahmer did nothing to distinguish himself from the other prisoners.

"I'd say he was just another run-of-the-mill prisoner who came in and did his time," says Michael J. Carr, superintendent. "I have a lot of documentation of him going to his job and spending a lot of extra hours at his job."

There was one problem when he was let out on a pass to visit his grandmother on Thanksgiving day, and returned smelling of alcohol. "He was given a balloon test for alcohol consumption, and the results were positive. He admitted going on a drinking binge," Carr's records show. It cost him two days of good time.

Of all of the people who knew Jeffrey Dahmer during his thirty-one years, no one—not one of them—ever thought of him as a killer.

"He's not well," says his eighty-seven-year-old grandmother, a retired school teacher. "The last time I saw him he was terribly thin. If he made a mistake, I'm sorry. But I love him dearly."

Dahmer loves roses, fancies tropical fish, and enjoys working on his home computer. To all outward appearances, he is the shy, soft-spoken bachelor. But underneath, according to a mental health professional who interviewed him, "This kind of guy is really an aberration, even of the abnormal. His behavior goes one step beyond...Each element of the case takes you one step farther into the bizarre."

# CHAPTER 21

## IS JEFFREY DAHMER CRAZY?

Jeffrey Dahmer is a serial killer. To qualify for that gruesome category, one must kill a number of people over an extended period of time. Three or more will suffice. Serial killers have been around a long time. It's only recently, though, that they have been scientifically studied. Many unanswered questions remain.

Unfortunately, in terms of prediction and criminal detection, there is not one type of person who becomes a serial killer. The inability to predict the profile of a serial killer with accuracy was demonstrated by the University of Louisville professor described in the first chapter of this book.

---

*This chapter was written by Gerson H. Kaplan, M.D., a psychiatrist practicing in Chicago. Dr. Kaplan has been on the staff of the Psychiatric Institute of the Circuit Court of Cook County for 31 years.*

Some serial killers are psychotic (crazy) but the majority are not. Many of these murders have obvious or grotesque sexual connections but some do not. Some of these killers are drifters, migrants with no steady job, or in some way on the margin of society. Others appear to be "solid" citizens who make a good appearance. They have steady jobs. They may be married. Some are very intelligent. Others are not very bright.

Some serial killers have the appearance of "psychopaths." Psychopaths usually have superficial charm and intelligence. They can be very convincing talkers. They have been described as "con artists." They are attractive. But underneath they are shallow and unreliable. They have no feelings for anyone but themselves. They are completely selfish. They are incapable of having long-term goals. They demand immediate gratification. They frequently are in trouble with the law. They depend on and are very destructive to their families. They have been described as having a "mask of sanity."

Most psychopaths do not kill. But many killers are psychopaths or have many psychopathic features.

Although they are diverse in many ways, serial killers do have some common characteristics. These features generally—but not always—are there. They share a history of childhood abuse, either physical or sexual, or both. They come from dysfunctional families—families with a lot of problems. The serial killer's parents do not get along. They may be separated or divorced. One or both parents are abusive. There is a history of childhood sadism, such as the torturing of animals and insects. The serial killer may be violent with his playmates. There is early (adolescent) abuse of alcohol or street drugs or both.

Serial killers are usually young white males. They tend to have charm. This lets them move in different parts of society and have access to their victims. They are skilled in picking vulnerable people to kill. They tend to dehumanize their victims. They do not see them as real people. This is understandable. It is easier to kill someone whom you do not perceive to be a person like yourself. Most serial killers have significant identity problems. This applies to basic identity issues, including sexual identity. This does not mean that all serial killers are gay or bisexual. It means that some serial killers are gay and some are bisexual but the rest have problems with their male identity. They are not sure who they are. They do not feel comfortable with a role in life. They certainly do not feel comfortable with themselves. In spite of superficial charm, they tend to be loners. They do not have close friends. They are unhappy people.

Such characteristics do not easily identify or distinguish a serial killer. Many thousands of men share them but are not serial killers.

Another feature is much more closely associated with serial killers. It is a common characteristic that tends to be ignored or taken for granted. Serial killers like to kill. Killing can be understood as an act of rage. A man who was repeatedly abused as a child now gets his revenge. This rage can be seen in the sadistic way that some killers treat their victims, both before and after death. The serial killer goes beyond rage. He has a need or compulsion to kill. It can be said he is addicted to killing. The killer finds relief from built up tensions when he kills.

If no psychological profile fits all serial killers, how can we explain why they kill?

It is possible that they have some underlying biochemical abnormality in their brains. But if this is so, it remains to be found. Alcohol and street drugs are commonly abused by serial killers, but this does not explain why they kill. These drugs can reduce inhibitions and excite passions and thus make it easier to kill. But millions of people do not kill who use alcohol and street drugs. Still, just as cocaine can be used to increase the pleasure of sex, so drugs can be used to increase the "pleasure" of killing.

There are a lot of ways to explain serial killers and most of them are being used. The abused boy identifies with the sadistic father and grows up to be a sadistic killer. He "chooses" to be the abuser rather than the victim. In the case of homosexual killers, the killing can be seen as a way of dealing with conscious or unconscious shame from engaging in homosexual relationships. If it is true, and I believe it is, that serial killers have profound identity problems, then it is possible that the act of killing is an attempt to remedy this defect. The killing can be seen as a way of getting a "high" to cure a sense of non-identity, or boredom, or depression, or anxiety. The killing is a way of holding together a personality that is in danger of falling apart. It is an attempt to feel by a person who does not feel. It is a pathologic attempt to give some "purpose" to a life without purpose. It can be a way to gain power or control in a person who feels he has no power or control.

The repetition of an act can be an attempt to come to terms with an original trauma. A common example is that of a person who has had an accident. He will describe the details of the accident with every person he meets for the next several days. By talking about the accident he is gradually accepting what happened to him. Some people are not good at talking about what is troubling them. If they have repressed (unconsciously forgotten) the trauma they are not able to talk about it. It is possible to understand the abused son who becomes an abusive parent as an attempt to come to terms with the trauma of his childhood. This same theory can apply to serial killers. Their killing can be seen as a very pathological attempt to cope with the trauma of childhood.

When a child is abused this act causes dramatic changes in the child's emotions or psychology. At the same time there are major changes going on in the child's physiology. These physiologic changes include dramatic changes in the brain chemistry. It has been theorized that some of these chemical changes are similar to the changes that occur when a person uses narcotics. Repetitive behavior can thus be understood as a type of addictive response in a traumatized individual. The chemical changes in the brain that occur when a person is put or puts himself in a situation similar to the original trauma can have an addictive quality. The serial killer will sometimes talk about it being easier to kill after he has killed for the first time. This is generally understood as a psychologic mechanism. The first killing breaks a profound ethical barrier and once broken the underlying feelings can erupt. Perhaps changes in brain chemistry also contribute to this pattern. Under stress the brain produces chemicals similar to narcotics. As we have noted earlier, serial killers like to kill. While the "pleasure" can be understood psychologically, it may also have a neurochemical basis.

Jeffrey Dahmer, like John Wayne Gacy, the infamous serial killer from Chicago, killed his victims after having sex with them. In Gacy's case bondage was part of the sexual involvement. Dahmer drugged his victims before killing them. Tying or drugging a person makes him an easy victim but it also provides a sense of power or superiority which can be pleasurable. Jeffrey Dahmer dismembered his victims after killing them. He took pictures of the dismembered bodies. There are many reasons why a killer dismembers his victims. It can be an attempt at concealment. It can be an expression of his anger toward the victim and who the victim symbolizes. It can be a way of getting further control over the victim. It can be a way of acquiring the strength of the victim, which can more easily be seen when the killer eats part of the victim. Some primitive cultures believe that by eating your victim you acquire his strength. Dahmer has stated that he had eaten at least part of some of his victims.

While this behavior seems consistent with what is known about Dahmer, this does not mean that it actually happened. Murderers have been known to lie. Serial murderers are no exception. Lying can be based on the wish to shock, to show people how extraordinary they are. Lying can be motivated out of self-preservation, a way to establish an insanity defense. The idea would be that if a person is a cannibal he must be crazy. Once caught, serial killers have been known to malinger, to fake a mental illness. The "Hillside Strangler," a serial killer from the West Coast, attempted to convince psychiatrists that he suffered from a multiple personality disorder. He tried to persuade them that one of his other personalities did the killing and he was not responsible. The average psychiatrist is trained to establish rapport, a relationship with each patient. He or she is taught to believe each patient. That type of trust is not helpful when doing forensic or criminal examinations. Serial killers are good talkers. They are very convincing. This trait helps them convince their victims that they will be safe with the killer.

Dahmer has told police he kept his victims' body parts because he did not want to lose his victims. This was a way of keeping close to them. It was a way of responding to the fear of rejection, of being left behind. He would always have them. The ultimate way to avoid losing something is to eat it. Then it becomes part of you. All this is consistent with his statements about killing his victims when they tried to leave. Dahmer's fear of losing his victims may be connected with his feelings that his parents favored his brother and that his mother had left Jeffrey when she gave birth to his brother. Jeffrey Dahmer has also stated that he had sexual contact with the dead victims and their dismembered body parts. This can be understood as a way of reliving the sexual contact he had with the victims before he killed them. The body part represents the victim just as another man might use a woman's underwear to represent the woman and then masturbate with the underwear.

A frequent question that is asked about the Dahmer case is, how could a human being behave in such a gruesome and disgusting manner? Not only did Dahmer dismember his victims and have sexual contact with their parts but he kept the dismembered bodies in the same apartment he continued to live in. He kept their skulls on display and saved their internal organs "to eat later." A tempting answer is to say that such behavior cannot be explained. There are, however, theories that attempt to explain such bizarre behavior. A classical theory suggests that people like Dahmer have a fusion of their sexual and aggressive feelings. In a healthy person there is fusion of sexual and loving feelings. In sadistic people something goes wrong and instead there is a mixing of sexual with aggressive or hateful feelings. An example would be the sadist who gets sexual pleasure by inflicting pain. They may be constitutionally different. They may be born with deviant sexual feelings. Perhaps they have had experiences that caused this deviant behavior. If a child is beaten by a parent, the child may hate the parent. At the same time the child still wants to love and admire the parent. The combination of these feelings may eventually lead to sadistic sexual behavior. A child who sees his parents having intercourse may perceive the act as the father violently inflicting pain on the mother. This can become the model for his future sexual behavior.

More specifically, in the case of Jeffrey Dahmer, there is evidence that he could not accept his homosexuality. The gruesome butchering of his homosexual partners can be understood as his way of trying to punish and deny that part of himself that he hated but that would not go away. The same people that gave him sexual pleasure also reminded him that he was somebody he despised.

When people hear the terrible things that Jeffrey Dahmer has confessed to doing, a frequent reaction is to say, "He must be crazy." When people see Jeffrey Dahmer sitting quietly in court, neatly dressed and groomed, a common reaction is to say, "He's not crazy." Both opinions can be wrong. Many psychotic individuals do not appear strange or bizarre. They appear normal. They do not talk to themselves or appear dirty or unkempt. However, because a person performs gruesome and bizarre acts does not necessarily mean he is psychotic. For example, there are men who married and have good jobs. They are not serial killers. They do not hear voices or believe there is a conspiracy to kill them. However, the only way they can reach orgasm is to have a woman urinate or defecate on them. There are other men who are also not psychotic but can only have an orgasm if a woman, who is naked, except for wearing long black stockings, ties them up and whips them. Bizarre bedroom behavior does not make a person psychotic. I have not examined Jeffrey Dahmer nor have I read any report of a psychiatric examination. I do not know if Jeffrey Dahmer is psychotic. My point is that dismembering bodies, saving body parts, engaging in cannibalism, having sex with corpses or parts of corpses is very disturbed, bizarre behavior but does not, in itself, mean Dahmer is crazy.

This issue will come up when he goes to trial. Legal insanity and psychoses are not exactly the same thing. Psychosis is a psychiatric term indicating a severe mental illness, a break with reality. Insanity is a legal term. To prove someone legally insane the defense has to convince the judge in a bench trial or a jury in a jury trial that the defendant suffers from a mental disease or defect — that he is psychotic (crazy). In addition they have to prove that this mental illness did one of two things. Either that this mental disease resulted in the defendant lacking substantial capacity to conform his behavior to the requirements of the law or that this mental disease made the defendant unable to appreciate the wrongfulness of his conduct. His mental illness must either prevent the defendant from controlling his behavior at the time of the crime or this illness must prevent him from understanding that what he did was wrong when he committed the crime.

The issue of legal sanity is distinct from the issue of legal competence. Sanity refers to the defendant's state of mind at the time of the crime. Competence refers to the defendant's state of mind at the time of the trial. To be competent the defendant must understand the charges against him, be familiar with court and trial procedures and be able to cooperate with his attorney. Jeffrey Dahmer's attorney has stated that his client is competent.

The defense will say that anyone who butchers his victims and then has sex with their body parts must be insane. The defense will point to Dahmer's cannibalism, his house of horrors, his living with the intolerable stench of decaying human flesh and conclude he must be com-

# STEP INTO MY PARLOR

pletely crazy and thus legally insane. The prosecution will emphasize that Dahmer planned his murders. He would go to gay bars with the idea of finding men to have sex with and then kill. They will point out that his behavior was cool and calculating and not wild or bizarre. They will mention that his behavior was so normal that he convinced three policemen that his fourteen-year-old victim should be returned to his "care." They will mention Dahmer's own statement that after killing one victim he went and got a suitcase, put the victim in the suitcase and then hired a taxi to transport the body. They will say this is the behavior of a cold killer, not a crazy man. Both the defense and the prosecution will hire mental health professionals, usually psychiatrists, to examine Dahmer and then testify in court. The experts for the defense will emphasize his mental problems that would render him legally insane. The experts for the prosecution will point out his strengths and say he was legally sane.

There has been criticism concerning the so-called "battle of the experts." Critics say that this proves psychiatrists do not know anything. If psychiatrists can examine the same person, at roughly the same time, and come to opposite conclusions than obviously psychiatry is not a science. What these critics do not understand is that the battle of the experts is built into the American trial system. If a bridge collapses causing loss of lives and money and there is a subsequent trial, the same battle of the experts occurs. Both sides hire engineers and architects to testify in court. No one is saying that their fields are not scientific, but the same disagreement occurs. The experts for the builders of the bridge testify that the materials and methods used were proper. The experts hired by the victims testify to the opposite. The American judicial system is based on the concept of a battle between two sides and

234

that truth will emerge from this battle. Sometimes, to re-solve this battle, the court (the judge) will appoint its own psychiatrists to examine the defendant. Since these ex-perts are not hired by either side their opinion is more in-dependent. In cases where the psychiatrists disagree, what usually happens is that the jury pretty much dis-counts all the psychiatric testimony and reaches a conclu-sion based on its own evaluation of the evidence.

What we know about Jeffrey Dahmer is consistent with the typical picture of a serial killer. He is a young white male of at least average intelligence. He comes from a broken home. There is a history of sexual abuse. He is described as being sadistic to animals in childhood. Al-though he was a loner, people found him personable. He drank heavily. He felt guilty about his homosexuality. He is described as a troubled, unhappy person.

Jeffrey Dahmer's parents had a bitter divorce when he was eighteen. This is about the time that he reportedly committed his first murder. Mr. Dahmer believed that his parents favored his younger brother. There are indications that Jeffrey Dahmer's mother was ill during the time she had Jeffrey's brother, who is six years younger. There are reports that Jeffrey felt neglected at that time. Jeffrey has stated that his mother had a nervous breakdown. Jeffrey Dahmer's father reported that Jeffrey was sexually abused by a neighbor when he was eight. Jeffrey denies that he was abused. This denial does not mean that he was not abused at that time. Sexual abuse is a very traumatic event. It is not unusual for a childhood victim to repress (unconsciously forget) this memory or to suppress (con-sciously forget) this trauma. As a child, Dahmer is re-ported to have stabbed small animals to trees. He used acid to remove the flesh from dead animals. He buried an-imals and marked their graves with crosses. He is described as being convincing and personable but he did not have close friends. People who knew him when he was growing up described him as seeking attention. Mr. Dahmer's probation officer describes a depressed unhappy man who is not accepting of his homosexuality. Dahmer grew up in a conservative setting where homosexuality was considered an evil. It is not surprising that he would feel shame in regard to his sexual orientation. He drank heavily as an adolescent and young adult. Different people reported a change in his personality when he drank. He became violent when intoxicated and several people were needed to hold him down. No one of the above features, by itself, indicates that Jeffrey Dahmer is a serial killer. Many children pull the wings off butterflies or torture dogs and cats, but they do not grow up to become murderers. Many children come from disturbed homes. Many children are abused. Many homosexuals are troubled with their sexuality. Many people have a change in behavior when they drink. There is a prominent jurist who, when drinking as a young man, would pretend to be Hitler and give long speeches in German. It is the total picture that indicates that Jeffrey Dahmer fits the profile of a serial killer. The problem is that there are many men with very similar profiles who are not serial killers.

It is very difficult to predict dangerous behavior. I once examined a man with no history of murder. He showed such a degree of obvious lack of concern for others that I predicted in writing that he would kill. Unfortunately, I was proven correct. That type of situation is rare and that type of person is not the common serial killer. Jeffrey Dahmer had an arrest record for indecent exposure, lewd and lascivious behavior, and second degree sexual assault. I think that on the basis of his known record of sexual offenses and his general attitude one could reasonably predict there could be more sexual offenses from him. But that record would not identify him as a serial killer. It is not surprising that professional people who had contact with Jeffrey Dahmer would not suspect his murderous behavior.

# CHAPTER 22

## A CITY IN TURMOIL

It was August 4. Healing Sunday.

Calling it "perhaps the most traumatic time in Milwaukee's history," Mayor John Olaf Norquist had asked the city's religious leaders to use their services that Sunday "to address the need for reflection on what has happened, to extend sympathy and support for the families of the victims, and to commit ourselves to working together to reunite our community."

"A vicious, cold-blooded, calculating killer has preyed upon our citizens," Norquist said. "He has also preyed upon the minds and hearts of the entire community."

---

*This chapter was prepared by Crocker Stephenson, who has been reporting on Dahmer for the* Milwaukee Sentinel, *since the first body was found.*

Now the young, first-term mayor—a soft-spoken son of a Presbyterian minister swept into office with campaign promises of racial progressiveness—stood before the congregation at Greater Galilee Baptist Church, one of the city's largest black congregations, located near the heart of one of the most segregated black communities of any major city in the United States, and reiterated his call for unity.

"We've had a terrible time over the last twelve days," Norquist told the congregation. "When we look at this, we have to look at it as a way to try to have some good come out of it."

But for many of the city's already alienated African Americans, looking beyond the horror of Jeffrey Dahmer meant only to stare into the face of hopelessness.

"Probably the most segregated place in Milwaukee is the churches on Sunday," scoffed Alderman Michael McGee, who the year before had created a Black Panther Militia and threatened to use violence if the city failed to significantly improve the plight of its inner city residents by 1995. "When you talk about healing, it's not going to take place here."

Long before Dahmer claimed his seventeen victims— most of them poor, most of them black—members of Milwaukee's minority community saw themselves caught in a web of racism, violence, poverty and ignorance so devastating as to be tantamount to genocide. Milwaukee is one of five "hypersegregated" cities in the United States, according to a 1989 study by the University of Chicago Population Research Center. By the close of the 1980s, the jobless rate for blacks in the Milwaukee area had climbed beyond 20 per cent. The black unemployment rate was five times higher than white unemployment. Milwaukee blacks were rejected nearly four times as often as whites for home loans at savings and loan associations—the worst disparity in the nation, according to a 1989 study.

Some thirteen children had died in fires in Milwaukee's rotting inner city housing stock during 1990. Eight more had died in fires during the first six months of 1991. Black Milwaukee Public Schools students were faring poorly compared to their white classmates, and the city's homicide rate, fueled by drugs and felt keenest in the city's black community, more than doubled between 1988 and 1990.

While virtually every large city in the country struggled with similar problems, the pain was deepened for Milwaukee's minorities by the growing prosperity, which seemed to leave them behind.

Milwaukee's economy remained strong during the recession, and its skyline glistened with new office towers, recreational centers and posh condos. At the same time, the inner city, including the neighborhood where Dahmer set up his butcher shop, grew bleaker, its people poorer, and their lives more desperate.

Dahmer, an avowed racist, was a freak, city officials said. He was not even a Milwaukee native, they said. An affliction, an accident of nature, they said. True enough.

But while Dahmer's murders sickened the city, it was the Police Department's investigation—particularly of the May 27 incident involving Konerak Sinthasomphone, the Laotian boy who had escaped from Dahmer's apartment, only to be handed back to the killer by police—that set the city on fire.

Racism seemed the only explanation for why the three white officers who handled the incident ignored the pleas of two black women and accepted Dahmer's explanation. To make matters worse, when one of the women saw the boy's picture in a story about his disappearance that ran in the *Milwaukee Sentinel* a few days later, her mother, Glenda Cleveland, called the police and begged for them to come take their statement. No one came. A few days passed and she called again. A detective told her he would look into it and get back to her.

"No one ever did," she said.

If there was some explanation for the way the three cops, working late and under stress in the Central City, handled the May 27 episode, what possible explanation could there be for the department's subsequent indifference.

There was simply no question in most people's minds that, had the incident occurred in Shorewood or Whitefish Bay, or any other affluent community, had the women been white and Dahmer black, had the victim been a fourteen-year-old white girl rather than an Asian boy, police would have handled the situation differently, and Konerak, as well as the four men Dahmer killed over the course of the next seven bloody weeks, could have been spared.

Hours after the mayor made his plea for unity to the city's black community, a virtually all-white crowd gathered in the City Hall Rotunda to show support for the Milwaukee Police Department.

The crowd of about 300, organized by a group of police officers' wives, wore blue ribbons pinned to their chests—a symbol of pride and solidarity, they said. Many carried picket signs that said, "Behind the Police All the Way," and "We Support Our Cops. Do You?" One boy carried a sign that said: "My Dad Is a Great Cop and There Are Many Like Him."

"The media and the chief have hung these three already," called out one angry woman. "The man who should be hung is Dahmer."

The crowd moved outside and marched around City Hall, cheering passing squad cars and pinning blue ribbons on anything that didn't move. A motorcycle cop rumbled by, raising his gloved fist in unity.

But if the march was meant to be a show of unity, then the absence of black police officers and their families was conspicuous.

"I didn't expect any to be here," one cop told a reporter.

Nor did the mayor or Police Chief Philip Arreola attend the rally. They wouldn't have been welcomed anyway. The chief and the mayor were considered traitors. An ugly "them or us" mentality had set in.

"There's no way, in any way, that we can go against the Police Department," Alderman Albert Anderson, who represents the city's white South Side, told the cheering crowd.

"Until we die, we stick together."

Police weren't the only group to feel besieged. The city's gay community, whose members were butchered by Dahmer, was now being victimized by an outbreak of homophobic hostility.

"People put in their minds that we're the perpetrators," said Scott Gunkle, president of the Lambda Rights Network, a gay rights group. "We are the victims."

The 219 Club, a gay bar on the city's Near South Side where Dahmer had hunted for some of his victims, had received bomb threats, and its patrons were pelted with eggs. The *Wisconsin Light,* a gay and lesbian newspaper, received an anonymous letter. It said: "I don't care if you queers die of AIDS or dismemberment."

The Dahmer case "really elucidated the kinds of division that exist in the community," said Representative Gwen Moore, in whose district Dahmer had lived.

"Black versus white. Heterosexual versus homosexual. The community versus police. The police chief versus the police union. That's what was so painful about it here."

Monday, two weeks after police discovered Jeffrey L. Dahmer's nightmare on 25th Street, the first truly ecumenical rally was held.

More than 400 people—blacks and whites, gays and straights, rich and poor—gathered in Juneau Park, a popular meeting spot for gays on the city's East Side.

There they held hands, lit candles and sang, many with tears in their eyes, "We Shall Overcome," before marching through the city to the square outside the jail that housed Jeffrey Dahmer.

Among the speakers that night was Shirley Hughes, the mother of Tony Hughes, a deaf mute Dahmer had slaughtered and dismembered. Her sad eyes stricken with grief, Hughes wore a picture of her son pinned to her shirt and clutched an old bible to her chest.

"I urge you. Please. Don't hold hatred in your hearts. Just pray to God for help," Hughes told the crowd. She paused. Tears began to pool in her eyes.

"Tony loved everyone, and everyone loved Tony," she said. Then she hung her head and wept.

Another speaker, Jeanetta Robinson, also urged the crowd to work toward justice and peace.

"Grief is hard to take," she said. "We must all work together, blacks and whites, homosexuals and heterosexuals, to get through this tragedy."

If only Robinson's idealism, or Hughes' faith were enough to banish the hate and anger that now gripped the city.

To some, it didn't seem likely. The ugliness was everywhere. Above the park's bathroom door, a few yards from where Hughes stood, supported in the arms of her three daughters, someone had scrawled in yellow paint: "Jeffrey Dahmer ate here."

The black community got a powerful morale boost with the Reverend Jesse Jackson's marathon one-day visit, his call on City Hall, and his march from the murder scene to the nearby church, but one neighborhood resident just shook his head.

"This won't mean anything with him making an appearance tonight and then going off," he told a reporter. "As soon as he leaves, everything will be back to normal."

Perhaps. But for that night, at least, there was a feeling among many members in the community that they would find in themselves the dignity and the strength to awaken from this nightmare and that the problems which were tearing at the city's gut could, somehow, be resolved.

But even as Jackson was rallying the city's minorities, the Milwaukee Police Department's rank and file were holding a solidarity test of their own.

With the city nearer to all-out rioting than it had been since the late 1960s, and with public trust in the department at an all-time low, the Milwaukee Police Association—peeved with Philip Arreola's decision to suspend the three cops involved in the May 27 contact with Dahmer—called on the chief, who had been in office a mere eighteen months, to resign.

Union leaders released the results of a survey that found that 93 per cent of the officers who responded had no confidence in their chief.

"The question that looms paramount is: Can the Milwaukee Police Department move forward with positive change, beneficial for the community and the police officers, with a police chief that does not enjoy the confidence of the majority of the rank and file officers?'' asked the union's local president, Bradley DeBraska.

The chief dismissed the action as ''an irresponsible vote by the union,'' a feeling that seemed to be shared by most Milwaukeeans.

''It's as if the union is completely out of touch with what has happened over the past two weeks,'' said one man watching the union's announcement on television. ''This is going to do nothing but widen the void between the department and the community.''

Jesse Jackson, in one of his speeches during his whirlwind visit, had called the union's vote ''mutiny.''

When Arreola took to the same podium at a Northwest Side church and vowed not to resign ''because we—you and I—have too much to do, and we need to do it together,'' it may have been the chief's finest hour.

He could not stay longer. He had to rush off to tape an episode for ABC's ''Nightline,'' where commentator Barbara Walters asked him to explain how his men had let Dahmer slip through their hands on May 27.

''I can only say it's inexplicable,'' said the chief, looking tired and drawn. ''I wish I could offer an explanation for that. It does pose some very traumatic and grave questions.''

With local, state and federal reviews planned, it seemed certain that some answers to those questions would be forthcoming. What remained to be seen was whether those answers would satisfy the Milwaukee community.

As the traumatic week drew to a close, and families began to bury their dead, the Police Department's handling of the Dahmer case had begun to overshadow the bloody homicides themselves, and the people of Milwaukee, now at perhaps the most uncertain hour in their city's history, were finding it increasingly difficult to find a common ground on which to stand.

As one mother put it, ''I used to tell my children that monsters aren't real and that, if they ever needed help, to ask a policeman. Now what do I tell them? What do I say to them now?''

On Friday, September 6, 1991, the other shoe dropped for police officers John Balcerzak and Joseph Gabrish, who had left Konerak Sinthasomphone in Dahmer's hands. Chief Arreola fired them from the force. The third officer involved, Richard Porubcan, was placed on one year's probation.

# CHAPTER 23

## THE MEN IN HIS LIFE

Here is a list of the known victims of Jeffrey Dahmer, in the order he said they were killed:

1. **Steven Mark Hicks**, nineteen, white, of Coventry Township, Ohio. Last seen June 18, 1978. His shattered bone fragments were found scattered around the yard of Dahmer's boyhood home in Bath Township.

2. **Steven W. Tuomi**, twenty-eight, white, of Ontonagon, Michigan. Last seen September 15, 1987, when he left his job in a Milwaukee restaurant. His remains were never found.

3. **James "Jamie" Doxtator**, fourteen, an American Indian, last seen in Milwaukee in January 1988. His remains were never found.

4. **Richard Guerrero**, twenty-five, Hispanic, disappeared in Milwaukee in March 1988. His remains were never found.

5. **Anthony Sears**, twenty-four, black, last seen March 25, 1989, in Milwaukee. His remains were found in Dahmer's Milwaukee apartment.

6. **Raymond Lamont Smith**, aka Ricky Beeks, thirty-three, black, of Rockford. Last seen in Milwaukee May 29, 1990. Remains found in Dahmer's apartment.

7. **Edward W. Smith**, twenty-eight, black, disappeared in Milwaukee in June 1990. His remains were never found.

8. **Ernest Miller**, twenty-four, black, last seen September 2, 1990, in Milwaukee. Remains found in Dahmer's apartment.

9. **David Thomas**, twenty-three, black, of Milwaukee. He was last seen March 7, 1991. His remains have not been found.

10. **Curtis Straughter**, eighteen, black, last seen in Milwaukee on February 18, 1991. His remains were found in Dahmer's apartment.

11. **Errol Lindsey**, nineteen, black, last seen in Milwaukee on April 7, 1991. Remains found in Dahmer's apartment.

12. **Anthony Hughes**, thirty-one, black, of Madison, last seen in Milwaukee May 24, 1991. His remains were found in Dahmer's apartment.

13. **Konerak Sinthasomphone**, fourteen, Laotian, last seen outside Dahmer's apartment May 27, 1991. His remains were found in the apartment.

14. **Matt Turner**, twenty, black, of Chicago, last seen June 30, 1991. His remains were found in Dahmer's apartment.

15. **Jeremiah "Jeremy" Weinberger**, twenty-three, Puerto Rican, of Chicago. He was last seen with Dahmer on July 6, 1991. His remains were found in Dahmer's apartment.

16. **Oliver Lacy**, twenty-three, black, of Milwaukee. He was last seen July 12, 1991. His remains were found in Dahmer's apartment.

17. **Joseph Bradehoft**, twenty-five, white, of Milwaukee. He was last seen July 19, 1991. His remains were found in Dahmer's apartment.

# CHAPTER 24

████████████████████████████████████

# GALLOWS HUMOR

Every tragedy is followed by sick humor. It was only a matter of time before someone would come up with a Dahmer joke. Very little time. Like the Chappaquiddick zingers that plagued Teddy Kennedy, the gross John Wayne Gacy gags, or the tasteless mots called "Geiners" that abounded nearly thirty-five years ago when authorities found Ed Gein's gruesome collection of body parts on his farm in Plainfield, Wisconsin, the void was suddenly filled with "Dahmers."

Gein, who died in a Wisconsin insane asylum in 1984, admitted to killing two people and to robbing countless graves for the body parts he fashioned into clothing or used for companionship and decorations for his home. As with Dahmer, it was the canabalistic elements of the Gein story that seemed to give rise to the greatest number of "Geiners."

What was Ed Gein's phone number? O-I-C-U-8-1-2.

Many of the crude Dahmer witticisms are Geiners, blatantly dug up, so to speak, to fit the new occasion.

"Why did the Defense Department call on Ed Gein? To ship arms to Vietnam."

"Why is Congress interested in Jeff Dahmer? They heard he was shipping arms to Iran."

At crime scenes and in courtrooms, in board rooms and on playgrounds, Dahmer jokes are told compulsively, repeated over and over until they budge us away from our terror.

Every wit and half-wit knows a Dahmer joke. Their popularity was noted in a *New York Times* editorial, which said "wisecracks that used to filter one at a time from Wall Street and Madison Avenue now flash instantly, NEXT PAGE after NEXT PAGE, on E-Mail or fax machines. Some have even made it into print and onto the air, then to surge through the young boy network."

What did Dahmer tell some late-arriving guests? "Sorry you couldn't be here earlier—everybody's eaten."

Violence and humor have always been curiously linked. A comedian goes out to knock his audience dead. When we laugh, we say his jokes are killing us. He slays us.

Humor is aggressive. We use it to master our fears. The comedian conquers his audience, the cartoonist lampoons presidents and kings, and even the feeblest of Dahmer jokes captures the killer and holds him up to public ridicule.

Some are spin-offs on Gein: What did Jeffrey Dahmer call dinner? "Gein Cuisine."

Others are tied to current events, such as when comedian Pee-Wee Herman was arrested for public masturbation in Florida: What did Jeff Dahmer say to Pee-Wee Herman? "Don't play with your food."

The only thing for sure, it seems, is that there will be no end to them. These are but a few, omitting the more blatantly racist examples:

Heard about the Dahmer club? It's for dis-members only.

Why did Dahmer put heads in the refrigerator? To see if the light really turns off.

What is Dahmer's favorite song? "The First Time Ever I Saw Your Face."

What is Dahmer's favorite song? "You Gotta Have Heart."

What's Dahmer's favorite book? A Farewell to Arms.

If ever you need help, don't ask Dahmer, "Can you lend me a hand?"

His favorite singing group is "The Talking Heads."

His favorite singing group is "The Fine Young Cannibals."

What's his favorite foods? Elbow macaroni, handburger, butt steak, peter bread, finger sandwiches, head cheese, head lettuce, Manwiches and scrambled legs.

What did the cops find when they looked into his shower? Head and Shoulders.

What kind of flower did Dahmer give his prom date? Tulips.

How much did Dahmer charge for a back rub? An arm and a leg.

Dahmer's landlord almost evicted him for playing hockey in his apartment after a neighbor reported seeing a face-off in his living room.

His mother asked how he liked his friends. "Stir-fried," he said.

Why was Dahmer so popular with his neighbors? He

kept an eye out for them, and was always willing to lend a hand.

Did you hear that Dahmer made bail? It cost him an arm and a leg.

Dahmer has designed a new freezer. It seats six.

When did Dahmer know it was time to go grocery shopping? When he went to the fridge and took a head-count.

What's Dahmer's favorite snack? A little head cheese, washed down with a Butt Lite.

Jeffrey Dahmer is a real competitor. He's always trying to get a leg up on the competition.

They asked Dahmer's high school teacher what kind of a student he was. She said, "He was a real cut-up."

One of Dahmer's former lovers said he finally broke off with him. "I just didn't have the stomach for it."

What three things do you find in Dahmer's refrigerator? Head cheese, a head of lettuce, and a Cheddar Head.

Dahmer's landlord is trying to lease out his old apartment. The ad says, "For Rent: Cozy efficiency apartment in Milwaukee's historic Near West Side. Comes with roommates—some assembly required."

Did you hear what they're going to rename Milwaukee? Hackensack.

Dahmer's other favorite song is, "I Left My Heart in San Francisco. . .and Akron, and West Allis, and Fresno, and Milwaukee. . ."

When somebody asked Dahmer how one of his friends was, Jeff answered, "Delicious."

Number one on Milwaukee's Top Ten list: "I Fall to Pieces."

What did Dahmer say when the cops arrested him? "Have a heart, fellows."

What did he ask his neighbor when he moved into

the neighborhood? "Know of any place around here to get a beer with a good head on it?"

Why didn't Jeff Dahmer need help in his work? It only took a skeleton crew.

What did he order at his favorite bar? "A beer with lots of body and no head."

Another thing you never want to hear Dahmer say: "You've got a good head on your shoulders."

Why did his friends stop hanging around with him? Because he was such a cut-up"

What has twenty-one legs and is always running? Dahmer's refrigerator.

Why was his apartment so busy? People were going there for used parts.

Heinz hired him as the new company spokesman for their slogan, "A sandwich is a sandwich, but a Manwich is a meal."

Dahmer's writing a book. It's called, I've Had My Fill of Men.

The crew they brought in to clean up Dahmer's apartment said it's going to take a lot of elbow grease.

What did Dahmer keep in his sewing basket? Belly buttons.

Dahmer doesn't have to worry about odors in his refrigerator. He always keeps an open box of Arm & Hammer on the shelf.

Why won't anyone play cards with Dahmer? He might come up with a good hand.

Why did Dahmer move to Milwaukee? To get a head.

What does Dahmer keep in his freezer? Eyes-cube trays.

What does Dahmer keep in his freezer? Eyes Cream.

Why did Dahmer turn out the way he did? When he

was young his mother gave him a cold shoulder. (Or a tongue-lashing—or a piece of her mind.)

Did you know Dahmer's looking for a new apartment? He needs more elbow room.

They've identified one of his victims as Bozo the Clown. They found his head in the refrigerator, his body in the bedroom, and his balls in Bucket No. 6.

# CHAPTER 25

# THE BOX AT THE AIRPORT

At three o'clock Thursday afternoon, August 15, 1991, a dog trained to sniff out drugs stopped at a cardboard box marked "computor parts" in the freight terminal at Milwaukee's Mitchell International Airport and wagged his tail. Something was in that box that wasn't supposed to be. "Good boy," his trainer said.

Sheriff's detectives cautiously opened the box and discovered a human skull and a loose assortment of bones.

"These sure as hell aren't computer parts. Call the medical examiner's office."

Jim Perla, an investigator for the Milwaukee County Medical Examiner, took one look into the carton and agreed, "These obviously aren't computer parts."

Perla took the skull and bones downtown, where pathologists thought they had a familiar look about them.

Indeed, they had. It turned out that they were all that was left of twenty-year-old Matt Turner, Jeffrey Dahmer's fourteenth victim.

The bones had been released to a Milwaukee funeral home, where someone simply tossed them into the cardboard box, slapped a label on it, and shipped it off to Turner's mother in Flint, Michigan.

And some people say cops are insensitive.

# CHAPTER 26

![separator]

# DAY XXXI
# AUGUST 22

Carolyn Smith's restless night ended about 3 a.m., August 22. She pulled herself from her bed and stood wearily in her still darkened bedroom, waiting for the day's first light, hoping it would bring some comfort. It didn't.

"It feels like a funeral," she muttered.

For Smith, who at times still found it hard to believe that her brother, Eddie, was really dead, it would be a particularly tragic and important day. The night before, she had gotten a phone call from the district attorney's office to warn her that today would be the day that Jeffrey L. Dahmer would be charged with her brother's slaying.

As she dressed for the early morning hearing, she taped a picture of her brother to her yellow and black blouse. She colored her lips a deep red—close to the same color of lipstick her brother liked to wear. She pulled the mass of her curly black hair away from her face and clipped it back so that it spilled onto her shoulders.

She wandered out of her house in a daze and caught a ride to the courthouse downtown.

By 7:30 a.m., the first-floor corridor outside Court Commissioner Audrey Brooks' courtroom had already filled with reporters, Sheriff's deputies, spectators and a handful of pickets protesting the police department's handling of the Dahmer investigation. A bomb dog sniffed around the chairs and the ashtrays as the reporters, some who had arrived as early as 6 a.m., scanned their papers and complained about the early hour.

Somebody thought that the scary-looking woman with a scar on her chin and a confection of black and blonde hair looked like the woman rumored to be Dahmer's girlfriend. Two reporters strolled over and asked her if she was connected in some way to the Dahmer case.

"I connected to a lot of case," the woman said. "The CIA is looking for me."

The two reporters hurried away.

About thirty members of the victims' families gathered in a nearby room. Babies and grandparents. Sisters and lovers. All eager to look at the man who had confessed to butchering their loved ones. A deputy frisked them for weapons, then they were escorted into the courtroom.

There they sat together quietly, some holding hands, most with eyes fixed on a door marked, "Do not open without permission from a baliff." Commissioner, lawyers and prosecutors took their positions, a deputy gestured, and the door opened. A long moment passed, and out came Dahmer.

His appearance had deteriorated since he had last been to court.

His blond hair was greasy and tangled. Blemishes had erupted on his nose and on his chin. His skin was pale. The bags beneath his eyes had deepened. He wore no T-shirt beneath his blaze-orange jail garb and the toes of his bare feet curled over the edge of his rubber sandals.

As during his previous two hearings, what little Dahmer had to say was uttered softly and without a trace of emotion. His face had congealed into a bland near-smirk that never altered, not even when District Attorney E. Michael McCann announced he was charging Dahmer with three additional counts of murder, bringing to fifteen the number of murder charges lodged against him.

When Brooks asked him if he understood that, if he was convicted, he faced fifteen life terms in a Wisconsin prison and an additional 150 years, Dahmer leaned toward the microphone on the table before him.

"Yes, I do, your honor," he said with the aloofness of someone who had just agreed to having freshly ground pepper added to his salad.

Then he pushed the microphone away and leaned back into his chair. He seemed to pay little attention to the remainder of the hearing. He hiked his elbows onto the armrest of his chair, stared down at his fingers and chewed his gum.

While Dahmer masticated, his attorney, Gerald Boyle, went to work.

First he announced that Dahmer would waive his right to a preliminary hearing, which meant the state would not have to outline its case against Dahmer.

"I would learn nothing that I don't already know," he told the court. "Number one, in my opinion, it would be a waste of time and, number two, it would not tactically help us.''

It could only hurt, in fact.

If the state had been required to give the court reason to believe Dahmer was responsible for the murders he had been charged with, prosecutors would simply introduce his gruesome confession. The media would have gone wild.

Then Boyle did an odd, but clever, thing. He voluntarily brought up Dahmer's mental competency, saying ''I have no reason to question my client's competency to proceed.''

Usually, a lawyer will bring up his client's competency only when it is in doubt. But in this case, Boyle took the unusual step of introducing Kenneth Smail, a forensic psychologist he had hired to keep tabs on Dahmer's mental condition. Smail also told Brooks that Dahmer was competent to understand the court proceedings.

Boyle then made it quite clear to the court that his statements concerning his client's current mental health were not meant to reflect, in any way, the condition of Dahmer's mind at the time the murders were committed.

By doing so, Boyle was making sure the issue of mental competency was preserved, with absolute clarity, in the court's record: He's not crazy now, though he may have been when he was frying up human biceps for dinner.

Boyle was covering his butt. He cited an earlier Wisconsin case in which an attorney had failed to raise the issue of his client's competency. The lawyer didn't think it was an issue. It became an issue years later when the defendant appealed and the case was remanded.

Boyle didn't want to be responsible if the state was forced to try Dahmer twice.

The hearing lasted all of nine minutes.

Bail was held at $5 million. Dahmer stood and two deputies led him back through the door he had entered by. The courtroom gallery was asked to remain seated until the victims' families had left.

They filed out without uttering a word and gathered in a room to receive copies of the amended complaint. It was a horrific keepsake of their day in court, spelling out the slayings of fourteen-year-old James E. Doxator, Richard Guerrero, and Edward Smith.

"Upon the statement of the defendant," the complaint said, "which statement is against his penal interest that in January of 1988 he met a young male he thought was Hispanic who was waiting for a bus in front of the 219 Club. . . (H)e approached him and asked him if he would like to make some money by posing in the nude, viewing videos, and having a drink at his residence. . . (T)he two of them went to that location by bus and they had sex and then he gave the young male a drink with sleeping potion and after he passed out killed him by strangling him; he dismembered him and smashed the bones with a sledgehammer and disposed of them; he did not keep any portion of this individual."

That was Doxtator. Dahmer said he remembered the boy because the child had two scars that resembled cigarette burns above each of his nipples. When police told the boy's mother, Debra Vega, about the scars, she knew her son was dead.

"Upon further statement of the defendant, that approximately March of 1988 he met a Hispanic male in the Phoenix Bar located on 2nd Street near the 219 Club. . . (H)e asked this man to come to his residence which at that time was his grandmother's house. . . (H)e asked the man to come to watch videos and take photos or engage in sex and the man came with him; they had oral sex at the house and then he drugged the man; while the man was drugged he killed him and dismembered the body and disposed of it completely without keeping any parts."

That was twenty-two-year-old Guerrero, who Dahmer identified from a picture Guerrero's family had placed in the paper when the young man vanished.

"Upon further statement of the defendant, that during the summer of 1990, approximately in July, he met a person whom he identified through a photograph as Edward W. Smith, DOB: 8-2-62, at the Phoenix Bar... (He) offered him money for sex and to pose for pictures; they took a cab to his apartment...(T)hey had oral sex and he gave Smith a drink which contained sleeping pills and then strangled him; he dismembered Smith and took four or five photos of him; he completely disposed of Edward Smith's body by placing it in garbage bags and at a later time he also got rid of the photos of Edward Smith; he further recalls that Smith wore a headband like an Arab."

The turban-like wrap Smith wore on his head was his trademark. Everyone knew him as "The Sheik."

Carolyn Smith stood in the hallway outside the courtroom. She was weeping, surrounded by television lights, cameras and microphones. The television people were hungry for a sound-bite. She gave them a good one.

"Today was the hardest day of my life," she said. "I feel like he's really gone now. Jeffrey Dahmer has destroyed a lot of things for us. And I don't think he feels any remorse."

Dahmer's aloof manner in court had angered several members of the victims' families.

"The man sits there so calm," said Roland Thomas,

father of victim David Thomas. "If he could just show some remorse."

Thomas lit a cigarette and stood on the steps of the courthouse, watching the cars zip by on West State Street.

"It hurts when someone you love dies," he said sadly. "It hurts worse when they are murdered. What this man did—it's pathetic."

David Thomas' pretty twenty-two-year-old sister, Leslie, stood nearby.

"Bitter," she said. "I feel bitter. He doesn't look like he has any remorse. The man is sick."

Leslie talked about the last time she had seen her brother.

She had tried to make him a sandwich, but she was out of Miracle Whip. Her brother loved Miracle Whip.

"That's all right, sis," he told her.

"I felt so bad. There was just nothing to hold his sandwich together. He said he was going to go out. And I said, 'Don't. Stay here. Come back and spend the night."

"He said, 'I'll be back.' And he never came back."

She grew angry.

"This is the first time I saw the man who did this to my brother. It made me sick. He should see all the pain behind his gruesome acts. And I don't think he's insane. Nothing could convince me that man's insane."

Insane or not, Carolyn Smith said, Dahmer "is worse than a monster."

Riding back to her home after the hearing, Smith struggled to explain the importance of having her brother's name mentioned in court and of having his murder accounted for in the complaint.

A part of it, she said, is that when Dahmer destroyed all traces of her brother's body, he destroyed any substantial way to come to terms with the young man's death. The complaint, though small and horrifying, is at least something connected to her brother's death that is concrete.

Still, she said, she wanted to know more. She wanted to know exactly how her brother died. She wanted to know exactly what Dahmer did to him.

"A detective said, 'You don't want to know. It's too disgusting.' But I do. I heard that, well—you know my brother liked to wear make-up. I heard Dahmer—you know—maybe treated him like a woman."

She shuddered.

A few weeks earlier, Smith had joined some other victim's family members at one of her brother's favorite gay bars. Patrons had been shocked by how much she resembled her brother. Same big dark eyes. Same smile. Same eager friendliness.

It was eerie, she said. Like he was still alive.

Smith stared at the dance floor. The music was turned up. She could see herself in the mirrors that surrounded the room. She pictured her brother there.

She pictured him alive. Dancing. Dancing.

"He loved to dance," she said as the car turned onto her street.

"That's been taken away, too."

# ADDENDUM

The following documents were filed with the Criminal Division of the Milwaukee County Circuit Court, in connection with the formal filing of murder charges against Jeffrey Lionel Dahmer:

1. An affidavit showing probable cause why he should be retained in custody.

2. Dahmer's waiver of the ten-day time limit for a preliminary hearing, and the setting of bond at $1,000,000.

3. A record of the hearing at which his bond was raised to $5,000,000.

4. A court affidavit outlining four charges of first degree homicide filed July 25, 1991.

5. The amended complaint of August 6, 1991, charging Dahmer with twelve counts of murder.

STATE OF WISCONSIN
CIRCUIT COURT                    MILWAUKEE COUNTY

CRIMINAL DIVISION

STATE OF WISCONSIN    )
                      )  ss.
MILWAUKEE COUNTY      )

————————————————————————————

## AFFIDAVIT

## DETENTION OF JEFFREY L. DAHMER D.O.B. 5/21/60

————————————————————————————

Affiant states he is a Lieutenant with the City of Milwaukee Police Department, Homicide Division, and that he is familiar with the events surrounding the arrest of a person by the name of Jeffrey L. Dahmer at 924 North 25th Street in the City and County of Milwaukee, State of Wisconsin and the investigation surrounding alleged homicides and evidence concerning homocides found at that location and that those reports reveal the following:

(1) That at approximately 11:25 p.m. on July 22nd, 1991 Milwaukee Police Officers Rauth and Mueller were flagged down by a citizen who had a handcuff on and indicated that he had been threatened by a person who was in Apartment 213 of 924 North 25th Street in the City and County of Milwaukee, State of Wisconsin.

(2) That Officers Rauth and Mueller with that citizen went to Apartment 213 at 924 North 25th Street in the City and County of Milwaukee, State of Wisconsin and there encountered the resident, Jeffrey L. Dahmer.

(3) That while inside that apartment, Officers Rauth and Mueller observed Polaroid photographs which included photographs of young males who were dead and in the process of being dismembered.

(4) That Officers Rauth and Mueller also observed a severed human head within the refrigerator in that apartment.

(5) That an investigation of the homicides at that scene led to the recovery of evidence which included a total of seven (7) severed human skulls and four (4) additional severed human heads on which the flesh remained.

(6) That the resident of the apartment, Jeffrey L. Dahmer, indicated that he had killed the persons whose heads and skulls he had and had dismembered their bodies.

(7) Dahmer further stated that he had met these individuals either at taverns or shopping areas and induced them to return with him to his home by offering money so that he could take pictures of them;

(8) Dahmer further stated that he would drug these individuals and usually strangle them and then he would dismember the bodies, often boiling the heads to remove the flesh so that he could retain the skulls.

(9) Jeffrey Dahmer further stated that he took Polaroid photographs of a number of these persons while they were alive, after he had killed them, and of their heads and body parts after he had dismembered them.

(10) Affiant further states that Milwaukee County Medical Examiner Jeffrey Jentzen has indicated that he has looked at the human remains seized by the Milwaukee Police Department from Apartment 213 at 924 North 25th Street in the City and County of Milwaukee, State of Wisconsin and that he (Jentzen) has determined that those re-

mains are the remains of at least eleven (11) distinct individuals.

Dated at Milwaukee, Wisconsin, this 24th day of July, 1991.

*Lieutonant David Kane*

Lieutenant David Kane

Subscribed and sworn to before me
this 24th day of July, 1991.

*R.O.D. who*

Notary Public, Milwaukee County
My Commission is permanent

*I find Probable Cause*

*Judge*

7-24-91
3:27PM

July 25, 1991
HONORABLE FRANK T. CRIVELLO PRESIDING

Carolyn Leverance, Court Reporter
Joan Smith, Deputy Court Clerk

District Attorney E. Michael McCann, Assistant District Attorney Carol White and Assistant District Attorney Gregory O'Mera present in court for the State of Wisconsin.

Defendant in person and in court with Attorney Gerald Boyle, Attorney Wendy Patrickus, Attorney Patricia Fricker and Attorney Scott Hanson.

Defendant given a copy of complaint. Defendant's attorneys waive reading of the complaint. Court reviewed complaint and finds probable cause to hold defendant for further proceedings. Defendant orally waives 10-day time limit for Preliminary Hearing through Attorney Gerald Boyle. Case adjourned for Preliminary Hearing to August 22, 1991, at 8:30 a.m., Branch PE.

BAIL: $1,000,000.00 CASH

AUG 6, 1991
HON. JEFFREY A. WAGNER PRESIDING,
Circuit Court Branch 38, sitting as Intake Court.

Court Reporter Tami Tichenor in court. Deputy Clerk James A. Schumacher in court.

Defendant in court with Attorneys Gerald Boyle, Wendy Patrickus, and Scott Hanson.

District Attorney E. Michael McCann, Assistant District Attorney Carol White, and Assistant District Attorney Greg O'Meara in court for the State. Amended Complaint charging 12 counts of First Degree Intentional Homicide, and 1 count of Habitual Criminality, in writing, received and filed, and copy of Amended Complaint given to the Defense. Defendant waived the reading of the Amended Complaint. Court advised the defendant of the maximum sentences, of his right to counsel, and of his right to trial by jury. Defendant waived his right to have a preliminary hearing within 10 days. Court reviewed the Amended Complaint and court found probable cause. Court reset bail at $5,000,000.00 Cash. Copy of letter to Attorney Gerald Boyle from District Attorney E. Michael McCann dated 8-5-91, received and filed. By stipulation of counsel, Court ordered the release of victims body parts to the families of the victims.

Court ordered case to remain calendared for preliminary examination on August 22, 1991 at 8:30 a.m. in the Preliminary Hearing Court.

CIRCUIT COURT
CRIMINAL DIVISION
STATE OF WISCONSIN        MILWAUKEE COUNTY
─────────────────────────────────────

STATE OF WISCONSIN,
Plaintiff                **CRIMINAL COMPLAINT**

vs.                      CRIME(S):
                         See Charging Section Below
Jeffrey L. Dahmer/5/21/60   STATUTE(S) VIOLATED
924 N. 25th St.          See Charging Section Below
Milwaukee, WI            COMPLAINING WITNESS:
        Defendant.       Kenneth Meuler
                         CASE NUMBER:
                         F-912542
─────────────────────────────────────

THE ABOVE NAMED COMPLAINING WITNESS BEING
DULY SWORN SAYS THAT THE ABOVE NAMED DE-
FENDANT IN THE COUNTY OF MILWAUKEE, STATE OF
WISCONSIN

**COUNT 01:   FIRST DEGREE INTENTIONAL HOMICIDE**

on or about June 30, 1991, at 924 North 25th Street, City
and County of Milwaukee, did cause the death of another
human being, Matt Turner a/k/a/ Donald Montrell, with
intent to kill that person contrary to Wisconsin Statutes
section 940.01(1).

**COUNT 02:   FIRST DEGREE INTENTIONAL HOMICIDE**

on or about July 7, 1991, at 924 North 25th Street, City and
County of Milwaukee, did cause the death of another human being, Jeremiah Weinberger, with intent to kill that
person contrary to Wisconsin Statutes section 940.01(1).

## COUNT 03:  FIRST DEGREE INTENTIONAL HOMICIDE

on or about July 15, 1991, at 924 North 25th Street, City and County of Milwaukee, did cause the death of another human being, Oliver Lacy, with intent to kill that person contrary to Wisconsin Statutes section 940.01(1).

## COUNT 04:  FIRST DEGREE INTENTIONAL HOMICIDE

on or about July 19, 1991, at 924 North 25th Street, City and County of Milwaukee, did cause the death of another human being, Joseph Bradehoft, with intent to kill that person contrary to Wisconsin Statutes section 940.01(1).

## COUNT 05:  HABITUAL CRIMINALITY

on January 30, 1989, Jeffrey L. Dahmer was convicted in the Circuit Court of Milwaukee County in Circuit Court Case Number F-882515 of the felony offenses of Second Degree Sexual Assault and Enticing a Child for Immoral Purposes in violation of 940.225 (2) (e) and 944.12 of the Wisconsin Statutes and that said convictions remain of record and unreversed and therefore defendant is a repeater pursuant to Wisconsin Statutes 939.62, and is subject to a total sentence of not more than ten (10) years on each count recited in addition to the mandatory life sentence for each count of First Degree Intentional Homicide.

Upon conviction of Counts One, Two, Three and Four, Class A Felonies, the penalty is life imprisonment as to each count.

Complainant states that he is a Detective Lieutenant with the City of Milwaukee Police Department and bases this complaint upon the following:

(1) Upon the statement of the defendant, which statement is against his (the defendant's) penal interest that:

(a) On June 30th, 1991 after the Gay Pride Parade in Chicago, he met a black male at the Chicago Bus Station and offered him money to pose nude and also view videos he (the defendant) had at his apartment back in Milwaukee; he (the defendant) with this black male returned to Milwaukee on a Greyhound Bus and then took a City Vet cab to his (the defendant's) residence in Apartment 213 at 924 North 25th Street, in the City and County of Milwaukee, State of Wisconsin; he (the defendant) gave the black male something to drink which had been drugged and that the man passed out and he (the defendant) used a strap to strangle the man then dismembered him and kept his head and put it in the freezer in his apartment and placed his body in a 57 gallon barrel that he had in his residence; further that he (the defendant) looked at a photograph supplied by the Chicago Police Department of Matt Turner a/k/a/ Donald Montrell and indicated that he thought this was the person that he had killed in this incident.

(b) The defendant further stated that on or about July 5th, 1991 he met a Puerto Rican male at Carol's Gay Bar on Wells Street in Chicago and that he offered the man money to come with him to Milwaukee to pose for him and to view videos; they took a Greyhound Bus from Chicago to Milwaukee and then took a cab to his apartment at 924 North 25th Street in the City and County of Milwaukee, State of Wisconsin; this man stayed with him for two days and on the first day they had oral sex and on the second day the man indicated that he wanted to leave and he (the defendant) didn't want the man to leave so he gave him a drink with a sleeping potion in it and strangled him manually and then took photos of him and dismembered him and then took more photos and kept the man's head in the freezer and body in the 57 gallon drum; he (the defendant) looked at a photo supplied by the Chicago Police Department of Jeremiah Weinberger and indicated that this was the man that he had killed in this incident.

(c) The defendant further stated that on or about July 15th, 1991 he met a black male on 27th Street between State and Kilbourn in Milwaukee and that the man stated he was going to his cousin's house; he invited the man to his residence to pose for photos and the man agreed to come and model; when they got to the residence, they removed their clothes and did body rubs and he gave the man a drink which had sleeping potion in it and when the man fell asleep, he strangled him and then had anal sex with him after death; he dismembered him and placed the man's head in the bottom of the refrigerator in a box and kept the man's heart in the freezer to eat later; he also kept the man's body in the freezer that he kept the man's identification which identified the man as Oliver Lacy, date of birth 6/23/67.

(d) The defendant further stated that on or about July 19th, 1991 he met a white male on Wisconsin Avenue near Marquette University and the man was waiting for a bus and had a six pack under his arm; he (the defendant) got off a bus at that location and approached the man and offered him money to pose and view videos and the man agreed and they returned to the defendant's residence at 924 North 25th Street in the City and County of Milwaukee, State of Wisconsin; they had oral sex and then he gave the man a drink with a sleeping potion in it and then strangled him with a strap while he slept; he dismembered this man and put his head in the freezer and his body in the same blue 57 gallon barrel where he had placed the bodies of the black male and the Puerto Rican male; he kept this man's identification card which identified him as Joseph Bradehoft, date of birth 1/24/66.

(2) Upon the statement of Dr. Jeffrey Jentzen, Medical Examiner for Milwaukee County, that on July 23rd, 1991 he was called by the Milwaukee Police Department to Apartment 213 at 924 North 25th Street in the City and County of Milwaukee, State of Wisconsin and inside the apartment at that location, among other evidence, he observed a refrigerator with a freezer section and that the refrigerator contained a head and the freezer section contained human body parts; also there was a floor standing freezer which was found to contain three human heads and other body parts and there was a 57 gallon drum which contained human body parts. Jentzen further stated that at the Milwaukee County Medical Examiner's Office these human body parts were examined and that fingerprints were lifted from hands that had been found at the scene and also attempts at dental identification was made; that Dr. L.T. Johnson whom he (Jentzen) knows to be a forensic odontologist did the dental examination and that fingerprint lifts were submitted to the Milwaukee Police Department Bureau of Identification for analysis.

(3) Upon the statement of Dr. L.T. Johnson, a forensic odontologist, that he (Johnson) at the Milwaukee County Medical Examiner's Office examined one of the human heads recovered from the freezer at 924 North 25th Street with known dental records of Jeremiah Weinberger and determined that the severed human head that he exam-

ined in comparison with those records was the head of Jeremiah Weinberger.

(4) Upon the statement of Wayne Peterson, that he (Peterson) is a Bureau of Identification technician and supervisor employed by the City of Milwaukee Police Department and that he (Peterson) made comparisons of fingerprints lifted by the Milwaukee County Medical Examiner's Office from body parts recovered at 924 North 25th Street on July 23rd, 1991 with known prints of various persons and was able to identify the prints of Oliver Lacy, Joseph Bradehoft, and Matt Turner a/k/a Donald Montrell as having been lifted from human body parts discovered in that apartment.

(5) Complainant further states that he has viewed a certified copy of Judgment of Conviction in Milwaukee County Circuit Court Case No. F-882515 and a copy of that Judgment of Conviction is attached hereto and incorporated herein and the aforementioned Judgment of Conviction indicates that the defendant was convicted of felony offenses in Milwaukee County within five years of the offenses listed in this complaint and that he (the defendant) is therefore a Habitual Criminal.

**** END OF COMPLAINT ****

SUBSCRIBED AND SWORN TO BEFORE ME
AND APPROVED FOR FILING JULY 25, 1991

E Michael McCann                    Kenneth Meuler
District Attorney                    Complaining Witness

CIRCUIT COURT
CRIMINAL DIVISION
STATE OF WISCONSIN        MILWAUKEE COUNTY

───────────────────────────────

STATE OF WISCONSIN, Plaintiff

**AMENDED CRIMINAL
COMPLAINT**

vs.

Jeffrey L. Dahmer/5/21/60
924 N. 25th st.
Milwaukee, WI
        Defendant.

CRIME(S):
See Charging Section Below
STATUTE(S) VIOLATED
See Charging Section Below
COMPLAINING WITNESS:
Donald Domagalski
CASE NUMBER:
F-912542

───────────────────────────────

THE ABOVE NAMED COMPLAINING WITNESS BEING
DULY SWORN SAYS THAT THE ABOVE NAMED DE-
FENDANT IN THE COUNTY OF MILWAUKEE, STATE OF
WISCONSIN

**COUNT 01: FIRST DEGREE INTENTIONAL HOMICIDE**

on or about March 26, 1989, at 2357 South 57th Street,
City of West Allis, County of Milwaukee, did cause the
death of another human being, Anthony Sears, with intent to kill that person contrary to Wisconsin Statutes section 940.01(1).

**COUNT 02: FIRST DEGREE INTENTIONAL HOMICIDE**

during the Spring or early Summer of 1990, at 924 North
25th Street, City and County of Milwaukee, did cause the
death of another human being, Raymond Smith a/k/a

Ricky Beeks, with intent to kill that person contrary to Wisconsin Statutes section 940.01(1).

## COUNT 03: FIRST DEGREE INTENTIONAL HOMICIDE

on or about September 3, 1990, at 924 North 25th Street, City and County of Milwaukee, did cause the death of another human being, Ernest Miller, with intent to kill that person contrary to Wisconsin Statutes section 940.01(1).

## COUNT 04: FIRST DEGREE INTENTIONAL HOMICIDE

on or about September 24, 1990, at 924 North 25th Street, City and County of Milwaukee, did cause the death of another human being, David Thomas, with intent to kill that person contrary to Wisconsin Statutes section 940.01(1).

## COUNT 05: FIRST DEGREE INTENTIONAL HOMICIDE

on or about February 18, 1991, at 924 North 25th Street, City and County of Milwaukee, did cause the death of another human being, Curtis Straughter, with intent to kill that person contrary to Wisconsin Statutes section 940.01(1).

## COUNT 06: FIRST DEGREE INTENTIONAL HOMICIDE

on or about April 7, 1991, at 924 North 25th Street, City and County of Milwaukee, did cause the death of another human being, Errol Lindsey, with intent to kill that person contrary to Wisconsin Statutes section 940.01(1).

## COUNT 07: FIRST DEGREE INTENTIONAL HOMICIDE

on or about May 24, 1990, at 924 North 25th Street, City and County of Milwaukee, did cause the death of another human being, Tony Anthony Hughes, with intent to kill that person contrary to Wisconsin Statutes section 940.01(1).

## COUNT 08: FIRST DEGREE INTENTIONAL HOMICIDE

on or about May 27, 1991, at 924 North 25th Street, City and County of Milwaukee, did cause the death of another human being, Konerak Sinthasomphone, with intent to kill that person contrary to Wisconsin Statutes section 940.01(1).

## COUNT 09: FIRST DEGREE INTENTIONAL HOMICIDE

on or about June 30, 1991, at 924 North 25th Street, City and County of Milwaukee, did cause the death of another human being, Matt Turner a/k/a Donald Montrell, with intent to kill that person contrary to Wisconsin Statutes section 940.01(1).

## COUNT 10: FIRST DEGREE INTENTIONAL HOMICIDE

on or about July 7, 1991, at 924 North 25th Street, City and County of Milwaukee, did cause the death of another human being, Jeremiah Weinberger, with intent to kill that person contrary to Wisconsin Statutes section 940.01(1).

## COUNT 11: FIRST DEGREE INTENTIONAL HOMICIDE

on or about July 15, 1991, at 924 North 25th Street, City and County of Milwaukee, did cause the death of another human being, Oliver Lacy, with intent to kill that person contrary to Wisconsin Statutes section 940.01(1).

## COUNT 12: FIRST DEGREE INTENTIONAL HOMICIDE

on or about July 19, 1991, at 924 North 25th Street, City and County of Milwaukee, did cause the death of another human being, Joseph Bradehoft, with intent to kill that person contrary to Wisconsin Statutes section 940.01(1).

## HABITUAL CRIMINALITY

on January 30, 1989, Jeffrey L. Dahmer was convicted in the Circuit Court of Milwaukee County in Circuit Court Case Number F-882515 for the felony offenses of Second Degree Sexual Assault and Enticing a Child for Immoral Purposes in violation of 940.225(2) (e) and 944.12 of the Wisconsin Statutes and that said convictions remain of record and unreversed and therefore defendant is a repeater pursuant to Wisconsin Statutes 939.62, and is subject to a total sentence of not more than ten (10) years on each count recited in addition to the mandatory life sentence for each count of First Degree Intentional Homicide.

Upon conviction of each count of First Degree Intentional Homicide, a Class A Felony, the penalty if life imprisonment.

Complainant states that he is a Captain of Police with the City of Milwaukee Police Department and bases this complaint upon the following:

## VICTIM ANTHONY SEARS, D.O.B. 1/28/65

1) Upon the statement of the defendant, which statement is against his (the defendant's) penal interest, that he met Anthony Sears (whom he identified in a photograph) at a club called LaCage; that a friend of Anthony

Sears drove him (the defendant) and Anthony Sears to the area of his (the defendant's) grandmother's house in the City of West Allis, County of Milwaukee, State of Wisconsin; that his grandmother's house is 2357 South 57th Street; that after they arrived at that residence, they had sex and he gave Anthony Sears a drink with sleeping pills in it; that he strangled him and dismembered the body; that he kept Anthony Sears' head and boiled it to remove the skin; further, that he kept the skull and painted it.

2) Upon the statement of Jeffrey Connor, an adult citizen, that he (Connor) was with Anthony Sears on the evening of March 25th, 1989 and on that evening they were at a bar on 6th and National; they closed the bar and that Anthony Sears had met a white male named Jeff who said that he was here from Chicago and was visiting his grandmother who lived at 56th and Lincoln; that he (Connor) then gave Jeff and Anthony Sears a ride to the vicinity of 56th and Lincoln where they (Jeff and Sears) got out of the car and walked southbound.

3) Upon complainant's personal knowledge of addresses in Milwaukee County and that the intersection of 56th and Lincoln is north of and in close proximity to the address 2357 South 57th Street in the city of West Allis.

4) Upon the statement of Dr. Jeffrey Jentzen, Milwaukee County Medical Examiner, that during the early morning hours of July 23rd, 1991 he (Jentzen) with Milwaukee police officers and other members of the County of Milwaukee Medical Examiner's Office was present at 924 North 25th Street in the City and County of Milwaukee, State of Wisconsin in Apartment 213; that he was present at that location when seven human skulls (three of which were painted) four human heads, and numerous other body parts were recovered; that all the human re-

mains recovered were transported to the Milwaukee County Medical Examiner's Office.

5) Upon the statement of Dr. L.T. Johnson, a Forensic Odontologist, that he (Johnson) made a comparison of the painted human skulls recovered from 924 North 25th Street in the City and County of Milwaukee, State of Wisconsin during the early morning hours of July 23rd, 1991 with known dental records of Anthony Sears and determined that one of the painted skulls is that of Anthony Sears.

## VICTIM RAYMOND SMITH A/K/A RICKY BEEKS D.O.B. 8/10/57

1) Upon the further statement of the defendant that approximately two months after he (the defendant) moved into Apartment 213 at 924 North 25th Street in the City and County of Milwaukee, State of Wisconsin he met a black male at the 219 Club and offered him money to be photographed and have a drink and watch videos; that the man agreed and came with him (the defendant) to 924 North 25th Street, Apartment 213; that at that location he (the defendant) gave the man a drink which was drugged and the man fell asleep; that he (the defendant) then strangled the man and removed the man's clothing and had oral sex with him; further, that he dismembered the body but kept the skull and later painted it; further, that he (the defendant) identified photographs of Raymond Lamont Smith as being photographs of the man to whom he had done this.

2) Upon the further statement of Dr. L.T. Johnson that he (Johnson) examined the painted skulls recovered at 924 North 25th Street in the City and County of Milwaukee, State of Wisconsin during the early morning hours of July

23rd, 1991 with known dental records of Raymond Lamont Smith and determined that one of the aforementioned skulls is that of Raymond Smith.

3) Upon your complainant's personal observation of a copy of the defendant's rental application for the living premises at 924 North 25th Street, Apartment 213; that the aforementioned rental agreement has an initial lease date of May 13th, 1990.

## VICTIM ERNEST MILLER, D.O.B. 5/5/67

1) Upon the statement of Vivian Miller, an adult citizen, that she (Miller) is the aunt of Ernest Miller and that on September 1st, 1990 Ernest Miller came from his home in Chicago to Milwaukee to visit for the Labor Day weekend and that he left her home during the early morning hours of September 3rd, 1990 and she has not seen him or heard from him since.

2) Upon the further statement of the defendant that during the summer of 1990 he met a black male (whom he identified through a photograph of Ernest Miller as being Ernest Miller) in front of a book store in the 800 block of North 27th Street in the City and County of Milwaukee, State of Wisconsin and that he offered the man money to return to his (the defendant's) apartment at 924 North 25th Street in the City and County of Milwaukee, State of Wisconsin; that when they returned to his apartment they had sex and then he (the defendant) drugged Ernest Miller and killed him by cutting his throat; further, that after taking photos of him, he dismembered the body and disposed of the flesh except for the biceps which he kept in the freezer; he also kept the skull which he painted after the skin was removed, and he kept the skeleton which he bleached.

3) Upon the further statement of Dr. L.T. Johnson that he (Johnson) has compared the painted skulls recovered on July 23rd, 1991 from the defendant's apartment at 924 North 25th Street in the City and County of Milwaukee, State of Wisconsin with known dental records of Ernest Miller and determined that one of the aforementioned painted skulls is that of Ernest Miller.

## VICTIM DAVID C. THOMAS D.O.B. 12/21/67

1) Upon the further statement of the defendant that he in the Autumn of 1990 met a black male in the vicinity of 2nd and Wisconsin in the City and County of Milwaukee, State of Wisconsin and offered the man money to come to his apartment at 924 North 25th Street; when they got to his apartment they drank and talked but he had no sex with this man because the man wasn't his type; that he gave the man a drink with a sleeping potion in it and killed him even though he did not want to have sex with him because he thought the man would wake up and be angry; that he dismembered the body but did not keep any of the body parts because the man wasn't his type; further, that he photographed the man while he was in the process of dismembering him.

2) Upon the statement of Chandra Beanland, an adult citizen, that she (Beanland) is the girlfriend of David C. Thomas and that she reported him missing on September 24th, 1990 to the Milwaukee Police Department.

3) Upon the statement of Brian O'Keefe, a City of Milwaukee Police Detective, that he (O'Keefe) contacted the family of David C. Thomas in the course of this investigation and specifically spoke with Leslie Thomas who identified herself as David C. Thomas' sister and that he (O'Keefe) showed Leslie Thomas the facial portion of the

photograph which the defendant identified as having been taken during the course of dismembering David Thomas; further, that the facial portion showed no injuries at the time it was shown to Leslie Thomas and that Leslie Thomas identified the person in the photograph as being her brother, David Thomas; that the Thomas family supplied a photograph of David Thomas sleeping which they had; further that the face in this family photograph appeared to him (O'Keefe) to depict the same individual as in the photograph the defendant had taken while dismembering this victim.

## VICTIM CURTIS STRAUGHTER D.O.B. 4/16/73

1) Upon the statement of Katherine Straughter, an adult citizen, that she (Straughter) is the grandmother of Curtis Straughter and that she last saw her grandson on February 18th, 1991.

2) Upon the further statement of the defendant that in February of 1991 he observed Curtis Straughter (whom he identified through a photograph) waiting for a bus by Marquette University and offered him money to come back to his apartment at 924 North 25th Street in the City and County of Milwaukee, State of Wisconsin; that Straughter did accompany him back and at the apartment he (the defendant) gave Curtis Straughter a drugged drink and had oral sex with him; the defendant then strangled him with a strap and dismembered the body; he also took photos and kept the man's skull.

3) Upon the further statement of Dr. L.T. Johnson that he (Johnson) compared the unpainted skulls recovered from the defendant's apartment with known dental records of Curtis Straughter and determined that one of the unpainted skulls was that of Curtis Straughter.

## VICTIM ERROL LINDSEY D.O.B. 3/3/72

1) Upon the statement of Yahuna Barkley, an adult citizen, that she (Barkley) is the sister of Errol Lindsey and that she last saw him on April 7th, 1991 when he went to the store and that she has not seen him since that time.

2) Upon the further statement of the defendant that in the Spring of 1991 he met Errol Lindsey (whom he identified by photograph) on the corner of 27th and Kilbourn in the City and County of Milwaukee, State of Wisconsin and that he offered Errol Lindsey money to return with him (the defendant) to his apartment at 924 North 25th Street in the City and County of Milwaukee, State of Wisconsin; that after they returned to his apartment he gave Lindsey a drugged drink and after he fell asleep he strangled Lindsey and then had oral sex with him; he then dismembered the body and saved the skull.

3) Upon the further statement of Dr. L.T. Johnson that he (Johnson) compared the unpainted skulls recovered from the defendant's apartment on July 23rd, 1991 with known dental records of Errol Lindsey and determined that one of the unpainted skulls is that of Errol Lindsey.

## VICTIM TONY ANTHONY HUGHES, D.O.B. 8/26/59

1) Upon the further statement of the defendant that in May of 1991 he met Tony Anthony Hughes (whom he identified through a photograph) who was deaf and mute in front of the 219 Bar on Second Street in the City and County of Milwaukee, State of Wisconsin; that he communicated with Hughes by writing and it appeared that Hughes could read lips; that he offered Hughes $50 to come to his (the defendant's) apartment at 924 North 25th Street in the City and County of Milwaukee, State of Wis-

consin to take photos and view videos; further, that he gave Hughes a drink with a sleeping potion and then killed him and dismembered his body and kept his skull.

2) Upon the further statement of Dr. L.T. Johnson that he (Johnson) has compared the unpainted skulls found in the apartment of the defendant with known dental records of Tony Hughes and determined that one of the unpained skulls is that of Tony Hughes.

3) Upon the statement of Shirley Hughes, an adult citizen, that she (Hughes) is the mother of Tony Hughes and that Tony Hughes came to Milwaukee from Madison during the late afternoon or evening of May 24th, 1991 and that she has not seen him since and further that her son, Tony Hughes, is deaf and mute.

## VICTIM KONERAK SINTHASOMPHONE D.O.B. 12/2/76

1) Upon the statement of Sounthone Sinthasomphone, an adult resident that he is the father of Konerak Sinthasomphone who was 14 years of age and that during the afternoon of May 26th, 1991 his son left home and did not return and he has not seen him since.

2) Upon the further statement of the defendant that he (the defendant) in late May of 1991 met a young Oriental male (whom he identified by photograph as Konerak Sinthasomphone) in front of Grand Avenue Mall in Milwaukee and that they went back to his (the defendant's) apartment at 924 North 25th Street in the City and County of Milwaukee, State of Wisconsin; that Sinthasomphone posed for two photographs while he was alive and that he (the defendant) gave Sinthasomphone a drink laced with a sleeping potion and that they then watched videos and while they were watching videos, Sinthasomphone passed out; that he (the defendant) then had oral sex with

Sinthasomphone and then he (the defendant) went to a bar to get some beer because he had run out; that while he was walking back from the bar located on 27th just North of Kilbourn, he saw Sinthasomphone staggering down the street and he (the defendant) went up to Sinthasomphone and then the police stopped him; that he told the police that he was a friend of this individual and that the individual had gotten drunk and done this before; that the police escorted them back to his (the defendant's) apartment and he told the police he would take care of Sinthasomphone because he was his friend; that they went into the apartment and after the police left, he killed Sinthasomphone by strangling him and then had oral sex with him and then he took more photographs and dismembered the body and kept the skull.

3) Upon the further statement of Dr. L.T. Johnson that he (Johnson) compared the unpainted skulls recovered from the apartment at 924 North 25th Street with known dental records of Konerak Sinthasomphone and determined that one of the skulls which was recovered from that location is that of Konerak Sinthasomphone.

## VICTIM MATT TURNER A/K/A DONALD MONTRELL D.O.B. 7/3/70

1) Upon the further statement of the defendant that on June 30th, 1991 after the Gay Pride Parade in Chicago, he met a black male at the Chicago Bus Station and offered him money to pose nude and also view videos at his apartment back in Milwaukee; he (the defendant), with this black male, returned to Milwaukee on a Greyhound Bus and then took a City Vet cab to his (the defendant's) residence in Apartment 213 at 924 North 25th Street, in the City and County of Milwaukee, State of Wisconsin; he (the defendant) gave the black male something to drink

which had been drugged and the man passed out and he (the defendant) used a strap to strangle the man and then dismembered him and kept his head and put it in the freezer in his apartment and placed his body in a 57 gallon barrel that he had in his residence; further that he (the defendant) looked at a photograph supplied by the Chicago Police Department of Matt Turner a/k/a Donald Montrell and indicated that he thought this was the person that he had killed in this incident.

## VICTIM JEREMIAH WEINBERGER D.O.B. 9/29/67

1) Upon the further statement of the defendant that on or about July 5th, 1991 he met a Puerto Rican male at Carol's Gay Bar on Wells Street in Chicago and that he offered the man money to come with him to Milwaukee to pose for him and to view videos; they took a Greyhound Bus from Chicago to Milwaukee and then took a cab to the defendant's apartment at 924 North 25th Street in the City and County of Milwaukee, State of Wisconsin; this man stayed with him for two days and on the first day they had oral sex and on the second day the man indicated that he wanted to leave and he (the defendant) didn't want the man to leave so he gave him a drink with a sleeping potion in it and strangled him manually and then took photos of him and dismembered the body; he then took more photos and kept the man's head in the freezer and body in the 57 gallon drum; he (the defendant) looked at a photo supplied by the Chicago Police Department of Jeremiah Weinberger and indicated that this was the man that he had killed in this incident.

2) Upon the statement of Dr. L.T. Johnson that he (Johnson) at the Milwaukee County Medical Examiner's Office compared one of the human heads recovered from the freezer at 924 North 25th Street with known dental re-

cords of Jeremiah Weinberger and determined that the severed human head that he examined in comparison with those records was the head of Jeremiah Weinberger.

## VICTIM OLIVER LACY D.O.B. 6/23/67

1) Upon the further statement of the defendant that on or about July 15th, 1991 he met a black male on 27th Street between State and Kilbourn in Milwaukee and that the man stated he was going to his cousin's house; he invited the man to his residence to pose for photos and the man agreed to come and model; when they got to the residence at 924 North 25th Street in the City and County of Milwaukee, State of Wisconsin, they removed their clothes and did body rubs and he gave the man a drink which had sleeping potion in it; when the man fell asleep, he strangled him and then had anal sex with him after death; he dismembered the body and placed the man's head in the bottom of the refrigerator in a box and kept the man's heart in the freezer to eat later; he also kept the man's body in the freezer; he kept the man's identification which identified the man as Oliver Lacy, date of birth 6/23/67.

## VICTIM JOSEPH BRADEHOFT D.O.B. 1/24/66

1) Upon the further statement of the defendant that on or about July 19th, 1991 he met a white male on Wisconsin Avenue near Marquette University; the man was waiting for a bus and had a six pack under his arm; he (the defendant) got off a bus at that location and approached the man and offered him money to pose and view videos and the man agreed; they returned to the defendant's residence at 924 North 25th Street in the City and County of Milwaukee, State of Wisconsin; they had

oral sex and then he gave the man a drink with a sleeping potion in it and then strangled him with a strap while he slept; he dismembered this man and put his head in the freezer and his body in the same blue 57 gallon barrel where he had placed the bodies of the black male and the Puerto Rican male; he kept this man's identification card which identified his as Joseph Bradehoft, date of birth 1/24/66.

## AS TO VICTIMS TURNER, LACY AND BRADEHOFT

1) Upon the statement of Dr. Jeffrey Jentzen, Medical Examiner for Milwaukee County, that on July 23rd, 1991 he was called by the Milwaukee Police Department to Apartment 213 at 924 North 25th Street in the City and County of Milwaukee, State of Wisconsin and inside the apartment at that location, among other evidence, he observed a refrigerator with a freezer section; the refrigerator contained a human heads and the freezer section contained human body parts; also there was a floor standing freezer which was found to contain three human heads and other body parts and there was a 57 gallon drum which contained human body parts. Jentzen further stated that at the Milwaukee County Medical Examiner's Office these human body parts were examined and that fingerprints were lifted from hands that had been found at the scene and also efforts at dental identification were made; that Dr. L.T. Johnson, whom he (Jentzen) knows to be a forensic odontologist, did the dental examination and that fingerprint lifts were submitted to the Milwaukee Police Department Bureau of Identification for analysis.

2) Upon the statement of Wayne Peterson, that he (Peterson) is a Bureau of Identification technician and supervisor employed by the City of Milwaukee Police Department and that he (Peterson) made comparisons of

fingerprints lifted by the Milwaukee County Medical Examiner's Office from body parts recovered at 924 North 25th Street on July 23rd, 1991 with known prints of various persons and was able to identify the prints of Oliver Lacy, Joseph Bradehoft, and Matt Turner a/k/a Donald Montrell as having been lifted from human body parts discovered in that apartment.

## AS TO HABITUAL CRIMINALITY

Complainant further states that he has viewed a certified copy of Judgment of Conviction in Milwaukee County Circuit Court Case No. F-882515 and a copy of that Judgment of Conviction is attached hereto and incorporated herein and the aforementioned Judgment of Conviction indicates that the defendant was convicted of felony offenses in Milwaukee County within five years of the offenses listed in this complaint and that he (the defendant) is therefore a Habitual Criminal.

**** END OF COMPLAINT ****

SUBSCRIBED AND SWORN TO BEFORE ME
AND APPROVED FOR FILING AUGUST 6, 1991

District Attorney                    Complaining Witness

# ACKNOWLEDGMENTS

The author is especially grateful to John O'Brien and Crocker Stephenson for their invaluable assistance and moral backing in putting this volume together under tremendous deadline pressure, to Dianne Banis for providing certain information that any book of this nature would have been incomplete without, and to Wayne Klatt for his expertise. Thanks to Sheryl O'Brien for her work in preparing a floor plan of the murder scene, to Kareema Ghani of the Milwaukee County Circuit Court's Criminal Division for her assistance in making necessary legal documents available, and to Lenore for maintaining a discreet distance while the writer worked. Thanks also to the scores of reporters who worked on the story, some of whom took calls at home on their days off, and whose countless articles helped put together a reasonable chronology of how this terror in Milwaukee could possibly have happened.

# INDEX

# OTHER BOOKS
# BY EDWARD BAUMANN

*Chicago Originals,*
with Kenan Heise

*Getting Away With Murder,*
with John O'Brien

*Murder Next Door,*
with John O'Brien

# ABOUT THE AUTHORS

Ed Baumann, a lifelong resident of Kenosha, Wisconsin, served with the Army Air Corps in New Guinea, the Dutch East Indies and the Philippines during World War II. He worked as a reporter or editor for the *Waukegan News-Sun, Chicago Daily News, Chicago's American, Chicago Today* and *the Chicago Tribune* before turning to full-time freelancing in 1988, when his peers honored him as Chicago Press Veteran of the Year. He is a past president of the Chicago Press Club, former chairman of the Chicago Press Veterans Association, a member of the Chicago Newspaper Reporters Association and Milwaukee Press Club, and winner of two Chicago Newspaper Guild Stick-O-Type Awards for investigative reporting. Baumann is the co-author, with Kenan Heise, of *Chicago Originals: A Cast of the City's Colorful Characters.* He and Tribune reporter John O'Brien have collaborated on

*Chicago Heist, Getting Away With Murder, Murder Next Door,* and the forthcoming *Teresita, the Voice from the Grave.* They are currently working on *The Polish Robbin' Hood,* the inside story of the Panczko burglary gang, better known in Chicago as the "guys who couldn't do nuttin right."

The phychological commentary on Jeffrey Dahmer (chapter 21) was written by Gerson H. Kaplan, M.D., a psychiatrist practicing in Chicago. Dr. Kaplan has been on the staff of the Psychiatric Institute of the Circuit Court of Cook County for 31 years.

The chapters on Milwaukee's anguish (chapter 22) and Dahmer's August 22 hearing were written by Crocker Stephenson. Mr. Stephenson is a staff writer and acting assistant city editor for the *Milwaukee Sentinel*.